Dad —
    Here's a little light
reading for you —
Drink lots of water —
it might be dry...
        Love,
            Susan
                Sept. 2002

Khrushchev Remembers

The
Glasnost Tapes

Khrushchev Remembers

The Glasnost Tapes

Foreword by
Strobe Talbott

Translated and Edited by
Jerrold L. Schecter
with
Vyacheslav V. Luchkov

Illustrated
with Photographs

Little, Brown and Company
Boston • Toronto • London

First Edition

Photographs are from the Time Inc. Magazines picture collection.

ISBN 0-316-47297-2
Library of Congress Catalog Card Number 90-52878

10 9 8 7 6 5 4 3 2 1

HC
Published simultaneously in Canada
by Little, Brown & Company (Canada) Limited

Printed in the United States of America

Contents

Foreword by Strobe Talbott   vii

1. Origins   1

2. The Great Terror and the Twentieth Party Congress   14

3. The Great Patriotic War   45

4. Unfinished Business   68

5. Comrades to the West   99

6. Comrades to the East   142

7. On the Brink: Berlin and Cuba   161

8. The Intelligentsia: Scientists and Writers   184

Appendix: Chronology of Khrushchev's Career   205

Index   213

Maps

The Soviet Union and Eastern Europe, 1939–1955   47

The Kharkov Disaster, 1942   61

Disputed Islands, Japan and USSR   91

The Cuban Missile Crisis: Range of Cuba-based Soviet Missiles   173

Photographs follow page 110.

Foreword

by STROBE TALBOTT

THE most important Russian word that Mikhail Gorbachev has introduced into English is *glasnost*. Usually translated as "openness," it really means the willingness of the Soviet Union to hear the truth about itself. With this book, *glasnost* has made possible the publication of new material from one of the most extraordinary archives of the twentieth century, the memoirs of Nikita Sergeyevich Khrushchev. Two earlier volumes have already established the memoirs as the single most comprehensive, candid, and authoritative firsthand account of the inner workings of the Kremlin leadership. Now there is more — all of it fresh and fascinating, much of it relevant to today's headlines about the upheaval in the Communist world.

It was twenty-two years ago that Jerrold Schecter, then the Moscow bureau chief of *Time* magazine, learned that the Soviet Union's most famous nonperson, the former first secretary of the Central Committee of the Communist party and chairman of the Council of Ministers, who was under virtual house arrest outside Moscow, had been dictating recollections of his career. Fed up with the wall of silence that his successors had erected around him and knowing that he was approaching the end of his life, Khrushchev decided to allow the tape recordings to be spirited out of the USSR so that they could be translated and published in the West.

In the months and years that followed, those of us who worked with Mr. Schecter on that project felt that we were part of a great adventure. We had an opportunity to mine a mother lode of some of the rarest and richest raw material of history. Here was the story, told in his own words, of a man who had ruled one of the two superpowers for more than a decade. As a member of Joseph Stalin's "narrow circle," he had risen in the Communist system during the Great Terror. But once he reached the top, he declared war on Stalin's ghost. In foreign policy, too, Khrushchev represented the best and the worst. He achieved an early form of détente with Dwight D. Eisenhower, then went to the brink of war with John F. Kennedy.

Nothing like these memoirs had ever before emerged from the Soviet Union. Hence the excitement within our own narrow circle of colleagues who were involved in the publication of *Khrushchev Remembers* in 1970: Hedley Donovan of Time Inc., Murray J. Gart of *Time*, Ralph Graves and David Maness of *Life*, the late Larned Bradford of Little, Brown, and myself, as translator and editor. I had the assistance of the late Yasha Zaguskin of Oxford, England, and, subsequently, Gregory Freidin, now a professor at Stanford.

However, even when we brought out a second volume, *Khrushchev Remembers: The Last Testament*, in 1974, based on additional material we received after Khrushchev's death, we had a sense of unfinished business. For one thing, while he labored away in the garden and sitting room of his dacha in the village of Petrovo-Dalneye, Khrushchev said over and over that he was primarily interested in addressing his monumental exercise in self-rehabilitation to his comrades in the Communist Party of the Soviet Union and to his fellow citizens of the USSR. The official press mentioned him once, six years after his ouster, in the context of a hoked-up repudiation of the first volume of the memoirs, and then again, in September 1971, in a brief announcement of his death that identified him only as a "special pensioner."

For nearly two decades, Khrushchev's memoirs remained in the category of *tamizdat* — supposedly subversive material "published over there," in the West, by the bourgeois capitalist press. We regarded ourselves as custodians of a treasure that should someday be accessible to Khrushchev's countrymen; in the meantime, we wanted it to be carefully preserved and at the same time available for study. It was in that spirit that after the publication of the second volume, Time Inc. presented all the tapes and transcripts in its possession to the Oral History Research Office and

the W. Averell Harriman Institute for Advanced Study of the
Soviet Union at Columbia University, then under the directorship
of Marshall Shulman. The Khrushchev archive consists of eighty
reels and sixteen cassettes of tape, as well as over three thousand
pages of transcripts, and it has been frequently studied and cited
by scholars.

How did we acquire the memoirs? In response to that obvious
and reasonable question, we always said, "From Khrushchev's family and friends." We knew it was not an answer likely to satisfy
anyone, except those whom we were honor-bound to protect. Journalists are often — and publishers are sometimes — obligated not
to reveal their sources, particularly when dealing with material
from the Soviet Union.

For that reason we were greatly constrained in what we could
say publicly, especially when the first volume was published in
1970. Our sources were under considerable pressure from the
authorities. We did not want to complicate their lives further.
Therefore, we kept quiet, not only about the provenance of the
tapes but about the measures we had taken to establish their
authenticity. An independent firm of recognized voiceprint
experts, Voice Identification Services of Somerville, New Jersey,
conducted an exhaustive spectrographic analysis. A spectrogram
was made every time there was any break or interruption in the
tapes — nearly six thousand different spectrograms in all. These
were carefully compared to, and found to match with, a sample of
Khrushchev's voice, recorded during an address he made to the
United Nations General Assembly. However, we agreed not to
reveal the existence of the voiceprints and the findings of the ana-
lysts as long as Khrushchev was still alive.

Partly for that reason, we had to listen silently to charges from
some Western experts that we had been duped into publishing a
massive piece of KGB disinformation — and to Soviet accusations
that the memoirs had been cooked up in the CIA's "kitchen of
fabricators."

The controversy over authenticity died down in 1974, when we
published the posthumous volume, *The Last Testament*, and
invited a panel of experts, including a number of skeptics, to a
conference at Columbia where they could listen to the tapes,
examine the transcripts, and study the voiceprint report.

Just as we were frequently in the position of knowing more than we could say, we also often guessed more than we knew for certain. For example, we had reason to believe that Khrushchev's son Sergei was a key figure in the preparation of the memoirs, but we had never had any direct dealing with him. Throughout what is now known officially as the "era of stagnation," when the men who had overthrown his father ruled the USSR, Sergei refused any public comment and was understandably laconic even in private encounters with foreign visitors.

I first met him in Moscow in June 1984. He was gracious but circumspect. He did, however, say that he hoped the day might be approaching when he could finally have something to say about the whole affair.

That day came in May of this year, with the publication by Little, Brown of Sergei's own book, *Khrushchev on Khrushchev.* He tells much, though not all, about how the memoirs were composed and how they came to be published in the West. He recalls how his father fumed over his relegation to oblivion and how he taped his side of the story so that it would be available if ever anyone was willing, and permitted, to listen. Several passages are worth quoting at some length here:

> As Father dictated one reel after another, he began to agonize about what would happen to his memoirs. "It's all in vain," he would say during our Sunday walks. "Our efforts are useless. Everything's going to be lost. As soon as I die, they'll take it away and destroy it, or they'll bury it so deep that there'll be no trace of it." . . .
>
> I tried to reassure my father as much as I could, but deep down I was inclined to agree with him. The fact that everything was quiet now didn't mean that it would continue that way forever. . . .
>
> I was haunted by a vision of beautifully produced, published volumes. . . .
>
> I found what I thought was a good way to send a copy of the memoirs abroad. It turned out to be much simpler than I expected. Still, aside from the physical problem of getting the memoirs out of the country, there was a moral consideration. It was no longer 1958, but it wasn't yet 1988.
>
> Only ten short years before, [Boris] Pasternak had drawn

thunder and lightning for giving his manuscript [of *Doctor Zhivago*] to an Italian publisher. . . .

Father was bolder than I. His were the memoirs of the first secretary of the Central Committee, he insisted, the confessions of one who had devoted his entire life to fighting for Soviet power, for a Communist society. The memoirs contained truth, words of warning, facts — they should be read by the people. Let them come out first abroad and at home later. The reverse would be better, but would we live that long?

In deciding to take this step, we crossed the threshold from legal to illegal activity. I felt uneasy. Where would it end? Arrest? Internal exile? It was no time to ponder the consequences; it was important to act.

Many of those who took part in the effort are still alive, and I still can't reveal details or the names of those who offered their assistance. Many of them asked me not to, and I'm not about to violate their confidence; not everyone wanted to become a hero of this book. I would like only to express my sincere thanks to those who helped preserve and publish Father's memoirs.[1]

In April 1988, I came across an interview that Sergei had granted to a Yugoslav newspaper, *Vjesnik*, in which he said, "I believe that my father's memoirs will eventually be published [in the USSR], and I am working on that." I got in touch with him on my next visit to Moscow, in June of that year, and told him that Time Inc. and the Harriman Institute would do anything they could to assist him. A month later, Henry Muller, the managing editor of *Time*, and John Stacks, the chief of correspondents, and I met with Sergei, his sister Rada, and their niece (who had been raised as an adopted sister) Julia. We offered to provide them with all the transcripts in our possession to supplement whatever material they had retained. They accepted and expressed their gratitude.

In 1989 and 1990, extensive excerpts appeared in a number of Soviet academic and popular journals. A special edition of the

1. Sergei Khrushchev, *Khrushchev on Khrushchev*, edited and translated by William Taubman (Boston: Little, Brown, 1990), pp. 238, 241, 248 250.

memoirs had also been translated back into Russian from the English edition, but it was available only to a small number of government and party officials. The Khrushchev family still has high hopes that several volumes of the memoirs, based on the original tapes and available to the general public, will be published before too long.

Even while awaiting the publication of a Soviet edition, we were aware of another respect in which our work was unfinished. It was evident from listening carefully to the original tapes in the early seventies that there had been deletions before they reached us. Khrushchev would be telling his tale, reliving the past with his characteristic gusto, and suddenly, maddeningly, there would be silence on the tape, sometimes lasting only a few seconds, sometimes for several minutes. More often than not, the gaps occurred at key points in the narrative. In 1973–1974, when we were working on *Khrushchev Remembers: The Last Testament*, the Watergate scandal was dominating the news; we joked among ourselves that our project must have fallen victim to the same "sinister forces" that Alexander Haig suggested had caused the famous eighteen-minute gap in the Oval Office tapes.

In some cases, it was possible to deduce what Khrushchev might have revealed in the missing sections. For example, recalling the Cuban missile crisis, Khrushchev said, "When Castro and I talked about the problem, we argued and argued." At that point there was an interruption, then the statement, "Our argument was very heated. But in the end, Fidel agreed with me." We could only conjecture that they had argued over who would control the missiles.

We could also guess at the reason for the deletion. Castro was still very much in power, and Khrushchev's collaborators in the project were already taking considerable risks; they did not want to press their luck by allowing the memoirs to reveal what might be considered state secrets about Soviet relations with foreign leaders still in office. Under Soviet law, it was a crime to publicize the proceedings of Politburo meetings. In several other places, Khrushchev seemed on the verge of criticizing his successors, particularly Leonid Brezhnev, when the tape went dead. In general, comments on Communist leaders still in office seemed to have been cut.

In his own book, Sergei Khrushchev confirmed what we had surmised: "Removed from the text were passages that might constitute military secrets and incidental references to people then in power in the USSR, and Father agreed to delete them" (page 251).

We also noticed how little discussion there was of Aleksandr Solzhenitsyn on the tapes that came to us. Khrushchev, after all, had been responsible for the publication in the USSR of *One Day in the Life of Ivan Denisovich*. Surely he must have devoted some time to that subject. However, his minion-turned-usurper, Brezhnev, had been responsible for the suppression of Solzhenitsyn's other works and the exile of the author himself. Therefore, we could easily imagine that some interesting commentary about Solzhenitsyn had been held back.

How many such passages were there? Exactly what was removed? Would the missing material ever be available? We did not know the answers to those questions until 1989, when we acquired tapes with the missing sections intact. They constituted a much larger body of material than we had expected — over three hundred hours. Some segments were brief yet intriguing — for example, Khrushchev's statement that he had heard Stalin confirm Julius and Ethel Rosenberg's "very significant" contribution to the Soviet atomic bomb project. But in the main, the contents proved to be more than just fragments of indiscretion on Khrushchev's part. They were, in many cases, remarkably coherent in form as well as new and interesting in substance. Here, for instance, was not just the missing passage from the account of the Cuban missile crisis contained in the published memoir, but a number of hitherto untold stories, including the startling assertion that in the midst of the showdown, Castro urged Khrushchev to order an attack on the United States. Here, too, was a detailed account of the Solzhenitsyn affair, filled with anger at Brezhnev's campaign against the novelist.

Another section provided considerably more detail about the Molotov-Ribbentrop pact of 1939 and its secret protocol "granting" the Baltic republics to the USSR. Still another reel included the inside story of the Soviet Union's postwar relations with Japan, including the revelation that some in the Kremlin (including Khrushchev) had been willing to make concessions on the four Japanese islands seized by the USSR in the closing days of World

War II. That issue remains the single biggest irritant in Japan's dealings with the Soviet Union today, yet there had been nothing on the subject in the tapes that provided the basis for the first two volumes of the memoirs.

As we knew, and as Sergei Khrushchev emphasized in his own book, his father was an irrepressible storyteller. Apparently quite a few of the stories he had told had been deemed so sensitive that they were not just censored selectively but withheld in their entirety. In almost all cases, it was easy enough to see why. In the early 1970s, the Soviet government was still systematically covering up and lying about the history of its relations with foreign countries, notably including Japan, as well as with constituent republics of the USSR, most dramatically the Baltics.

By 1989, much had changed in Soviet internal and foreign policies alike. The reformist government of Mikhail Gorbachev was now distancing itself from the obstreperously orthodox regime of Fidel Castro. The Kremlin was prepared to denounce the Molotov-Ribbentrop pact and to concede, at least in principle, the Baltic republics' right of secession. Gorbachev was also eager for improved relations with Japan, and there was speculation about possible Soviet concessions on the northern islands. It was also no longer dangerous to his survivors for Khrushchev to be quoted as saying, "It was a mistake to send our troops into Czechoslovakia. Now the wise and logical thing is to take them back out."

Much of the new material is remarkably germane to current events. In addition to passages that make timely reading against the backdrop of headlines about Lithuania's bid for independence, there are tirades against the inefficiencies and inequities of the Soviet economy that sound very much like speeches Gorbachev himself has made to the Congress of People's Deputies and the Supreme Soviet. It is clearer than ever that Khrushchev's attempts to reform Soviet agriculture and industry constituted a precedent for *perestroika*; his cultural thaw was the forerunner of *glasnost*; his drastic and controversial curtailment of the size of the Soviet armed forces was the antecedent of Gorbachev's attempt to demilitarize Soviet society. When Khrushchev says that Soviet interests should be "defended within limits, and along lines that [do] not harm other countries," he is anticipating Gorbachev's policy of nonoffensive defense and mutual security. No wonder Gorbachev has, on a number of occasions, paid homage to Khrushchev as an innovator and a precursor.

For all these reasons, it soon became evident that we had the makings of a new book. Anyone who read the first two volumes of *Khrushchev Remembers* will, we hope, find *The Glasnost Tapes* a worthy sequel.

IN preparing this volume, Jerrold Schecter worked closely with Vyacheslav Luchkov, a scholar from Moscow. They had the assistance of Margarita Luchkov on the transcription of the tapes, Carl Sandstrom on the translation, and Jef Olivarius McAllister on the editing. We are all grateful to Roger Donald of Little, Brown, who supervised the publication with skill, patience, and encouragement.

Messrs. Schecter and Luchkov have given priority to distilling the freshest material and keeping repetition from the earlier books to an absolute minimum. It was Khrushchev's habit to tell the same story over and over again, with different points of emphasis and varying degrees of embellishment. The tapes that we received in 1989 contained numerous such retellings. In quite a few cases, there were passages that had not been in the tapes on which the first two volumes were based; yet they covered the same ground as the earlier tapes, and the new material was not sufficiently substantial or compelling to merit inclusion in *The Glasnost Tapes*. Those outtakes are, of course, part of the now considerably expanded collection of tapes and transcripts that resides at Columbia and is open to scholars. We appreciate the assistance of Robert Legvold, now the director of the Harriman Institute, during the past year.

There are no indications in the new tapes that anything else has been deleted or held back. We believe that the Khrushchev archive is now complete. However, our work of editing and publishing the memoirs — of making them available to a wide readership — is still not done.

Ideally, it should be possible to read Khrushchev's memoirs in a form that is both comprehensive and coherent. Now that the massive, untidy original is finally together under one roof, the edited, published version should be together between one set of covers. The scope and significance of the material itself require that kind of treatment. Therefore, we intend in due course to bring out a definitive edition of the memoirs, in both Russian and English, that will weave together the various strands now dispersed among the three books and that will include the still unused fragments in the original. That will be a big, time-consuming job, but it is necessary if we are to fulfill the obligation to Nikita Khrushchev and to history that we undertook twenty-two years ago, when Mr. Schecter first made contact with the family and friends of a special pensioner.

Khrushchev Remembers

The
Glasnost Tapes

1

Origins

FOR a long time my comrades have been suggesting, even urging, that I write down what I remember. My generation has lived through interesting times: revolution, civil war, the transition from capitalism to socialism, the Great Patriotic War, the development and strengthening of socialism — an entire epoch. It was my lot in life to have taken part in the whole process. Much has happened during these years that many do not understand. Nor do I understand everything completely myself.

I understand the concern of comrades who are so insistent that I write my memoirs. At some point, after a lot of time has passed, every word uttered by those of us who lived in our period will be an invaluable guide to those who come later. I feel very fortunate to have traveled the path that I did, and I have been involved in the social and political reconstruction [*perestroika*] of our country.

I was lucky. I was part of the process, from the smallest cell of our party organization right on up to the highest level — to the party's Central Committee and the Politburo, to the offices of chairman of the Council of Ministers and first secretary of the Central Committee, and to membership in the Presidium of the USSR Supreme Soviet.

My career has been one of great responsibility and great difficulty. I had an opportunity to participate in finding solutions to many problems and then in implementing those solutions. That is why I feel it my duty to give my opinion, to share my understanding of what happened.

I know at the outset that no opinion will please everyone. Nor is pleasing everyone my goal. I want my point of view to survive, and to be known, along with all the others that will be recorded and stand as our generation's legacy. We are people of one body — the party, the Politburo, the Presidium of the Supreme Soviet, the Central Committee, the Council of Ministers. While our views might coincide on some issues, they will differ on others. This is only natural. That's how it was and that's how it will always be. The truth is born through quarrels. Even within the same party, among people who share the same principled position — that of Marxism-Leninism — there can be different understandings, interpretations, and nuances in the solution of a problem. The times often demand a flexible approach to solving problems. I know that we will have differences of opinion, possibly even opposing views. As a retired politician I see this quite clearly now that I have plenty of time to sit back and observe the world.[1] This does not trouble me. I rely on those who will be my judges. The judges will be the people, who will read and understand this material and draw their own conclusions.

I am not suggesting, and I do not believe, that what I have to say is the final truth. Not at all. Each person will make up his own mind, comparing and weighing various points of view on a given issue.

That is all I want. Only a fool thinks everyone is stamped from the same mold and that anything not conforming to the mold must be heretical, or worse, criminal. No, let history be the judge. Let the people decide.

This is the position from which I would like to be heard. For this reason I ask the reader's forgiveness beforehand for those of my thoughts that may seem to be wrong. Well, so what? It is my point of view. That is the way I see and understand things; that is the way I write.

I don't wish to keep silent or gloss over certain aspects of reality. I don't wish to smooth out the rough spots or to polish our reality.

---

1. Nikita Khrushchev held power as first secretary of the Communist Party of the Soviet Union from September 1953 until he was ousted in October 1964. He began dictating his memoirs in 1966 and continued the project, off and on, until his death, in September 1971.

It does not need polishing, because it is such a grandiose monument. I was fortunate enough to live at a particular juncture in history when an old order, based on capitalism and land ownership, was replaced by a new way of life. We tore down and discarded the old way, and we are building new practice on top of new theory.

Theory is important, yet theory without practice is worthless. Based on the most progressive theory — Marxism-Leninism — we are paving the way for practice. This is a complicated process. Extremely complicated. This is why our path includes mistakes and outrages, some deliberate, some innocent.

As they say, let our descendants forgive us. They will understand that our experience was the first of its kind in the world. First attempts are always unique. We should be judged according to the circumstances in which we lived and worked. It is only now that I have finished my work and can begin to produce memoirs. This is necessary so that the good that came out of our time — the results of our efforts, the efforts of the party and the working class, the fruits of the peasants' labor — should not be lost. We must not repeat the mistakes of the past. I would even go so far as to say we must not commit the same crimes that were made in the name of the party.

I will have to dictate my memoirs without access to archival materials. Getting to them will be difficult for me. In my situation, such materials are not available. I want simply to be truthful and to provide the facts. In future generations, anyone who is interested in what I say here can check up on me. The facts can be found in the minutes and protocols of meetings. In the future it will be possible to study them in full detail. Now the archives are closed. But I feel that the majority of such materials should be open, because there is nothing about them that should be kept secret.

After Stalin's death, when we had acquired some distance from the period of his leadership, we discovered the party archives that had been unknown to us. It was then that we lost the faith that we had built up in Stalin. When he was in power everything done by him or under his guidance seemed to us to be unshakably and singularly correct. Only after he died did we begin to think critically about the past and, to the extent it was possible, check what we remembered against the records in the archives.

WHEN my grandfather got out of the army, where he had served twenty-five years in the guard, he settled down to a peasant's life.[2] He had three daughters: one of them, Aksiniya, or Ksenya for short, was to become my mother. While she was still a young girl, Ksenya went to live with her older sister, Aleksandra, in Tishkino. Like all country folk, she earned her living working for the landowner, scrubbing floors. Aleksandra could sew and she taught Ksenya.

The son of a friend of my grandfather's, with whom he had served in the army, married Ksenya and took her away to Kalinovka [near the Ukrainian border], his native village. He was my father, Sergei Khrushchev. No sooner did they get there than his father made him leave. According to the custom of the day, the father drove the eldest son out of the house when he was married, not giving him any land or gifts for his marriage. My mother and father left and settled elsewhere, but they lived in poverty. They had no land, and my father went off to the Donbass [the Donets Basin, 275 miles southeast of Kalinovka], where he first worked as a common laborer on the railroad. He sorted railroad ties, leveled the embankments, drove stakes, and dug drainage ditches. When that seasonal job ended he worked in a brick factory. He mixed the clay and laid bricks until he had gained enough experience to be allowed to work the kiln. This work, too, was seasonal, and he left. He finally arrived in Yuzovka to work in the mines.[3]

First he worked as a laborer, then he went down the mine shafts to haul out the coal, pulling a cart by hand. Soon, he had saved up enough money and returned home to the village. About this time [1894] I was born.

2. Before the reforms of Czar Alexander II (1818–1881), peasants and burghers were liable for military service, and those who had the misfortune to be conscripted had to serve for twenty-five years.

3. The Yuzovka Metal Factory and Yuzovka — or Hughes-ovka — were named after the owner of the factory, the Welshman John Hughes. Yuzovka was later called Stalino and is now Donetsk. See Theodore H. Friedgut, *Iuzovka and Revolution*, vol. 1, *Life and Work in the Donbass, 1869–1924* (Princeton, N.J.: Princeton University Press, 1989).

There were two children in the family, myself and my sister, Irina Sergeyevna. My father came to the village on one of his visits and saw how his family was living. At that time I was already six or seven years old, and had begun to go to a three-year parochial school. The teacher was a deacon who would hit the children hard on the forehead and the hands with a ruler. He made us learn by rote, especially when we studied the textbook of God's laws. Such teaching methods did not foster any love of learning in me.

My father, seeing that life in the village was hard, returned to the mines. Some time later he met with the owner of the mine, who asked him, "Sergei, are you a bachelor or have you got a woman?"

My father answered, "I've got a wife, and small children too."

"Would you like to bring your wife here?"

"Of course, I'd like that," my father replied.

The owner took our address and sent off some money, which he deducted from my father's pay. Soon we arrived — my mother, myself, and my sister.

In Yuzovka I began to go to a real school, but we did not stay for very long, about a year and a half. Then we all went back to Kalinovka.

My father had saved some money, and we returned to live with my grandfather. He received us warmly, for we now had the means to pay for ourselves. I again went off to school, where one of the teachers was Lydia Mikhailovna, the woman whom I remember as my first real teacher.

Lydia Mikhailovna was not a believer, and she never went to church. For this the peasants of the village never forgave her. Although they had great respect for her, the fact that she did not attend church made them feel something was wrong with her.

I remember that I first saw banned books at Lydia's house. Once I called on her and she introduced me to her brother, who was visiting from the city and was lying in bed. Apparently Lydia had spoken favorably about me to him. "This is that boy I told you about. He is asking me for forbidden pamphlets," she said. Her brother smiled and replied, "Give him these. Perhaps he'll make some sense of them, and then when he's grown up he'll remember."

I was very quick at math. I could quickly grasp any problem they threw at me and solve it in my head. I often stood in for Lydia Mikhailovna when she had to go into the city or run her own errands. She trusted me to conduct the math class. I taught basic arithmetic to the other children.

When I finished school, only four years in all, Lydia said, "Nikita, you should study further. Don't stay here in the village; go to the city. A person like you must study. You should become educated."

These words struck a chord deep inside me, but my father's money had run out and my grandfather chased us out of the house again. We ended up in a clay hut with a dirt floor and tiny windows. My grandfather was fond of me. At night he let me sleep above the stove in his log cabin. My father went to the next village to work as a farmhand for the landowner. My mother went too. She was now a laundress and sewed clothes for the other peasant women. I went to work there too, as a shepherd boy. I tended the sheep and received five kopecks a day.

My father soon grew tired of farm work and went back to the mines in Yuzovka. He was an experienced worker and they took him on right away. When he left, he told me that as soon as he had gotten settled he would send money for me to follow him. Sure enough, after a while my father did send some money, and my grandfather took me fifty versts [thirty-three miles] in a horse-drawn cart to the train station. He bought me a ticket and saw me off. I was all of thirteen years old. After transferring twice I arrived in Yuzovka.

Fresh off the train, I asked around and made my way to the mine and to my father. I had long dreamed of becoming a fitter because the work appealed to me. However, first I was sent to apprentice in the boiler shop, with the blacksmiths. I worked for half a year in the shops and was finally offered the choice of becoming a lathe operator or a fitter. I chose fitter. When asked why, I answered, "A lathe operator makes only single parts, while a fitter assembles all the parts and breathes life into the whole machine so that it begins to work."

After brief training, I was given my own vise and tools and began to work in the shops as a fitter. Thus, I became a worker at the age of fifteen. After this my father sent for my mother and sister, and the whole family was together in Yuzovka. I worked in the shops and my father worked in the mines.

It is interesting to note that at the mine there was no financial office, not even a single accountant or payroll clerk. The owner did it all himself. He handed out the pay, calculated production figures, and kept track of it all. He really did control the entire mine, acting as manager, bookkeeper, and cashier. He knew how much each worker should get and he paid them.

Later in life, when I entered the workers' school and first heard about political economy, I immediately grasped the concept of capitalist means of production, recalling everything that went on at the mine. In *Das Kapital*, Marx described exactly the same setup.

I began to read Bolshevik newspapers. First there was the *Zvezda* [Star], and then *Pravda* [Truth]. There were always people handing out papers at the gates to the workshops and mines. I dashed out on my break to buy a paper for five kopecks, and then ran back in to read it in the shop. There was a man named Fomenko who worked with me. He was a revolutionary at heart, a literate man who read forbidden material and who made a great impression on me and my view of the world.

One day Fomenko said to me, "So, Nikita, did you buy your paper?"

"I did," I answered.

"Let's have a look at it," said Fomenko. When I dug into my pocket for the newspaper, it was not there. Instead I found a large hole, through which I had evidently lost the paper walking across the yard.

Fomenko smiled and said, "Nikita, you've learned to buy newspapers but not to take care of your property. That's what you need to work on now, for thrift is one of life's basics."

Working in the mines, and as yet having no contact with Marxists, Bolsheviks, or Social Democrats, I often argued with my coworkers about political issues we learned about reading the newspaper or pamphlets. One day the issue was, "What would you rather have, power or education?" Opinions were split, and the arguments were heated. One of my comrades, who eventually became a prominent Bolshevik, and I both said that we would rather have power, of course. With power, we would take control of the schools. The universities and high schools would be in our hands and we could then easily obtain an education. If we had only education, it would still not mean we had power.

The workers said that I spoke well, and therefore they chose me to act as their spokesman before the owner when they wanted to obtain some improvement or benefit. They often sent me to him with ultimatums because they said I had the courage to stand up to the owner.

One day the shop workers banded together and decided to petition the owner for a pay raise and for time-and-a-half pay for work on holidays and weekends. They chose me to carry their demands. They decided that if the owner did not give them what they wanted, they would walk out.

When I laid everything out for the owner, the head engineer said, "We will not honor your demands."

"Then we'll all walk off the job," I told him.

"Fine, walk off," the engineer answered.

When I returned to the shops and told the workers of the boss's answer, they wavered. I was still single, but many of them had families to support. Many of them decided to stay on the job. I said, "We decided to walk off, and I delivered our ultimatum to the owner. You may stay, but I will leave."

I actually left the mine and soon was hired at another mine, which had no opening for my specialty. I worked as a lift operator, raising and lowering workers through the mine shaft.

My father had a friend who was a shoemaker and who was willing to take me on as an apprentice. He promised my father that he would make a good shoemaker out of me. My father said that being a shoemaker was a good deal: "You've always got a roof over your head and money in your pocket because everyone wears boots, and everyone wants good boots. A shoemaker can always make a good living."

After we moved to Yuzovka my father had another idea — to make me a store clerk. My father liked how polite the clerks in the company store were to workers, always trying to please them and offering them the best goods. In general, there was no one more courteous or more polite to the workers than the clerks. Of course, this attitude toward the workers was meant to make them buy more in the store and that meant more money for the mine owner.

I hated clerks, and it disgusted me to see them run out of the shops on payday. They would grab workers by the arm and buy them drinks, then drag them to their stores so that they would buy something.

When my father said that he wanted me to become a clerk, I categorically refused. I even told my father that if he was going to force me to become a clerk I would leave home. My father did not insist, and I went to work in the mines.

The mine owner's wife was a Frenchwoman who was bored with life in the backwater town of Yuzovka. The owner was Russian and had people to talk to, but his wife was completely alone. She liked to dress well and would mingle with the workers. One day she said to them, "Did you know that the miners at the neighboring mine are striking and demanding an increase in pay? My husband is a fair man, and if he were to see you strike and demand an increase, he would probably give it to you."

Well, the miners took her advice and announced their intention to strike. The owner really was a smart man and said to them, "I'd gladly give you an increase in pay, but the mine owners have an agreement. It says that we shouldn't have differences in wage rates. So if all the owners of mines where there are strikes going on increase their wages, I'll do the same for you. If they don't, then I'm sorry, but I won't increase your wages either." When other striking miners got their raises, the owner of our mine made good on his word and increased wages, but only for men with families; the single men did not get raises.

After the outbreak of World War I, the miners in Yuzovka went out on strike more and more often. They began to fight for better living conditions, better housing, and higher wages. They were often successful. I was not yet politically aware, but I intuitively sided with the Bolsheviks.

At one of the regional conferences in the Donbass to which I was a delegate, I met Kaganovich, who had also come as a delegate from a group of mines.[4] The conference decided to elect one del-

4. Lazar M. Kaganovich (born 1893), a Ukrainian Jew, was Khrushchev's mentor and helped him climb the party ladder and promoted him through the Ukraine and Moscow party apparatus all the way to the Central Committee. Kaganovich was first deputy chairman of the Council of Ministers after Stalin's death, in 1953, and supported Georgi M. Malenkov in the succession struggle. First Secretary

egate from each individual mine to meet at a large conference, which would be conducted by the Bolsheviks in this industrial mining area. This large conference was attended by myself and Kaganovich, who by that time was a party member.

Actually, when I first met Kaganovich his last name was not Kaganovich, but Kantorovich. Much later, when I had become secretary of the party district committee, and Kaganovich was the general secretary of the Ukraine, we ran into each other at a plenum. I recognized him, but his name was different. I was looking at a man that very much resembled the Kantorovich that had visited us in the Donbass. At one of the meetings I asked Kaganovich, "Excuse me, please, but were you ever named Kantorovich?"

He was surprised, and asked, "And did you know someone named Kantorovich?"

"Yes, I did. He visited us once, and we were at some meeting together."

Kaganovich said, "Yes, I really did have the name Kantorovich then. Now my name is Kaganovich; it is my real name."[5]

In the mining region I was widely considered an activist worker and was trusted. One day when I returned home from work, I was told that someone had stopped in from another mine to see me while I was out. The man asked if I could pay him a visit. I got on my bicycle and rode off to the neighboring mine but found that the man was out since he was working the night shift. "All right," I said. "Ask him to meet me at the pond at lunchtime tomorrow, at one o'clock. I will come on my bicycle."

The next day I rode over to the pond and found a man already there, lying on the grass. I walked up to him and said, "Are you so-and-so?"

"Yes," came the answer.

Khrushchev accused Kaganovich of being part of the so-called Antiparty Group in 1957 and expelled him from the Presidium. In 1990 Kaganovich was still living in retirement in a Moscow apartment.

5. In underground revolutionary life, name changes were used to confuse the authorities. Later, Jews within the Communist party often changed their names to appear to be of Russian nationality and avoid anti-Semitic discrimination. In the Soviet Union, Jews are considered a separate nationality. Internal passports list "Jew" as a nationality, similar to Russian, Armenian, and others.

"Were you looking for me?"

"Uh-huh. You're Nikita, right?"

"That's right, I'm Nikita."

"Well," said the man, "I've heard that you are an activist. We need a very trustworthy man who has good handwriting and is very literate. Do you know of anyone?"

"Yes, I know such a person. He works with me in the mine."

"Very well, please ask him to come here tomorrow."

The next day I sent my coworker over and he copied down in his best handwriting the resolution of the Zimmerwald Conference.[6] The copy was run off and distributed to the workers and miners in the Donbass.

That man later, by the way, counted himself as a party member since 1915, because he copied the Zimmerwald resolution. I was known as something of an activist, but I did not become a party member until 1918. When people asked me why I did not join earlier I explained that in those days joining the party was not the same as it is now. No one campaigned or tried to convince you to join. There were many different movements and groups, and it was difficult to keep them all straight.

When the revolution took place I decided on my position immediately. I took the post of deputy secretary to the local party committee.[7] Later, I left Kalinovka to join the army. First, I was a Red Army soldier. Then I was made commissar of a construction platoon, and later of a battalion. As commissar of the construction battalion I was chosen by the troops to take a two-month course for political workers. After completing the course I was appointed a political instructor in the political division of the Ninth Army.

That was about 1922.[8] An order came down that all former work-

6. The Zimmerwald Conference of European socialists, held in Switzerland on September 5, 1915, discussed the importance of peace as a preface to world revolution but did not support Lenin's slogan urging "the transformation of the imperialist war into civil war." See Edward Hallett Carr, *The Bolshevik Revolution*, vol. 3 (London: Pelican Books, 1953), pp. 562–565 and 588–589.

7. Khrushchev refers to his position in the *ukom*, or party committee of the *uyezd*, a district, the lowest administrative unit in Russia at that time.

8. The civil war against the Bolsheviks' efforts to consolidate power continued from 1917 to 1922 and included intervention by Great Britain, France, and the United States after Russia withdrew from World War I in March of 1918. Allied intervention lasted until 1920. Japanese intervention in the Far East began in December 1917 and continued until October 1922.

ers and miners in the coal region were to be demobilized and returned to their mines. I was included. In the division headquarters, a clerk said to me, "So, you're a miner? Good. You can go with the working army, as commissar of a labor brigade. You are just what we need at the moment — a commissar!"

At first I resisted the assignment. The clerk and I swore at each other. "Who do you think you are?" I shouted.

"And who do you think you are?" he replied.

I ended up going. The living and working conditions were terrible. There were no uniforms and no changes of clothes. The men went unwashed and unshaven and were overworked. There was not enough food.

At that time I was living with a peasant family — not exactly rich, but well-off. I stayed in their house, where I had my own small room in the back. There was little food and I went hungry. Food was so scarce that I began to starve and my body began to swell.

The peasant family — father, mother, son, and daughter-in-law — were usually eating when I returned from work. I tried to come back as late as possible so as not to whet my appetite too much. One evening when I returned home, the son came to my room and said, "You know, we see that you are starving. My wife and I made you some food. Here, please eat." I refused at first but then ate hungrily.

The couple, the wealthy peasant's son and daughter-in-law, continued to feed me every evening. Sometimes it was kasha, sometimes milk and bread. Thanks to them I slowly began to regain some of my strength.

On the day before a holiday — I think it was May Day — the command center sent the labor brigade an official commendation for work well done. The commander and I thought hard and decided not to call the men together just to announce the message of appreciation, because there was nothing to eat and they were so weak and poorly dressed. Instead, we decided to bring the men together the following day to celebrate the holiday and announce the command center's commendation then. In reality, a better form of thanks would have been to send the men new shirts or more bread.

Soon after that came an order to transfer to another area, along with a supply of new uniforms. The men were loaded into troop trains and were off.

A friend of mine who had become the director of a mine in Yuzovka invited me to come to the mine and work. "Just get over here and we'll take care of the rest," he said. I left the labor brigade and went to the mine. Eventually I became the mine's deputy director. That was sometime in 1923. About this time one of the mine directors in the Donbass came up with the idea of establishing a mining institute in Yuzovka. The institute did not come into being immediately, and it was decided to establish some kind of worker training program. I applied to my superiors to be allowed to participate in the program, but at the same time they appointed me director of the mine. I firmly refused the appointment, but the managers wouldn't give in.

I went to the director of mines for the Donbass, who had also applied for a program, and said, "You are an educated man, you've finished high school, and now you have applied to study at the mining institute. But you won't let me go. I don't think that's right. Why won't you let me go? I've finished only four years of school, and can add, subtract, multiply, and divide. You're educated and are going to study further, but you won't let me continue my education." As a result of all my urging, I was allowed to attend the worker training program in 1923 in the Donbass.[9]

9. From Yuzovka, Khrushchev moved to the Ukraine party apparatus with the help of Kaganovich and then on to Moscow, where he rose through the party ranks in the 1930s. See the appendix for a chronology of Khrushchev's career.

2

The Great Terror and the Twentieth Party Congress

I saw Stalin's wife, Nadezhda Sergeyevna Alliluyeva, before her end. It was, I think, at the celebration for the October Revolution.[1]

There was a parade, and I was standing by the Lenin mausoleum with a group of Moscow city party activists. Alliluyeva was there too. We were standing next to each other and we talked to each other. It was a cold, windy day. As usual, Stalin was wearing his military greatcoat. The upper button was left open. I remember she glanced at him and said, "My man didn't take his scarf. He will catch cold and get sick." I could tell from the way she said this that she was in good humor. At the end of the parade I went home.[2]

The next day Kaganovich invited the party secretaries for a meeting and said that Nadezhda Sergeyevna had died suddenly. I asked myself, "How can it be? I just talked to her. Such a beautiful woman." However, it happens, people die.

Then again, in a day or two, Kaganovich gathered the same group and said, "I'm speaking on Stalin's behalf. He asked me to bring you together and tell you what happened. She did not die

1. Nadezhda Sergeyevna Alliluyeva, Stalin's second wife, died on November 9, 1932. (The October Revolution took place on October 25, 1917, under the Old Style calendar, then in effect in Russia. When the Gregorian calendar, used throughout Europe and the United States, was adopted by Russia in 1918, the anniversary of the revolution became November 7.)

2. Khrushchev knew her as Nadya when they both attended the Industrial Academy in Moscow in 1929–1930. Alliluyeva studied textile chemistry and was a party group organizer. Khrushchev was secretary of the party organization. Khrushchev considered Nadya's favorable reports on him to Stalin "my lucky lottery ticket," which helped him escape the purges and rise in the party hierarchy.

naturally. She committed suicide." Of course, in front of the group he didn't go into details, and we didn't ask him anything.

We buried her. Stalin seemed to be suffering at the graveside. I do not know how he felt inside, but outwardly he mourned.

It was later, after Stalin's death, that the cause of her death became known to me. Of course, this is not documented. We just asked Vlasik, chief of Stalin's bodyguards, what caused Nadezhda Sergeyevna's death.[3] He said that after the parade everybody went to Voroshilov's big apartment for dinner. After parades they always went to Voroshilov's to eat.[4]

It was a limited group of people: the marshal of the parade and members of the Politburo and a few others. They went there directly from Red Square. In those days parades and demonstrations lasted for a very long time. Everyone drank at the dinner, of course, as is the custom in such cases. Stalin was alone there. Finally, everyone left. So did Stalin. But he didn't go home.

It was late. Who knows what time it was. Nadezhda Sergeyevna got worried: "Where is Stalin?" She started searching for him by phoning out to the dacha in Zubalovo [outside Moscow] — not where Kaganovich's dacha is now and not where Mikoyan lived recently, but another half kilometer, across the ravine. So, she called there and asked the duty officer, "Is Stalin there?"

"Yes," he answered, "Comrade Stalin is here."

"Who is with him?"

He named the woman.

3. Nikolai Vlasik, Stalin's first and most enduring bodyguard, began his Red Army career sleeping outside Stalin's door and rose to the rank of lieutenant general. A short, uneducated peasant, Vlasik was barely literate and was infamous for eliminating Stalin's "enemies" and for holding parties in his apartment on Gorky Street with naked women and "so many bottles of wine they said a truck was needed to carry them away in the morning," according to a former Kremlin Guards officer, Peter Deriabin.

4. Kliment Y. Voroshilov (1881–1969) was people's commissar of military and naval affairs at the time. He was a cult figure used to promote the Red Army, "the first Red officer." A political general rather than a professional soldier, he was blamed for the heavy losses sustained by the Soviet Union in the Winter War of 1939–1940 against Finland and for the failure of the Red Army to adequately prepare for World War II. He was demoted and kept on by Stalin "as a whipping boy," according to Khrushchev. After Stalin's death, Voroshilov was elected chairman of the Presidium of the USSR Supreme Soviet, a post he held until he retired on the grounds of ill health in 1960.

In the morning — I don't know exactly when — Stalin came home and Nadezhda Sergeyevna was no longer alive.

She didn't leave a note; or if there was one, it never was revealed to us.

The other woman was the wife of Gusev, who had also been present at the dinner. When Stalin left he took Gusev's wife with him. Gusev was from the military, but I didn't know him, nor do I remember meeting his wife.[5] Mikoyan told me she was a very beautiful woman.[6]

So Stalin was sleeping with her there at the dacha, and Alliluyeva learned that from the duty officer. Vlasik said, "The duty officer was a fool, inexperienced. She asked him and he just told her everything."

Well, later there were rumors that maybe Stalin killed her. I heard these stories, and Stalin, of course, knew about them from his agents. In a word, this side of the story is not clear, but the other side seems to be more certain. Although Vlasik might have been misinformed, he was, after all, a bodyguard.

How did Stalin and Nadezhda Sergeyevna get along? I can only judge on the basis of some things I heard. Sometimes when Stalin was a little drunk he would tell us: "I lock myself in my bedroom, and she knocks on the door and cries, 'You are an impossible man. It is impossible to live with you!' But I just lock the door and sit there while she continues to call me rude, callous, and inhuman."

He also told us that when little Svetlanka got cross at him she

5. There were at least three Gusevs of importance in the military at this time. Sergei Ivanovich Gusev (1874–1933) — his real name was Yakov Davidovich Drabkin — was a colleague of Lenin's and an outstanding military leader of the revolution. When he died, in 1933, he was buried with military honors in Red Square. During the purges his name was expunged from the history of the party and the civil war, and it remained so until his rehabilitation in 1964.

Dmitri N. Gusev (1894–1957) was an instructor at the Frunze Military Academy.

Nikolai I. Gusev (1897–1962) served on the general staff.

6. Anastas I. Mikoyan (1895–1978), the most powerful Armenian in the Soviet Union, was known in the West as the Soviet Union's top traveling salesman. People's commissar of internal trade, and later of foreign trade, he toured the United States to study food production methods in 1936 and again in 1959. Mikoyan fell out of favor with Stalin during the dictator's final years, but he remained close to Khrushchev and rose quickly with Khrushchev as a powerful Politburo adviser. His son, Sergo, and Khrushchev's son Sergei are close friends.

repeated her mother's words that she heard once: "I will complain against you."[7]

"Who are you going to complain to?" Stalin asked.

"To the cook," Svetlanka replied.

I also remember once coming to Stalin's after Nadezhda's death and seeing a beautiful young woman with dark skin there. She was from the Caucasus. When I entered, she disappeared like a mouse. I was told later that she was a tutor for Stalin's children; but she was not there for long. Later she vanished. She was there on Beria's recommendation. Beria knew how to pick tutors.[8]

THE early years were romantic times, but now a petit bourgeois mentality had taken over the party. In those days we did not have thoughts about dachas and fancy clothes. All our time was spent on work. There was no time to read. Molotov asked me: "Comrade Khrushchev, do you have time for reading?" No, I replied. Molotov confessed that he didn't have time for reading either.[9]

The Trotskyites had been ousted from the party, so they did not have to spend time on party activities. Therefore, they obtained better academic degrees. As a result, Stalin grew critical and

7. Svetlanka is the diminutive for Svetlana, the name of Stalin's daughter. Svetlana Alliluyeva defected in 1967 to the United States, where she wrote a best-selling autobiography, *Twenty Letters to a Friend*. She said she never wanted to return to the "profoundly corrupt" Soviet system. Unhappy in Wisconsin, where she married American architect William Peters, she moved to Cambridge, England, in 1982 with their daughter, Olga. In 1984 Svetlana regained her Soviet citizenship in Moscow and said she had never had a happy day in America. By December 1985, however, she petitioned Mikhail Gorbachev to leave the Soviet Union again, and in April 1986 she returned to America. Since 1986 she has lived in England and in Spring Green, Wisconsin.

8. Lavrenty P. Beria (1899–1953) was promoted by Stalin as a reliable Georgian informer and inquisitor to be head of the secret police during the late 1930s and World War II. Beria fully deserved his reputation as Stalin's bloody right hand. A shocking number of his sexual crimes against young women were exposed when Beria was tried and executed after Stalin's death.

9. Vyacheslav M. Molotov (1890–1986) was born with the name Scriabin. He took the name "Hammer" as a young revolutionary and attached himself to Stalin from the early days. Lenin once called him "the best filing clerk in Russia." He became foreign minister in 1939 and was known for his stubbornness as a negotiator and his obsequious behavior before Stalin. After Stalin's death he opposed Khrushchev, and he was ousted in 1957 as a member of the Antiparty Group.

vengeful toward them. He kept saying: "Why do they have this privilege of a better education?" At the same time, within the party apparatus there was the appearance of disrespect, even contempt for educated people. "Only idlers have a higher education," was the standard saying.

I remember there was a clash between two lines on how to develop Moscow. The rightists emphasized the importance of providing Moscow with consumer goods, so they were called "cotton cloth Muscovites." My group wanted to emphasize the development of the city as an example of construction and industrialization.

As early as the 1930s there were agents and informers who provided the party and the militia with information on what people were saying about the party line and party functionaries.

I remember that at the Seventeenth Party Congress [in 1934] I watched how Stalin voted. Very demonstratively, in front of everyone, he took the ballots with the candidates' names for the Central Committee and, without even glancing at them, went up to the box and dropped them in. This was particularly striking to me. I only later realized that not a single one of those candidates would have been named without Stalin's blessing.

I remember something else that made a striking impression on me. Before the voting, Kaganovich instructed us, the relative newcomers to Moscow, on how we should treat the candidates' ballots. Of course, this was strictly confidential, a secret session, so that others would not get wind of what we were up to. Kaganovich suggested, for example, that we cross out so-and-so, and so-and-so. He was on bad terms with Molotov and Voroshilov, so he asked us to cross their names off the ballots. He said this was to ensure that Stalin did not receive fewer votes than either Molotov or Voroshilov, or any other Politburo members, if there happened to be any votes against Stalin.

We understood this politically, but it left me with a distinct bad taste in my mouth. How could this happen in a collective like ours, such a select group? Kaganovich was a member of the Politburo; he was secretary of the Central Committee and responsible for the Commissariat of Transportation. To think that such an authority figure would suddenly ask us to do something so unworthy of a party member! Voting as ordered, in other words.

It was an unfortunate moment and one that caused considerable discussion among those of us who were trying to understand the situation. I was especially concerned, and Misha Katzenelenbogen was very open with me. He was a very intelligent man and was then secretary of a regional central committee and involved in agriculture. He was Jewish, and as they say, Jews don't know anything about agriculture. But Katzenelenbogen — Stalin changed his name for him to Mikhailov — was very capable when it came to agricultural issues. I had a great deal of respect for him. Katzenelcnbogen was, in my eyes, an authority on the ins and outs of party politics. I admit I was a bit of a hick, while he was more experienced and had spent more time hanging around with the Moscow bunch than I had. So he tried to explain things to me.

In examining the start of the purges, the Shvernik Commission[10] also showed interest in how the voting was carried out at the Seventeenth Party Congress and whether the votes were "cooked." The Shvernik Commission investigated whether the results reported by the counting commission corresponded to reality, or whether there were some other results. Some of the members of the counting commission had managed to stay alive, and they were questioned.

One name remains in my memory — that of Comrade Adreasian. I knew him well. He worked as the secretary of the Oktyabrsky region party committee in Moscow at the same time that I was secretary of the Krasnaya Presnya party committee and then later, when I was the secretary of the Moscow city party committee. Comrade Adreasian was a close friend of Comrade Mikoyan. They attended the theological seminary together before the revolution. Adreasian did his share of time in the camps of Siberia, for fifteen or sixteen years.

10. In 1956 Nikolai M. Shvernik, chairman of the Party Control Commission, was named to head a special commission of the Central Committee of the Communist Party of the Soviet Union to investigate the 1934 murder of Sergei Mironovich Kirov, Leningrad first secretary, which triggered the purges. The investigation lasted several years, and according to Roy Medvedev, *Let History Judge* (New York: Columbia University Press, 1989), p. 335, more than three thousand people were interviewed. A document summarizing the commission's conclusions was prepared but never published. According to a member of the commission, when Khrushchev read the conclusions he locked the document in his safe and said: "As long as imperialism exists in the world, we will not be able to publish this document."

The members of the counting commission at the Seventeenth Party Congress said that the number of votes cast against Stalin was not 6 as had been reported to the congress, but 160 or 260 votes. I do not remember exactly, but both numbers were too big for Stalin to swallow, particularly if you take into account Stalin's position, his character, and his vanity. Yet only 6 negative votes were declared.

Who interfered with the counting? Without Stalin's approval nobody would dare to do such a thing. So everything falls into place. Stalin was a clever man. He understood who might cast the votes against him at the Seventeenth Party Congress. Only the cadres from Lenin's time could have voted against him. He could not possibly believe that Khrushchev, or the likes of Khrushchev — young cadres, who rose through the ranks under Stalin and who deified him, hanging on his every word — would vote against him. However, the older cadres who had known Lenin well, and in whose memory Lenin's testament was still fresh, could not tolerate the situation. Stalin, by the time of the Seventeenth Party Congress, had gained so much strength that he stopped paying attention to the old cadres and started showing his true character, about which Vladimir Ilyich Lenin had warned in his testament.[11]

Stalin understood that the old cadres who were in the leadership were displeased with him and wanted to replace him. At the Seventeenth Party Congress the secretary of the North Caucasus territory, B. P. Sheboldaev, went to see Kirov. I knew Sheboldaev but was not close to him. I knew him as a party secretary, as an old Bolshevik and an important politician. They used to tell about his significant role in 1917 in the czar's army on the Turkish front, where he carried out active party work among the soldiers.

11. Lenin's testament is the letters he wrote in 1923, when he tried to head off a split in the party after his death. The relevant passages: "Comrade Stalin, having become general secretary, has concentrated enormous power in his hands; and I am not sure that he always knows how to use that power with sufficient caution. . . . Stalin is too rude, and this fault, entirely supportable in relations among us Communists, becomes insupportable in the office of general secretary. Therefore, I propose to the comrades to find a way to remove Stalin from that position and appoint to it another man who in all respects differs from Stalin in one superiority — namely, that he be more tolerant, more loyal, more polite, and more considerate to comrades, less capricious."

So this Comrade Sheboldaev said confidentially, "Kiroi" — that's what Kirov was called by the people close to him — "there is talk among Lenin's old cadres that the time has come to return to Lenin's testament. We must move Stalin to some other position, as Lenin recommended. We must put in his place a man who will treat those around him more decently. The people in our circle say that you should be made the general secretary." The report of such a story was given to the Shvernik Commission and to the Central Committee. How Kirov responded, I don't know. But the report continued that Kirov went to Stalin and told him all about the talk with Sheboldaev. Stalin was said to have listened and replied simply, "Thank you, Comrade Kirov."

Such a curt statement by Stalin was typical of his character. In this "thank you" there was no hint of whether he was really thanking Kirov or threatening him. So that was the end.

This was just one of the episodes that became known to us in the course of the investigation into the origins of the extermination of party and other cadres in 1937, 1938, and 1939. This episode, however, helps to draw back the curtain on how the meat grinder got started.[12]

The Shvernik Commission decided to inquire into Nikolayev, the murderer, in order to understand what motivated him.[13] They checked his background, how he committed the crime, and all the documents that were left. One thing in the commission report stuck in my memory and excited me tremendously. Shortly before he shot Kirov, Nikolayev was arrested by Chekists outside the Smolny Institute, where Kirov's office was located. The square was closely guarded because it was frequented by members of the Politburo and the leadership of the Leningrad city and regional party committees. Probably, Nikolayev looked suspicious to the guard. He was arrested, searched, and found to be carrying a gun.

12. B. P. Sheboldaev was arrested and shot in 1937 when Stalin decided that the North Caucasus territory party organization headed by Sheboldaev was not reliable. See Roy Medvedev, *Let History Judge*, p. 669.

13. Leonid Vasilievich Nikolayev was a disgruntled, thirty-year-old Communist party member; he was arrested on two occasions with a loaded revolver in his briefcase and released before he shot Kirov in the back of the neck at 4:30 P.M. on December 1, 1934, killing him. See Roy Medvedev, *Let History Judge*, pp. 334–346, and Robert Conquest, *Stalin and the Kirov Murder* (New York: Oxford University Press, 1989), pp. 7–13.

In spite of this incriminating evidence, he was released. I pay special attention to this. How could it happen?[14]

When Nikolayev later shot Kirov, he actually penetrated Smolny through the doorway that was used only by Kirov. Nikolayev killed Kirov on the landing as he was coming up the stairway. His bodyguard had lagged behind. So Nikolayev must have been given access to Smolny. He was probably sent to the square to commit the terrorist act by some high-ranking people, but he was arrested by low-ranking people from the same organization who, understandably, had not been informed. He was then released on an order from the top.

When the commission continued its investigation we received a report that shocked me and all the members of the government. The commission came across a rumor that when Stalin demanded that Nikolayev be brought before him — with Molotov and Voroshilov present — Nikolayev fell to his knees and told Stalin that he had acted on orders. That this actually happened is difficult for me to accept, and equally difficult to deny. He no doubt carried out an order. Of course, there are no documents concerning this.

This rumor, reported by the Shvernik Commission, that Nikolayev begged for mercy on the basis that he was following orders, has a certain logic. After all, Nikolayev was not a big man. Maybe he figured he would be allowed to live because he had only carried out his mission. He was a fool, because in order for the mission to remain really secret he had to be exterminated. Nikolayev was exterminated.

As I say, according to the same rumor, Voroshilov and Molotov were there when Nikolayev told Stalin he had acted on orders; but we were not so naive as to ask Voroshilov and Molotov if that was so. They both would have angrily denied it, because otherwise they would be admitting their participation in the plot and in the murder of Kirov. They were not stupid enough to admit that, and we were not so naive as to ask.

But I do know this: when Stalin, Voroshilov, and Molotov were in Leningrad to investigate Kirov's murder, Stalin ordered the

14. At the Twenty-second Party Congress, in 1961, Khrushchev said publicly that Nikolayev was arrested twice with weapons on him and then released "upon someone's instructions." Khrushchev described the circumstances of Kirov's murder but drew no conclusions.

commissar who was personally responsible for guarding Kirov that day to be brought to him for interrogation. I think the newspapers reported it — in any case party activists were told — that when they took this commissar to Stalin the truck crashed into a house and the commissar was killed. Something went wrong with the steering.

Much later, when our commission started its investigation, attention was drawn to the accident. It was recommended that the commission question the people who were escorting the commissar. We wanted them to tell us about the circumstances of the accident. They started looking for the three men who had been in the truck escorting him, two in the back with Kirov's bodyguard, one up front in the cab with the driver. It turned out that the three were not alive anymore. They had been shot. This aroused still more suspicion in us. We were convinced that it hadn't occurred by chance. I remember suggesting, "Shouldn't you look for the driver?" But I held no hope of finding him when I saw how the whole affair had been organized. No doubt the driver had been dealt with too.

Fortunately, as it turned out, the driver was alive after all, and we questioned him. He gave us all the details. "We were on the way, myself and a Chekist sitting next to me. All the time he urged me to go faster so we could deliver the arrested man sooner. At a certain street, while turning, or maybe without turning, I do not know, he tried to grab the wheel out of my hands and steer the truck into the corner of a house. I was young then and strong. I grabbed the wheel back from him. We only dented the fender. There was no accident, but I heard a thump behind us in the back of the truck. Later they said that during the accident the arrested commissar died."

I was astonished. Sometimes a murder is carefully plotted but not everything is foreseen and a trace is left. As a result, the whole crime is unraveled. That's the case with the driver.

Then we started looking for [F. D.] Medved, the NKVD head for the Leningrad region, on the chance that he would tell us something.[15] They say he was Kirov's closest friend. They used to go hunting together, and their families were friendly. We found out

15. NKVD is the Russian abbreviation for the People's Commissariat of Internal Affairs, which handled all police matters, including state security, at that time.

that Medved had been exiled somewhere in the north. He was not guilty of any particular crime, he was just in exile. Later, he was shot. This also shed some light. Here was a man close to Kirov who probably had some theories of his own concerning Kirov's murder.

Later, the commission reported to me that one of the medical workers in a labor camp hospital in the north, where Medved was treated, had received some kind of message to pass on to the organs [common euphemism for secret police] because Medved said he feared he would be exterminated. He wanted his knowledge — his secret — to be known. However, the commission failed to find the person with whom he talked. His prediction came true. Medved really was shot.

And Nikolayev, who was he connected with? They used to say that he was once a Trotskyite. The Shvernik Commission had ample opportunity to review all kinds of documents concerning Nikolayev's connections, but they did not find the Trotskyite charge to be true.

I do not think, of course, that Stalin directly, personally, ordered Nikolayev to kill Kirov. No, Nikolayev was too small for that, but I have no doubt that Stalin was behind the plot. This murder had been organized from the top.

I think that it was organized by Yagoda on Stalin's instructions. Secret instructions one-on-one, from Stalin's mouth to Yagoda's ear, so that nobody would know anything. That's how it was.[16]

Now I come to the main question. Why did Stalin choose Kirov to be murdered? It was absolutely clear to me. Kirov was a person close to Stalin, close in the sense that he was sent to Leningrad after the Zinoviev opposition, which was supported for the most part by the Leningrad party organization, had been defeated.[17]

16. Genrikh Grigorevich Yagoda was chairman of the NKVD from 1934 to 1936. He had the dubious distinction of managing the first great treason trial (that of Zinoviev and Kamenev in 1936) and introducing an organized forced labor system to construct the White Sea Canal. In September 1936, Yagoda was arrested and charged with conspiracy, espionage, and treason. He was shot in March 1938.

17. Grigory Yevseyevich Zinoviev was a key organizer of the Bolsheviks under Lenin. Although he opposed Lenin's policy of a Bolshevik seizure of power, Zinoviev held high party positions. In the internal power struggle after Lenin's death, Zinoviev, whose power was in Leningrad, was ousted by Stalin and deprived of all his offices. He was sentenced to ten years in prison for "moral complicity" in the assassination of Kirov and was tried again at the show trials

Kirov fulfilled an important mission in Leningrad, turning the party organization into a good, active group that served as a support for the Central Committee and fully implemented its decisions and those of the Seventeenth Party Congress. Kirov deservedly got credit for this. Kirov knew how to handle people. He was a brilliant orator who worked as hard as he could for the party and for Lenin's ideas. Kirov was very popular with the party and the people. Therefore, a blow against Kirov would hurt the party and the people.

That's probably why Kirov was marked for sacrifice. Kirov's death would provide a pretext for shaking up the country and getting rid of the undesirables who were out of favor with Stalin. How to get rid of them? By calling them "enemies of the people" and accusing them of "raising their hands against Kirov." That was the phrase used later when they were arrested. So Kirov's death was needed for Stalin to take the law into his own hands and crush the old Bolsheviks. Then he broadened the purge further to include the leadership of the party, economy, and army, as well as ordinary people.

Stalin used Kirov's death to alarm the country, to make it accept the terror so that he could annihilate the flower of our Communist party, our army, our Soviet intelligentsia, and ordinary people as well. So many people were eliminated that Stalin nearly destroyed us.

My transfer from the Ukraine [back] to Moscow [in 1949] was a continuation of this. Stalin told me directly: "Things are going badly here. In Leningrad we have treason. And in Moscow we are in bad shape too. We want to have real support for the Central Committee in Moscow. We're requesting your transfer from the Ukraine. You've had enough of the Ukraine, you've been sitting there too long. You've turned into the chief agronomist of the Ukraine. Come to Moscow, you are needed more here."

I went to work in Moscow as the Moscow party committee secretary and I was also made a Central Committee secretary. Stalin immediately handed me a document that was evidently fabricated,

---

before his execution in 1936. L. B. Kamenev, another high-ranking party official, was a skilled theorist and the first editor of Lenin's *Collected Works*.

despite the signatures on it. The document said there was a plot in Moscow against Stalin and the leadership. It was exactly as it had been in Leningrad, where the investigation started and where they were preparing a trial.[18] Actually, a trial in Stalin's time was no trial at all. It was an execution, a torture chamber. In Moscow the "plot" was supposedly headed by G. M. Popov, a Central Committee secretary and the secretary of the Moscow party committee. Later he was chairman of the Moscow City Council. I took over everything from him.

When I familiarized myself with the document, I told Stalin that it was a fabrication. "In any case," I said, "the people who are named in this document as part of the plot are, I am sure, the most honest and devoted Communists. Therefore, this is a provocation." I was so certain when I spoke to Stalin that it soothed him and there was no action taken as a result of this document.

But it would have been enough for me to say only one thing in response to Stalin's question "Have you familiarized yourself with the document?"

"Yes, I have," I could have replied.

"Well, what do you think?" This is what Stalin would usually ask, looking into your eyes.

"Yes, this is a serious document, a very serious document," I could have said, and of course those people would have been immediately arrested. The interrogations would have started, and in a day or two they would have confessed that they were agents of foreign countries. Then a trial would start. It would not stop with a trial, because Stalin's paranoia was inflamed, the meat grinder would have started to turn.

People may say, "Here is Khrushchev puffing himself up again." But I am genuinely, and with all honesty, expressing my opinion without trying to exaggerate. I knew Stalin well, and I am absolutely sure it would have happened exactly the way I describe it.

I remember when Stalin told me that sticks should be given to workers to beat the Jews who he insisted were behind the strike

18. The Leningrad Affair, in 1949–1950, was yet another of the purges that marked the last years of Stalin's life. Politburo member N. A. Voznesensky and A. A. Kuznetsov, secretary of the Central Committee, were shot. About three

in a Moscow factory. Stalin was a dyed-in-the-wool anti-Semite. He gave me direct instructions to make short work of the Jews in the Moscow party organization. If I had followed these orders it might have happened. But there was something that held Stalin back. It was probably world public opinion. It would have been too dirty an affair.

The terror was bad enough as it was. Like thunder out of the clear blue sky came the arrests of Tukhachevsky, Yakir, and Uborevich, followed by the commander of the Moscow military district, a Lithuanian, a good leader, a colonel in the old army. We all thought he was a good Communist.[19]

It was quite a psychological blow. I knew Yakir very well and was close to him. He worked in the Ukraine and I would meet him in the Donbass at party or republic conferences, or at party congresses for the Ukraine. When I worked in Kiev during 1928–1929, the city was considered to be quite important militarily because it was essentially a border city. Yakir traveled frequently to Kiev and let me in on what he was doing. Now all of a sudden Yakir was a traitor, an enemy of the people.

When I went to work in Moscow [in the 1930s], I got to know Comrade Semyon Zakharovich Korytny, who was already there. He had worked in Kiev at the same time as I had and later, when I was secretary at Krasnaya Presnya, he was elected head of the organizational department of the Krasnaya Presnya regional committee.

When I was elected second secretary of the Moscow city committee, Korytny, I believe, became secretary of the Krasnaya Presnya regional committee. Later he was a secretary of the city party committee. It was here that he was arrested and also met his end. He was a very good and exceedingly loyal man, an able worker.

Korytny was married to Yakir's sister. She is still living but is very ill. She is a wonderful woman. Whenever Yakir would visit

---

thousand senior Leningrad party members were arrested and many were shot. See Robert Conquest, *The Great Terror* (New York: Macmillan, 1968), p. 498.

19. The first arrests were in late 1936 and early 1937. Marshal Mikhail Tukhachevsky, a brilliant organizer and strategist, was deputy people's commissar of defense. General Iona Yakir, a civil war hero and recognized talent, was commander of the Kiev special military district. General I. P. Uborevich, a civil war hero, was commander of the Byelorussian military district at the time of his arrest.

the city, he would drop in on his sister. We would all go out to Korytny's dacha. I was living at that time at a dacha in Ogarevo [outside Moscow]. A few days before his arrest Yakir was in Moscow. He and I had walked and talked for a long time. He was basically a good comrade. I simply could not fathom it. How could he be an enemy of the people? Yet at the same time I chastised myself for having spent so much time with him and not having been able to spot him. But Stalin could see it all clearly!

Stalin himself had high praise and much respect for Yakir. I know that for a fact. Yakir had a note from Stalin. Stalin was very stingy with written compliments. But somehow, I was told, he considered Yakir worthy of a handwritten note praising his personal qualities. Yakir deserved it. He really was a decent man.

I also had great respect for Tukhachevsky. He summoned me once — invited me, actually, since neither of us was in a subservient position with respect to the other. I remember him saying, "What do you say we go see some new machinery?" We went and both saw for the first time a conveyor-belt excavating machine. Tukhachevsky impressed me then. I felt he was the soul of the army. It seemed to me that if anyone in the armed forces knew his job, it was Tukhachevsky and [Yan] Gamarnik. Gamarnik was first deputy of the Peoples' Commissariat for War and specialized in military economics, logistics, and military construction. It was common knowledge that the location for building the city of Komsomolsk-na-Amure had been chosen on Gamarnik's initiative. After traveling to the Soviet Far East he recommended to Stalin the establishment of a base in case of war with Japan.

Now suddenly Yakir, Gamarnik, and this whole group were enemies of the people. We could not believe that they were just the victims of slander. After all, there was an investigation, and a trial involving very authoritative figures. Marshal Yegorov was among the judges. Later he too would fall victim to the excesses.[20]

When the cases of Moscow party members and nonmembers were being discussed and their sentences were being reviewed,

20. Yakir's arrest, trial, and hasty execution along with Tukhachevsky and other important generals was announced in the press on June 11, 1937. Marshal A. I. Yegorov, chief of the general staff and a hero of the revolution, was arrested and killed in the next round of assaults on the military command, which took place in the second half of 1937 and 1938.

there was only one man who spoke out in their defense. His name was Aleksei Viktorovich Shchusev. I knew him well and respected him. He was a fascinating man, although most of us viewed him with a great deal of skepticism. We considered him an old czarist architect because he had built churches on appointment to the czar. We felt he could not have changed since then. Shchusev had quite a quick tongue. He said exactly what he thought, but what he said did not always change the way people thought or felt.

When calls were made at a party meeting for condemnation and appropriate sentencing, Shchusev stood up and said: "So a suggestion has been made to condemn Yakir. I personally am from Kishinev, and I knew Yakir's uncle, who was a doctor and a very respectable gentleman. So I cannot accept that this man's relative is a criminal." This was most unusual back then.

I have to admit that at the time I was indignant. It would be easiest for me to say today that in my heart I sympathized with Shchusev, but that's not true; I did not. As far as I was concerned, Stalin's word was law. We were all convinced that Stalin could do no wrong. We were outraged and condemned those arrested.

In the Moscow area we had a secretary of the Komsomol [Young Communist League] regional committee whom I really liked. He was a young man, lively and full of enthusiasm, an excellent organizer who fit right in. One morning when I came in to work, I was told that this secretary had gone hunting — it was springtime — and had accidentally shot himself. I was very sorry for him and was at a loss to understand how such a thing could have happened.

I called Stalin right away. I told him that we had just had some unfortunate news, that a very good secretary in the Komsomol regional committee had shot himself. Stalin answered calmly, "That's understandable. He did it because Kosarev has been arrested." Kosarev was the secretary of the Komsomol central committee. Stalin may even have told me that the arrest of our secretary had been around the corner.

Now I was really shocked. In the first place, Kosarev was someone I felt to be above suspicion. He was a young man from a working-class family and he was a worker himself, employed at a Moscow factory. Suddenly Kosarev too was an enemy of the people. How could it be? What turned him into an enemy of the people? Still, no one expressed suspicion that anything was amiss, or that a mistake had been made. If the Central Committee, or Stalin, did something, it was irreversible and therefore was based on reality. It weighed heavy on my heart that the capitalist countries' intelligence had penetrated so deep into the party and the Komsomol, infecting even the leadership. Kosarev was considered the leader of the entire Komsomol.[21]

Events began to unfold quickly after that. I remember learning suddenly that Jan Rudzutak, a respected candidate [nonvoting] member of the Politburo and a pleasant person, was arrested. He had been very accessible as a Politburo member, always agreeing to come to city and regional meetings or to meetings at factories whenever we asked.[22]

Nineteen thirty-seven was a hard year. It was to have been the year for elections in all the party organizations. The meetings tended to be very lively, even heated. The party was already completely demoralized. I am speaking of the leadership below the level of the Central Committee. Managers did not feel they were managers. There were verbal instructions that all candidates for party leadership positions had to be checked out before they could appear on the ballot. Were they associated with any enemy of the people — that is, with anyone arrested as an enemy of the people? In other words, the secret police, the Chekists, had to give candidates the stamp of approval. It followed that candidates were basically installed rather than voted in, from the point of view of intraparty democracy. The Chekists were supposed to be under the control of the party, yet it was turning out just exactly the opposite. The Chekists were beginning to control the party and its elected bodies. But screening for a party position by the Chekists was no guarantee, because those cleared by the NKVD might still be arrested the next morning and perish without a trace.

It was also mandated that all candidates for lower-level elected

21. Aleksandr Kosarev was denounced for obstructing the war against enemies of the people in 1938. He was arrested, given a fifteen-minute trial, considered lengthy during the Great Terror, and executed.

22. Rudzutak repudiated his confession at his trial before the Military Collegium of the Supreme Court. His counteraccusations and his affirmation of total loyalty went unanswered. Stalin refused to talk with him and he was shot. Rudzutak's repudiation of his confession was read by Khrushchev in his secret speech to the Twentieth Party Congress, in 1956.

offices had to be approved by the upper-level party offices. This meant that the upper-ups went over the lists of candidates, with the help of the Chekists, before voting took place.

There was one sad instance, I remember, during a Moscow party conference. I made a summary report, then there were debates. The conference participants had all been very involved and full of ideas, despite the trying times. The prevalent view was that we had reached a stage in our development where our enemies and the capitalist intelligence agencies had been unable to break us through direct efforts from the outside, so they must be making every effort to infiltrate and destroy us from within — by recruiting party members, by planting their own people, and so on.

The insubstantial nature of these arguments was clear, because the members who suffered the most were the oldest ones, those who had been through the underground or the first years of the revolution and the civil war. It made no sense, therefore, that these individuals would have succumbed to temptation and been recruited by foreign intelligence.

While I can say this now, I didn't speak at all at the time. I saw everything through the eyes of the Central Committee — that is, through Stalin's eyes. I also spoke with his mouth. I would repeat what I heard from him.

One day, probably in 1937, Comrade Stalin called me up and said, "Come to the Kremlin. There are some Ukrainians here, and I'd like you to show them the city." I went over to the Kremlin right away and sure enough, there were Kosior, Postyshev, and Lyubchenko. Lyubchenko was already chairman of the people's commissars in the Ukraine; he had replaced Chubar. Chubar had come to work in Moscow, where he was deputy chairman of the Council of People's Commissars, Molotov's deputy.[23]

"So," said Stalin, "they'd like to see Moscow. Let's take them

23. S. V. Kosior had been first secretary of the Ukrainian party since 1928. P. P. Postyshev was second secretary of the Ukrainian party and a candidate member of the Politburo. V. Chubar was a colleague of Khrushchev in his early days in the Ukraine. He was appointed prime minister of the Ukraine in 1923 and joined the Politburo at the same time as Mikoyan in 1935, in place of the murdered Kirov.

around." We all went out and got into Stalin's car. Everyone fit into one automobile. We drove and talked. The relationship among us couldn't have been better or more full of party camaraderie. Of course, we never got out of the car; we saw the city through the windows.

During the ride Postyshev asked, "Comrade Stalin, there were some good traditions, things that the people believed in. Children especially were overjoyed to see the Christmas trees. But the custom has been criticized recently. Is there any way to give the children back their trees?"

Stalin reacted favorably, answering, "Take the initiative yourself. Write letters to the press voicing the suggestion, and we'll support you."

That's the way the children got their trees. Postyshev wrote to *Pravda*. *Pravda* supported his idea, and other papers quickly picked up on it and echoed the suggestion. I wanted to relate this episode because it demonstrates how good our relationship was, how attentive Stalin was to Kosior, Postyshev, and Lyubchenko. Postyshev was later transferred to Moscow and became secretary of the Central Committee.

At one point domestic affairs took a turn for the worse. The people started to talk about how a critical situation had developed in the Ukraine. Kaganovich went to the Ukraine and stayed for several days. As a result of Kaganovich's trip, Postyshev again returned to the Ukraine.

Kaganovich reported that Kosior was a good party and political leader, but weak as an organizer. He had allowed the leadership under him to become soft and undisciplined. They needed to be disciplined, brought back up to snuff: Postyshev was the best man to send to bolster Kosior.

As Postyshev went to the Ukraine, the arrests continued, reaching farther out to encompass more and more victims. Important people were arrested. I remember finding out that Vareikis had been arrested. I knew Vareikis from the party congresses; he worked in the Central Black Earth region as party secretary for the province, then he was secretary of the Far East territory.[24] To put

---

24. I. M. Vareikis was secretary of the Far East territory at the time of his arrest in 1937.

it simply, Vareikis had clout. I remember that the accusations against him came directly from Stalin. Stalin explained how Vareikis had been an agent of the White Guard who had penetrated the Red Army.[25] And so it went, on and on. We were all shaken. Again, how could such a thing happen?

Widespread arrests of important figures continued for some time. Again there was a hitch of some kind in the Ukraine leadership, and I believe Kaganovich was sent there for a second time. The next thing we knew, Lyubchenko shot himself after a stormy plenary meeting of the Ukraine central committee. Lyubchenko had been criticized. Although he was an important Ukrainian worker, Lyubchenko had unquestionably blotted his record with some serious political transgressions. He was in his day quite an admirer of Petlura.[26] I saw a photograph showing him seated with some followers of Petlura's, perhaps even Petlura himself. We knew about this when I worked in the Donbass. That's why at all congresses in the Ukraine, when voting for the central committee, the Donbass delegation always rejected Lyubchenko. I personally felt that Lyubchenko was a perfectly capable man who had honestly distanced himself from Petlura and now stood on firm party ground. He was an excellent worker.

But these accusations were dragged up again and held against him at the plenary session. He went home during a recess. When the session resumed, Lyubchenko had not returned. The members decided to check on where he was. They sent people to his home. There they found him and his wife, dead in their beds. It was believed that Lyubchenko had made a pact with his wife to shoot her and then turn the gun on himself.

This was also an enormous shock. We tried to explain it by rationalizing that Lyubchenko was a former follower of Petlura, and that he hadn't been able to shed his past. There were other explanations too, such as that some foreign intelligence agency had gained control over him and forced him to work for them.

25. In 1937 Vareikis had protested the arrest of Marshal Tukhachevsky. Stalin called him to say that "only an enemy of the Soviet regime could defend Tukhachevsky and others." A few days later Vareikis was urgently summoned to Moscow and arrested. See Medvedev, *Let History Judge*, p. 532.

26. S. V. Petlura, the celebrated Ukrainian nationalist leader, who was dedicated to an independent Ukraine and fought against its incorporation into the new Soviet Union.

Incidents like this only served Stalin's purpose, aiding him in his campaign against the enemies of the people, helping him defend all that the revolution had accomplished. On and on it went.

It was after this, I think, that Stalin sent Kaganovich back to the Ukraine. Kaganovich returned with information that was in neither Kosior's nor Postyshev's favor.

Kaganovich described how he had gathered the party's most loyal members together in the Kiev opera house, where he questioned each one individually, insisting, "Let's have it, who knows what about any enemies of the people?" It was a ludicrous kind of people's court. Yet people came forth and said anything they could think of.

As Kaganovich told us, he found out that there was one woman whose last name was Nikolaenko — a party member, an active worker on the cultural front. She was supposedly fighting against enemies of the people but received no support. Kaganovich was only too glad to help. He summoned the woman Nikolaenko, who came and began to identify enemies of the people. The consequences for those she named were devastating.

Today it is shameful to recount, but it really happened. This is why I want to tell what I know, so that such despicable acts never happen again. Yet at the time, all this madness was seen in a positive way.

Kaganovich told the story to Stalin, and at some meeting Stalin said that there were small people who made huge contributions to the cause of our party. One such person was this woman Nikolaenko, in the Ukraine, who had helped the party to uncover the enemy in a big way. The anecdote found its way into the press. Nikolaenko was immediately placed on a pedestal as a fighter for the revolution against enemies of the people.

At the end of 1938, at a Komsomol plenum, a woman named Olga Mishakova denounced Kosarev and his friends. Soon thereafter Kosarev was arrested, while Mishakova remained a Komsomol secretary and was put on the party honor roll as a fighter whose example was to be followed. She was a fighter who had no remorse for anyone.

We now can see clearly that such individuals were not in their right minds. Mishakova, without a doubt, must have had some kind of psychological defect. Nikolaenko was simply crazy. I learned that much later, when I retired. I had lost track of her and thought that she must have passed away years before. She sent me a New Year's letter, and its content needed no expert psychoanalysis. Any reader would have seen that the author of the letter was mad. She was insane.

There was another episode, very typical, from my point of view. I was with Stalin in his office one day in the Kremlin. The phone rang and he went to answer it. I could not hear what he was saying because I was on the other side of the room, and he spoke quietly anyway. He hung up and said to us in a calm voice, "That was Chubar, crying. He says he is not guilty and that he is an honest man."

When he said this, his voice expressed humanity and compassion for Chubar. I knew Chubar and liked him. He was a simple, honest man, an old working-class Bolshevik whom I had known when he was in the Donbass, still the chairman of the central committee of the stone and coal industry, where he had replaced [Yuri] Pyatakov. Chubar was an approachable man, with simple ways and a tendency toward self-criticism. When he transferred to Moscow we continued a good relationship. For this reason I was heartened to see the sympathy with which Stalin seemed to treat him. Apparently, I thought, Stalin doesn't believe whatever material they have on him. I thought Chubar was in no danger of being arrested.

But I was wrong. I can say now that Stalin was a complete stranger to me. The next day I learned that Chubar had been arrested. Then there was neither hide nor hair of him.[27] It was as if he'd vanished into thin air. Much later, after Stalin's death, I turned to the secret police to try to find out what had happened. I asked them to tell me who had been in charge of Chubar's case and who had interrogated him. I wanted to find out what he had been guilty of. The public prosecutor, [R. A.] Rudenko, told me that Chubar had been guilty of nothing, that there was no material on him that could have been used against him.

They told me the name of the chief investigator for Chubar's

27. Chubar disappeared in the summer of 1938 and was executed in February 1939.

case. I suggested to the members of the Presidium that we invite the investigator to speak to us.[28] "Let's see what kind of man he is, and how he did his job. Why did Chubar plead guilty, and what was the basis for having treated him so savagely?"

The man who came before us was surprisingly young. He was quite agitated when we began to ask him questions.

"Did you interrogate him? Was Chubar your case?" I asked. The man answered affirmatively, and so I continued. "How did you conduct your investigation? Of what was Chubar accused, and how did he come to acknowledge his guilt?"

The investigator said, "I don't know. I was called up and told that I would be conducting the Chubar case, and they directed me simply to beat him until he confessed. So that's what I did, I beat him until he agreed to confess."

When I heard this, I felt both angry and bitter. I was unsure how to react. Everyone agreed that we had to investigate the investigator, that he had to be tried. There was an investigation and the man was brought to court. But by then I had already reached the conclusion that although what we were doing might be correct legally, in practical terms it was not. If you take a look at the situation that prevailed at that time, you find that the investigator was just an ordinary man. He had no idea how to carry out an investigation, and he was politically naive. He believed in the party and in Stalin. They used him as a tool. He was told that these men and women were enemies of the people and that they were not acknowledging their crimes. He was told to beat confessions out of them, and that's what he did. Investigations were not carried out using intelligence, but rather by using a stick. Everyone investigated during that period got the same treatment.

STALIN was partial to jesuitical, provocative methods of conversation. I remember Stalin once asking me to come to the Kremlin, to a particular square that was being laid out near the Tainitsky garden. I went right away, of course. As soon as I entered the Kremlin I saw Stalin, Voroshilov, and Molotov walking along, admiring the reconstruction work.

28. The Presidium replaced the Politburo at the Nineteenth Party Congress, in October 1952.

I approached and saw Stalin's face, expressionless as usual. He looked at me and said, "You know, Antipov was arrested."

[N. K.] Antipov was a prominent politician from Leningrad, a people's commissar for the mails and a member of the Central Committee.

"No, I didn't know," I answered.

"He had some evidence of some kind against you," said Stalin, staring into my eyes with that blank look of his.

I stared back at him, not knowing what to say. Then I answered, "No, I did not know Antipov was arrested, nor do I know with what he has been charged. But I do know that Antipov would not, indeed could not, offer any evidence against me, because I never have anything to do with him. The extent of our acquaintance is tipping our hats in the hall and our work together at party meetings."

Stalin turned, lowered his head, and started to talk about Moscow, the real reason he had called me in the first place. He asked me some questions. As he did so I think he was trying to read in my eyes how I was going to act. It just so happened that my external appearance, my face and my eyes, gave him no reason to suspect any link between me and Antipov. Well, what if — after all, it's entirely subjective — he had somehow gotten the impression that I was trying to hide something? Would it only have been a matter of time, then, until we had a new enemy of the people?

We walked a bit more, and then he said he had no more questions for me; so I left. Later, of course, I couldn't stop thinking about the questions he had asked me. I felt like asking what basis Stalin had for coming after me like that. The explanation lies in his utter irresponsibility and complete lack of respect for anyone other than himself.

There was another time when Stalin behaved that way. It was during the period when they started arresting Comintern [Communist International] members in Moscow [1936]. Polish representatives, as far as I know, were all arrested and shot. The information was given to us that Pilsudski somehow planted those Poles as his agents.[29] A hunt for Poles started, and when there were

---

29. General Józef Pilsudski (1867–1935) was a Polish nationalist leader who became president of an independent Poland in November 1918. He opposed

no more Poles they grabbed everybody who occupied a position of importance.

Once when I came to Moscow, Stalin told me that I was a Pole. I went to a Central Committee meeting. We were standing around with Yezhov.[30] As soon as Stalin came in he walked in our direction, pushed his finger into my shoulder, and said, "What's your name?"

"Comrade Stalin, it seems to me that I am Khrushchev," I replied.

"No, you are not Khrushchev," insisted Stalin. He always spoke in such a brusque way. "You are not Khrushchev. Such-and-such person says that."

Stalin mentioned a Polish name unfamiliar to me. "How can you say that, Comrade Stalin?" I replied. "My mother is still alive. The plant where I worked . . . my village of Kalinovka in Kursk region . . . Check them."

"This is what Yezhov says," Stalin replied.

Yezhov started to make a denial. Stalin immediately called Malenkov as his witness. Stalin said Malenkov told him that Khrushchev is not Khrushchev, but is a Pole.

Malenkov also started making a denial. To put it simply, the matter took such a turn that in the hunt to find Poles they started turning Russians into Poles.

Those were the only times something like that ever happened between us. Stalin apparently thought better of me than of others. Perhaps he trusted me more. As a result, I was never subjected to the measures he took against the most honest and faithful people, loyal to the working class and to the party of Lenin.

I remember Stalin, probably feeling his own impending death, sitting at the table, puffing up his breast like a turkey and expounding on who would succeed him. He went through all the names of the Politburo members, characterizing them in this or that way, and drawing conclusions. The characterizations were not insulting, of course.

He dismissed Beria. Beria could not be chairman of the Council

---

Soviet domination of Poland after the Bolshevik Revolution and remained a powerful figure in the Polish government until his death.

30. Nikolai Yezhov replaced Yagoda as head of the NKVD in 1936.

of Ministers because he was not a Russian. He was Georgian. The position needed a Russian.

Khrushchev? Well, Khrushchev was a country boy. We needed a member of the intelligentsia. Who else? Kaganovich? Kaganovich wasn't Russian, he was a Jew. Voroshilov? Too old.

In general, Stalin did not have a good relationship with Voroshilov. Voroshilov had failed when he was people's commissar of defense. The army had been caught without enough weapons. Although the guilt was Stalin's to a large extent, Voroshilov was the one who answered for it.

Then Stalin named [Nikolai] Bulganin future chairman of the Council of Ministers. Of course, none of the other Politburo members discussed Stalin's choice or made any comment, but each felt in his heart that it was a miserable choice. No one thought seriously that that was the way it would end up.

After Stalin's death Bulganin became the people's commissar of defense. He did not inspire confidence in us that he would be able to manage the position well. He was not a military man, nor was he especially quick-witted in military matters or anything else. I couldn't understand at all the reason for Stalin's relationship with Bulganin. Stalin had promoted him and given him the rank of marshal, although he clearly did not deserve it by virtue of his participation in the war, or because of his experience. Bulganin had never commanded anything or anyone, and he simply could not command.

Later, after Malenkov, Bulganin became chairman of the Council of Ministers for a short while [1955–1958]. But it only proved he was not ready for the post. Although he was unquestionably loyal to the party, and an honest, sensible man, he simply was unexperienced. Insufficiently prepared, I would say, in the moral sense to occupy such a high post. Thus life had actually borne out the opposite of what Stalin had believed.

BEFORE the Twentieth Party Congress [in 1956] there were still people labeled "enemies of the people." They were pariahs. They were no longer deprived of their civil rights, but morally they were dispirited. We were still so spellbound by Stalin that we could not find the courage to do what we should. We already had doubts that not everything about Stalin was right. There were doubts whether all the arrests and executions were justified, or at least to what extent they were justified. But we were afraid to lift the curtain and look backstage.[31] During Stalin's life it was always hidden from us. Stalin kept it closed off. Only he told us what was going on. "Today we also arrested this man. Today we shot that one. Today we found those two were enemies of the people. . . ." The Central Committee and the Politburo barely functioned. There were no discussions, to say nothing of reports in the proper sense of the word. Whatever Stalin said was correct; they were words of genius. He said all that was necessary in the interests of the revolution, in the interests of victory and anything else of importance.

When Stalin died there were literally a million agents. One agent watches another agent, and all of them report. If you are an agent then you have to justify your existence with activity. They reported. Everything was overflowing with paper. People were arrested and sentenced. The prisons were filled up and all the agents' mouths had to be fed besides.

When we approached the Twentieth Party Congress we faced the question head on. Some people had been freed right after Stalin's death. Beria had raised the matter.[32] "Let us free them," he said. He suggested adopting a law that would have given the Ministry of Internal Affairs [MVD] the right to decide at its discretion

31. Robert Conquest, in *The Great Terror*, estimates 20 million dead, "which is almost certainly too low and might require an increase of 50 percent or so, as the debit balance of the Stalin regime for twenty-three years." See pp. 525–535. In *The Great Terror: A Reassessment* (New York: Oxford University Press, 1990) Conquest assesses the figure of 20 million dead again and notes it is now given in the USSR. "And the general number of 'repressed' is now stated (e.g., in the new high-school textbooks) as around 40 million, about half of them in the peasant terror of 1929 to 1933 and the other half from 1937 to 1953." Conquest criticizes Western Sovietologists who began to assert that the Terror had claimed far fewer victims. See pp. 484–489.

A KGB report issued on February 13, 1990, acknowledges that 786,000 people were shot to death as enemies of the people in the Soviet Union from 1930 to 1953. During this period 3,778,234 people were sentenced for counterrevolutionary activity or crimes against the state. The cases of more than 850,000 people were posthumously reconsidered by the KGB and the prosecutor's office from 1988 to 1990, and all but 12,000 of them were cleared.

32. After Stalin's death, in March 1953, Beria briefly took over the Ministry of Internal Affairs (MVD). The MVD had the responsibility for all security functions. After Beria's execution, in 1953, it was broken up and superseded by the KGB, the Committee for State Security.

where prisoners should return when their sentences ended: either to their former homes or places of work, or to a new prescribed area. Beria and the MVD were supposed to decide that. I protested that part of the idea and everybody supported me. As a result Beria withdrew this recommendation. At first only criminals were freed: killers, burglars, scoundrels, a whole army of corrupt people. When they returned to their homes they resumed stealing and killing. The people started grumbling that we had let out only the genuine criminals, who continued their dirty business.

By that time Beria had already been exposed and sentenced, and the responsibility to explain [the prisoner release policy] fell on us. We saw that it was not the right thing. While it had been done on Beria's suggestion, it was still a government decision. There was also a decision by the Central Committee. We, of course, were responsible for the decision.

What were we to do about the political prisoners, who served their time in strict isolation, in prisons, and in exile? I raised this issue at a meeting of the Presidium of the Central Committee. "Comrades, after all, why shouldn't we look into how justified the arrests and executions were? We are approaching the congress. We have to know the truth." Before that I called the procurator, Comrade Rudenko, to my office and asked him, "Have you looked through those cases?"

"Yes, I have," he replied.

"What is your opinion? What can you say about them? How justified were the arrests?" I asked him.

He told me that in proper juridical terms there were no facts to justify the arrests, to say nothing of the executions. Everything was done on orders from above. It was done on whim.

I said, "All right, and what about those people who were tried in open trials? I was present at the trial of Rykov, Bukharin, Yagoda, Zinoviev — probably Kamenev was with them also.[33] What about those people? What were their crimes?"

Rudenko smiled and said, "No, there were no crimes there

---

33. Khrushchev is referring to the famous show trial of March 1938 in which N. I. Bukharin, Lenin's close associate, and A. I. Rykov, Lenin's successor as prime minister of the Soviet Union, were convicted and executed with disgraced NKVD chief Yagoda. Zinoviev and Kamenev were convicted with fourteen others at an earlier trial, in 1936, and then shot.

either. There is no criminal evidence in the materials. This was also done arbitrarily on instructions. This is an abuse from the point of view of criminal trial procedure. The people who organized the trials extorted confessions."

I myself had heard how those people gave evidence, confessing to the crimes with which they were charged, I told him.

Rudenko looked at me and smiled again. "Well, that was the art of those who carried out the investigations and the trials."

I believe they probably tortured people. They reduced them to a state where they had only one choice: to end the abuse and suffering. The only possible way to achieve that was through confession. The next step then was a trial, followed by swift execution.

I told the Presidium of the Central Committee of the opinion of the procurator. Then it was decided to establish a commission. I suggested we make the Central Committee secretary [Pyotr] Pospelov the head of the commission. I thought of it this way: first, he is a secretary. For many years [1940–1949] he had served as editor of *Pravda*. He was considered a man close to Stalin, otherwise he would not have been *Pravda* editor. Pospelov was slavishly loyal. When it was announced that Stalin died he was more upset than the others. Pospelov broke down sobbing. Beria even had to bring him around by saying, "What's the matter with you? Cut it out."

We thought that Pospelov would be a good choice as the chairman of the commission, because we felt this would create a sense of confidence in the report of the commission. The Pospelov Commission called in many people and questioned them, including those who carried out the investigations and arrested people. They looked through all the documentation on the basis of which people were sent to prison and executed. Then the commission prepared a report signed by all its members. From the report it was clear that we had to deal with incredible abuses of power. Stalin had done things that none of us had imagined.

We raised this question with the members of the Presidium of the Central Committee, who met during the congress. There was categorical opposition on the part of the troika of Molotov, Voroshilov, and Kaganovich. During our discussions I insisted that we should inform the congress, that we could not avoid telling the congress.

"This is not a small matter," I said. "This is a matter of thousands and thousands of people who perished or who were executed, and of millions of people who were in exile and in prisons. These problems have to be faced. If we do not speak the truth at the congress, then we will be forced to tell the truth after some time. But then we will not be reporting; we will be people under investigation, because then we will be accused as accomplices. If we did not participate directly, then we covered up this abuse after Stalin's death, when we already knew that it was an abuse of power," I said.

There was opposition, so I then said, "At the party congress each member of the Presidium is free to have his opinions known. He is freed of the collective discipline imposed on him as a member of the Central Committee and as a member of the Presidium of the Central Committee."

Those who opposed me probably understood that I wanted to make a report at the congress, to speak about all this. So they said, "All right, let's present a report."

"I find it necessary," I replied. Then I suggested that the report be presented by Comrade Pospelov. He had studied the materials. He had prepared the commission's report. Besides, the congress was already under way and there was no time for anyone else to prepare a presentation. It would be easy for Pospelov because he had already been working on a report for several months.

Some people pointed out that the congress might not understand why First Secretary Khrushchev, in his review of the Central Committee's work, failed to say anything. Why was Secretary of the Central Committee Pospelov now delivering a report on this issue? Does it mean that there are divisions in the leadership on this matter? So it was suggested that I should present the report instead of Pospelov.

I did so. It was Pospelov's report modified. I read it at the congress [in a special closed session], and then we gave it out to the heads of delegations present so they could study it. Comrade Bierut received it and sent it back to Warsaw.[34] This document was particularly bitter for Poles to read because it described how the Polish Communist party was dissolved and what kind of accusations were made against it. Those accusations were groundless.

34. Boleslaw Bierut was the head of the Polish Communist party when he died in Moscow in March 1956, after Khrushchev's secret speech on Stalin's crimes. He was succeeded by Edward Ochab.

The leadership was shot by Stalin. It was a tragedy for the Polish Communist party.[35] Other Communist parties also did not escape this fate, although not on such a scale as the Polish party.

After Bierut's death there were divisions in the Polish leadership, and as a result copies of the speech became accessible to the public. I was told that in Poland you could buy two copies in the market for one ruble. In this way it became available to the forces of world reaction. Naturally, they gobbled it up and used it.

Deep emotional concern was felt by the French and Italian Communist party delegations. It was apparent to me that they were more concerned than other fraternal parties. That was understandable. They were large, mass proletarian parties, and they still are. Both Togliatti and Thorez had been present at the open trials.[36] By their presence and the reports they made afterward they verified that the crimes had been committed and the prosecution cases were proven. Now everything was turned upside down.

Taking this into account, we felt compelled to exclude [from rehabilitation] those people who were prosecuted in open trials. However, we said they committed no crimes, that they were sentenced arbitrarily, and that the sentences were not based on crimes to which they confessed at the trials.

I, of course, am sorry that I wasn't able to complete the investigation of all those cases and gather all the relevant materials, which I was told were many and rich. However, while I was in the leadership I failed to conclude this business. So what? What one person fails to do will be done by another. If the other also fails, then a third person will achieve the goal. As they say, the right cause will finally triumph.[37]

35. The Polish Communist party was virtually exterminated by Stalin when he purged its members living in Moscow from 1937 to 1939.

36. Palmiro Togliatti (1893–1964) was an Italian editor and longtime leader of the Italian Communist party. Maurice Thorez (1900–1964) was the founder of the French Communist party. He unswervingly followed Stalin and the Soviet line.

37. It was not until 1988 that those condemned and executed in the purge trials were rehabilitated. The case of Bukharin, whose widow memorized his last will and testament and kept silent for more than forty years, was the most dramatic. Finally, in February 1988 he was declared innocent and posthumously restored to party membership, becoming a person who could be mentioned and honored in the press and in history books.

3

The Great Patriotic War

I want to record some reminiscences about the war — why we were so badly prepared, how the fighting developed, and what the outcome was for our country and the world. I know these subjects well. I'm particularly familiar with events on those fronts where I was a member of the military council, in the Kiev military district, then on the southwest front, later at Stalingrad and Rostov. I was present for the recapture of Rostov, the Battle of the Kursk Bulge, the crossing of the Dnieper River, and the liberation of Kiev. After that I participated less actively because Stalin told me that I should devote more time to the restoration of the economy and the organization of state and party organs.

I will start with the story of the pact we signed with the Germans on August 24, 1939, but first some background. I went hunting with Voroshilov the day before Ribbentrop [Joachim von Ribbentrop, the German foreign minister] arrived. When I got back from the hunt I went straight to see Stalin. I brought a duck to add to the pot, as they say. Stalin was to have had a gathering of all the Politburo members that were in Moscow at the time. I came in and told him about our trip, of course, and boasted about my luck. He was in a very good mood, and joked with me.

He was of a mixed mind about hunting. Sometimes he would get all fired up to go out, but other times, when he was in a different mood, he would speak out against hunters. He did not condemn hunting the way other people do, for the unnecessary taking of life, but rather because he felt it was a colossal waste of time. Even though he did not go hunting, he wasted a lot of time himself. I think no one from the higher levels of government, no other leader, wasted more time than Stalin. He wasted it at the table, eating and drinking over lunches and dinners.

Sometimes Stalin would say unflattering things about Lenin on this business of hunting. Everyone knew that Lenin loved to hunt and hunted often. True, as some writers later said, Lenin went hunting to spend time with people. But that was not the main reason. The main thing for him, as for every hunter, was that he loved to do it. It was a passion with him. That's why he went hunting. He even hunted while he was in exile.

Anyway, when we met at Stalin's around 3:00 A.M. on August 24, I had cleaned my prize from the previous day for our table. Stalin told me that Ribbentrop would leave in the morning. He had come bringing a draft agreement on friendship and nonaggression and we had signed the agreement.[1]

Stalin was elated. Tomorrow those British and French representatives would find out what had happened and would leave right away. They were still in Moscow. Stalin fully understood the significance of the agreement he had signed and understood that, as he put it, "Hitler wants to trick us, but I think we've gotten the better of him." He said then and there that the document we signed would give us Estonia, Latvia, Lithuania, Bessarabia, and Finland. The fate of those territories would be up to our discretion. We would make our own agreements with those countries about the territories involved. Hitlerite Germany did not figure into the picture at all for us — that was up to us.

Stalin also mentioned Poland. He said that Germany was going to attack Poland, to seize it and make it a protectorate. The eastern portions of Poland would go to us — those portions now [1969] settled by the people of Byelorussia and the Ukraine.

Of course we were in favor of the agreement, although I had misgivings. Stalin, I sensed, understood how I felt. He presented

1. Ribbentrop arrived in Moscow at 1:00 P.M. on August 23, 1939, and signed the pact at 2:00 A.M. on August 24, following a marathon negotiating session with Molotov and Stalin (the date of the signing is generally given as August 23). After the signing ceremonies, which ended around 3:00 A.M., Stalin sped off to his dacha at Kuntsevo, outside Moscow, for a late supper with Khrushchev, Bulganin, Mikoyan, and Voroshilov. Such a schedule was standard for Stalin and his cronies. For a full account of the session in the Kremlin, see Anthony Read and David Fisher, *The Deadly Embrace* (New York: W. W. Norton, 1988), pp. 254–257.

The Soviet Union and Eastern Europe, 1939–1955

Territory annexed by USSR through Molotov-Ribbentrop pact and World War II

Warsaw Pact allies, 1955

FINLAND

Leningrad

Tallinn

ESTONIA

DENMARK

SWEDEN

BALTIC SEA

Riga

LATVIA

LITHUANIA

Vilnius

N

KALININGRAD REGION

Berlin

Minsk

E. GERMANY

Warsaw

POLAND

Pinsk

USSR

W. GERMANY

Prague

CZECHOSLOVAKIA

Lvov

Kiev

N. BUKOVINA

Bug River

Vienna

Uzhgorod

Dniester River

AUSTRIA

Budapest

RUTHENIA

BESSARABIA

Kishinev

HUNGARY

Prut River

MOLDAVIA

Tiraspol

Trieste

TRANSYLVANIA

Odessa

ITALY

YUGOSLAVIA

Belgrade

ROMANIA

Bucharest

ADRIATIC SEA

Danube River

BLACK SEA

ALBANIA

Sofia

BULGARIA

Tirana

GREECE

TURKEY

G.W.WARD

the arrangement as a game of who was tricking whom, who got the better of whom.

We saw the situation this way: War would break out, but now it would not be a war of the West against us, with us fighting Hitler alone. The agreement made it sound like Hitler would be starting the war, that he would attack Poland — he had already taken Czechoslovakia — and, in this way, France and England would have to come out and fight him first. This was good for us, both militarily and morally.

So we would remain neutral. I thought that this was the best position for us. I understood it and approved, since England and France wanted to pit Germany against us, one-on-one. They were hoping to rid themselves of the German threat at the expense of our blood and territory, at the expense of our riches.

Poland's policy at this time was also unwise. It did not want to hear about joining forces with us against Germany. We essentially had no recourse. We had a chance to get our head out from in front of our enemy's rifle, a choice we were pushed into by Western powers. That was our justification for the pact. That is still the way I see it today. However, it was a very difficult step to take at the time. For us Communists, antifascists, a people who stood on philosophical and political ground diametrically opposed to Hitler, to suddenly join forces in this war — how could we? Certainly the average citizen saw it that way. It was even difficult for us to fathom and to digest. But we were forced into it, and we were getting something out of the deal too.

Hitler would make his move on September 1, 1939. Actually, that was not specified in the pact, but rather just stated by Ribbentrop.

On September 1, when the Germans attacked Poland, our troops were concentrated on the border. I remember because I was with them, as a commander. The members of the military council were stationed on the border.

I was with the troops that were to move in the direction of Ternopol [in the Polish Ukraine. Semyon K.] Timoshenko was right there too. Timoshenko was the commander of the Kiev military district. When the Germans were approaching the territory that the pact gave to us, our troops went into action. Poland by then had almost ceased its resistance.

The Polish army had been crushed, destroyed. Poland had been utterly unprepared for the war.

What a farce! All because of Poland's pride and disregard for our proposal to join forces.[2] What a shameful failure of Poland's government and military machine!

We crossed the border [on September 17]. For all intents and purposes there were no troops to oppose us. We moved in, and marched to Ternopol. I met up with Timoshenko and went through the town.

NOWADAYS many people keep asking whether we knew that Hitler would attack us. To put it simply, were we taken by surprise? Or did we know something, and maybe more than something, in advance? There are supporters of both points of view.

To argue that we did not expect a German attack is just plain stupid, particularly coming from military people who were close to the general staff. No one with an ounce of political sense should buy the idea that we were fooled, that we were caught flat-footed by a treacherous surprise assault. Even to suggest such a thing is irresponsible. Yet just such phrases have often been used in newspaper articles, which means that they serve a certain political purpose. They're used to cover up for those who were responsible for the preparations of the army and the country, and who failed in their responsibility. People are trying to justify either themselves or Stalin — his genius, his foresight, and his vigilance. If he really was vigilant, where was the treachery?

Yet still, even now, some of Stalin's lackeys are trying to whitewash him by blaming Hitler for fooling us, for breaking the Molotov-Ribbentrop pact, and so on. This is a formula either for fools or for people who are completely incompetent in politics. I'm not talking about military politics — I mean the most elementary understanding of how the world works. Never, nowhere in history,

---

2. While Stalin and Molotov were negotiating with the Germans for the Molotov-Ribbentrop pact, British and French military delegations were in Moscow for talks with Defense Commissar Voroshilov on military cooperation against a German attack in Europe. The Russians insisted on the right to send their troops through Poland and on cooperation from the Poles, who were approached and rejected these conditions, since they feared Stalin's intentions toward Poland.

was there ever an amicable agreement between two states that included provision for one side to attack the other. What has always happened is that one side later finds a reason for an attack. But whatever the pretext, the real justification is usually a feeling of superior strength on the part of whoever strikes first. Hitler had that sort of superiority, and he simply created the conditions for attacking at will whomever he wanted.

I don't deny — in fact, I can confirm — that our intelligence should have been better. Nonetheless, the basic elements of Hitler's plan to attack the Soviet Union were well known. As the saying goes, sparrows were chirping about it at every crossroad. Hitler and the Nazis were yelling at the top of their voices about how they wanted to rid the world of Communists and communism.

What could have been a clearer warning than the book Hitler himself wrote, *Mein Kampf?* He set forth the task of eliminating bolshevism, eliminating communism, extermination of Slavs, or at least let's say reducing them in numbers. So if Hitler decided to sign a treaty of friendship and nonaggression with the USSR, then it was obviously a political ploy, a ruse to deceive Stalin, to deceive the Communist party of the USSR and public opinion. Hitler believed he was riding a victorious horse. Having neutralized his main enemy in the East, the USSR, and positioned himself to defeat and occupy Poland, he could deal with his various opponents one by one. I believe Hitler also hoped the treaty would sober and subdue politicians in the West, particularly in England and France, forcing them to accept the aggressive policy of German imperialism. Hitler also probably hoped that France and England would write off Poland. France and England had treaties with Poland obligating them to come to her assistance in case of attack. Perhaps those treaties would be consigned to oblivion, freeing Hitler's hands to direct his efforts against the USSR. He considered his main enemies to be communism, the USSR, and the Slavic people. He wanted to come to terms with the West and then to redraw the map of the world, reclaiming Africa and other territories that Germany lost as a result of World War I.

As for Stalin's decision to sign the treaty, that was also a political maneuver. He thought he was deceiving Hitler, turning him against the West. I don't think either Stalin or Hitler took the treaty seriously. Each was pursuing his own goals. Hitler's were those that we knew from *Mein Kampf*. Stalin understood correctly what Hitler was up to, but he thought he could deflect the blow of the German army away from the USSR and direct it at the West, and in that way buy time. Of course, the West, meanwhile, did everything it could to turn Hitler against the East.

When I say "buy time," I mean that it was understood the treaty would not save us from attack — it would only give us a chance to catch our breath. Stalin may have had some hope that once Hitler attacked Poland, England and France would enter the war and these two powers would then crush Germany. But I doubt it, and I certainly don't remember any direct statements or discussions along those lines.

Many say that the treaty with Hitlerite Germany allowed us to do what we wanted with Estonia, Latvia, Lithuania, Finland, and Romania. Naturally, we understood that there were concessions to us in the treaty and that they were to our advantage. I want to say this straightforwardly. The access we gained to the Baltic Sea significantly improved our strategic situation. By reaching the shores of the Baltic, we deprived the Western powers of a foothold that they might use against us — and that they actually had used during the civil war — for establishing a front against the USSR.[3]

Romania occupied Bessarabia after the October Revolution and behaved in a hostile and provocative manner toward the USSR. Romania kept causing trouble along the border. Shots were fired at our bank of the Prut River. In a word, there was always tension in that area. As for the Finns, they carried out unrestrained propaganda against the Soviet Union. There could be no doubt that Finland was eager to join in a campaign against the Soviet Union. Therefore, it was unquestionably useful for us to make an agreement with these five states — the Baltics, Romania, and Finland — that solved the territorial issues in our favor. That was our goal in making the treaty with Germany. But the point I want to stress is that the treaty did not exclude war; it did not exclude an

3. Khrushchev is referring to the Allied efforts to conquer the Baltic states, which were controlled by the Germans during World War I and after the armistice. In 1920 the Soviet Union regained the Ukraine as a result of the Polish-Soviet war, but it was forced to recognize the independence of Latvia, Lithuania, Estonia, and Finland. The Soviet Union annexed Latvia, Lithuania, and Estonia as the result of a secret protocol in the Molotov-Ribbentrop pact of 1939.

attack against us from the West. It just gave us some time to get ourselves prepared.

Did we take advantage of that opportunity? No! I think the main cause of our lack of preparedness was the extermination of military cadres [during the purges in the 1930s]. Thousands of people perished. I'm not speaking here about all those party cadres, engineering personnel, workers, or intellectuals who were killed as enemies of the people, or crammed into camps and prisons. I'm talking about our military personnel. So many were executed that the high command as well as middle and lower echelons were devastated. As a result, our army was deprived of the cadres who had gained experience in the civil war, and we faced a new enemy unprepared.

History records the names of the victims. It's a big list, all exterminated. The new officers, on whose shoulders fell the heavy burden of organizing the defense, were honest people; they were loyal, good Communists. But they had no experience in commanding troops. By the time the Germans were getting ready to attack us, Voroshilov was minister of defense. He was responsible for the state of the armed forces and their preparedness, for military personnel, for intelligence, for the availability of weapons. He turned out to be a total loss.

There was plenty of reason to expect a large-scale war, a European war, perhaps one that America would enter at a certain stage. Perhaps that war would exhaust the strength of the German state and undermine its military power. We also thought — I believe correctly — that all this would be to the advantage of the USSR, because Germany and its ideology were primarily aimed at communism and the USSR as well as at progressive forces inside Germany and worldwide.

Nor should we forget the situation that was developing in the Far East. Japan's behavior was disgusting. Not even that word says enough. Japan aggressively probed for weak points in order to strike a blow against the USSR and to tear away our territory in the Far East. Later, when the Japanese seized Manchuria and advanced far into China, they started thinking about a deeper raid against the USSR. Japan launched an offensive across Mongolia at the Khalkhin-Gol [River], where there was heavy fighting with our forces.[4] The operation was carried out very well. Zhukov was exceptional. It ended with the complete destruction of the Japanese troops. The defeat of the Japanese at Khalkhin-Gol only served to spread the dangerous bacillus of complacency to an even greater degree. Our country was unassailable! We had destroyed the Japanese samurai!

THE Japanese were sobered by the losses they suffered there and gave up their aggressive designs against the USSR. However, at that time they started conspiring with Hitler to form the Berlin-Rome-Tokyo Axis.

Japan's grand strategy was to acquire territories in the Pacific, but that did not diminish our own anxiety. Japan remained a potential enemy capable of striking a blow against us. That's why we always kept plenty of troops in the Far East.

This was the situation when a number of us gathered at Stalin's dacha on August 24, 1939, after Ribbentrop signed the treaty. When we arrived at Stalin's, there were others — Comrade Mikoyan and, of course, Beria and Molotov. (Malenkov was not invited to Stalin's.) We had dinner. Stalin was in high spirits. He was glad that the treaty had been signed. He said, "Well, we deceived Hitler for the time being," or something like that, showing he understood the inevitability of war and that while the treaty postponed the war, it only gave us some time.

We all listened to Stalin. There was no real discussion of the situation at the governmental level, no political deliberation in the Politburo. I know because I was a member of the Politburo. We did not analyze the condition of our armed forces and other elements that should have been taken into consideration if we were

4. From July to September 1939 the Soviet Union and Japan fought a small-scale war along the Mongolian-Manchurian frontier in the vicinity of what is now called the Ha-lo-hsin River, on the eastern approaches to Mongolia. Although little publicized at the time, it was the largest tank battle in history until World War II. The Soviet commander, Marshal Georgi K. Zhukov, demonstrated for the first time the decisive but costly military tactics that he was to use against the Germans. Zhukov overwhelmed the Japanese with superior manpower, artillery, and tanks on August 20, 1939, and by August 31 he had driven them back across the frontier.

going to counter the imminent military danger facing the USSR. Nor did Stalin ever tell us what was in the intelligence reports. All this put us at a disadvantage. I'd even call it another abuse on the part of Stalin. He took everything on his own shoulders. He decided everything himself, and he decided poorly, as the beginning of the war showed.

I should also describe how Stalin reacted when Hitler moved against France [in 1940]. The French and British troops [in France] were defeated. Marshal [Philippe] Pétain capitulated, and German troops entered Paris. Hitler moved with lightning speed, saving his strength, even increasing his fighting capacity. The war in the West was a rehearsal for one in the East.

I happened to be in Moscow at that time. I remember being with Stalin. He was extremely nervous. I rarely saw him like that. Normally, he could hardly ever sit still during meetings. He had the habit of pacing. On this occasion, he was racing around, cursing like a cab driver. He cursed the French. He cursed the English. How could they allow Hitler to defeat them, to crush them? I took this as a sign of his great anxiety that the war in the West was coming to a close in Hitler's favor. Now only the English were putting up a fight from the British Isles. But Hitler had no real worry that England would interfere with his plans. The British had run from the Continent as fast as their legs could carry them. They lost a huge amount of military equipment, and many of their troops were taken prisoner. With Poland, France, Denmark, Holland, Norway, Luxembourg, Hungary, Yugoslavia, and Romania all occupied, now it was the USSR's turn. Stalin understood that war was inevitable.

Stalin not only saw the superiority of the German army — he knew that the Germans sensed our weakness particularly well because of the war we had fought with Finland. I had firsthand knowledge of what happened, including the strategic miscalculations on our side. The very day the war with Finland started, I was in Moscow with Stalin. He didn't even feel the need to call a meeting. He was sure all we had to do was fire a few artillery rounds and the Finns would capitulate. Instead, they rejected our terms and resisted. There was still a false sense of confidence on our side: a few days would pass and we would polish off the Finns. But that didn't happen either. Many of our troops were ground up by the Finns. Only with great effort did we manage to break through and overrun the fortified Mannerheim Line.

Here we have to give credit to Comrade Semyon Timoshenko. He had commanded the Kiev military district until he was made the commander in the war with Finland. Later he was appointed minister of defense. But the point is, little Finland made us pay such a large price in our offensive — our Baltic fleet was helpless against the Finnish navy — that the Germans could see that the USSR was a giant with clay feet. Hitler must have concluded that if the Finns could put up such resistance, then the mighty Germans would need only one powerful blow to topple the giant.[5]

Stalin lost his nerve after the defeat of our troops in the war against Finland. He probably lost whatever confidence he had that our army could cope with Hitler. Stalin never said so, but I came to this conclusion watching his behavior. After the Germans had already moved their army from the western front, Timoshenko and I sent Stalin a request for permission to mobilize several hundred thousand collective farmers who would dig antitank trenches and build field fortifications. Stalin said that would be a provocation and should not be done. Meanwhile, he was scrupulously fulfilling all the conditions of the Molotov-Ribbentrop treaty. We were obliged to ship Hitler a certain amount of petroleum, grain, and some other things. So while those sparrows kept chirping, "Look out for Hitler! Look out for Hitler!" Stalin was punctually sending the Germans trainload after trainload of grain and petroleum. He wanted to butter up Hitler by living up to the terms of the Molotov-Ribbentrop pact!

In return, the Germans presented the Soviet navy with an unfinished cruiser and promised all kinds of technical assistance to get it ready for service. But by then, Hitler had already set a date for attacking the USSR, so the Germans must have figured the

5. The Winter War of 1939–1940 resulted from the Soviet invasion of Finland when Soviet demands for Finnish territory were refused. The Soviet troops met unexpected resistance from the Finns, led by Marshal C.G.E. Mannerheim, a former czarist general, who was responsible for the Mannerheim Line of fortifications in depth, which forced heavy Soviet casualties before the Finns were overwhelmed by superior numbers.

cruiser wouldn't be completed in time to take part in the war. It was just another diplomatic maneuver to calm us down, to lull us into a false sense of security — and at the same time to intimidate us. And the tactic worked.

When Stalin summoned me to Moscow in the days leading up to the German attack, I felt my presence there was pointless. I would have been better off back in the Ukraine, where there was a lot of work to do; but I couldn't leave. Stalin kept ordering me to postpone my departure. "Wait," he said. "Don't be in such a hurry. There's no need to rush back." Why? Because he was in such a state of confusion, anxiety, demoralization, even paralysis. This was criminal inactivity on the part of Stalin and the other people who were directly responsible for the defense of our country. But Stalin had the most to answer for.

Three or four days before the beginning of the war in June 1941, you could feel the static, the discharge of tension, in the air. I told Stalin, "I have to go. The war is about to break out. It may catch me here in Moscow or on the way back to the Ukraine."

This time Stalin said, "That's right, that's right. Just go." I left on Friday, and on Saturday I was in Kiev. By then Stalin himself understood that the war was about to begin. So how can anyone still say it was a surprise attack?

The war started on Sunday, June 22. The day before, I received a warning from Moscow through the chief of the Kiev headquarters, General M. A. Purkayev. He said that an enemy attack was expected. Later I found out that a German soldier had fled across the Bug River. He had told us that the war would start the next day at 3:00 A.M.

Our situation was disastrous from the very beginning. Stalin failed to designate which plants should produce rifles, artillery, ammunition, tanks, and armored vehicles, so there simply weren't anywhere near enough weapons. When Malenkov told me that they had to send Osoaviakhim[6] rifles with holes in the barrels to Leningrad and there was nothing available for Kiev, it was like a

---

6. Osoaviakhim is the Russian acronym for a society established in 1927 for the military training of civilians. By 1939 it had more than 12 million members. The chairman of its central council, R. P. Eideman, was one of the leading Red Army commanders sentenced to death with Marshal Tukhachevsky in 1937.

thunderbolt out of the clear blue sky. I visited the front lines with Comrade Zhukov, who came to Kiev on orders from Stalin. Our command post was near Ternopol. We immediately could tell there was a shortage of arms. We had too few planes, too few tanks.

We rightly criticize the czarist government's lack of preparedness for World War I; we talk about how, by the second or third year of the war, Russia didn't have enough rifles for its soldiers. Well, in 1941, we didn't have enough on the third or fourth day of the war! I got on the phone myself and called Moscow from Kiev to ask for rifles. "There are no rifles," I was told. "Forge broadswords and knives. Prepare bottles with inflammable mixtures." The whole thing was a disgrace. Our army and our people had been brought up on slogans like "Not a single step back!" and "Not one inch of land to the enemy!" Another was "Fight on foreign territory!" It meant we were supposed to carry the war to the enemy if he attacked us. How were we supposed to do that?

A later battle, our defeat at Kharkov, illustrates what kind of commander Stalin was. During 1942, Hitler planned only one big offensive along the southern front. He would push in the direction of Stalingrad and the northern Caucasus. After occupying Stalingrad he would turn the left flank of his attacking forces to the north and thus extend his control far around Moscow, cutting it off from the east and forcing our troops to capitulate.

Our troops captured the plans for the operation along with documents from German headquarters, outlining the offensive. There was no guesswork on our part; the operation was laid out on the maps and described in the documents. The offensive was to commence north of Kharkov.

I was a member of the military council under Timoshenko. It was our front that would bear the brunt of the German attack. We sent the captured material to Moscow along with suggestions on how to counter the Germans. The high command studied the maps, drew its conclusions, and reported to Stalin.

Stalin called to talk to Timoshenko. He also spoke with me and told me how Hitler was trying to confuse us. In an insulting and humiliating way, he said, "You don't understand. Hitler is leading you around by the nose. He has other plans. He planted those documents. This is a trick."

I pointed out that Germans are a very punctual people, and that I thought they were really going to attack in our direction. I had no reason to see any larger plan of Hitler's, a plan that he may have had behind the operation. His idea was simply to move further east. I, along with others in command at the southwest front, knew that the Germans would move in that direction. Only the timing of the movement was in question and would depend on circumstances. We knew this before we saw the plans being considered by Hitler for the operation.

Time passed and we received almost no support. We were given enough equipment and one division to be used only to cover the ravaged area south of Kharkov, where our troops had already been crushed. But we received absolutely nothing to make a stand against the German invasion being prepared to the north of the city. The general staff was utterly convinced that the Germans would not be carrying out such an operation, that they were planning to push in another direction.

This other direction was supposedly against Moscow, on the western front, and so troops were reinforced there. I know that we needed to do all in our power to block the Germans' path to Moscow, but we also should have been on the lookout, and maintained our military posture over all sections of the front. That was important and needed to be done. That's what the general staff is for. That's why we have intelligence; that's why we have the multitude of resources necessary to correctly determine, analyze, and deduce the enemy's plan and to formulate a defense. This is just what the general staff was unable to do. As a result, they gave Stalin an incorrect orientation and he acted accordingly.

At the same time, we started an offensive of our own against the Nazis. We encountered no resistance. This fact, together with the captured German plans, indicated to Timoshenko and me that the Germans were gathering their forces for a major move. The logical thing to do was to halt our offensive and reposition our troops to withstand the German assault; but Stalin insisted on continuing the offensive. Timoshenko tried in vain to persuade the general staff that this would allow the Germans to encircle our forces; it would lead to catastrophe.

I tried to speak to Marshal [A. M.] Vasilevsky, the head of the general staff, but he said that Stalin had made the decision. Then

I talked directly with Stalin. Two German fighter planes that were to take part in the advance had come down at our airstrips. Stalin phoned me and asked, "So you still think that the Germans will move in this direction?"

I answered, "Yes, Comrade Stalin, I still think so."

"They are just tossing those planes to you to throw you off!"

"They are just sacrificing them? Two pilots?" I responded. "They were probably inexperienced; they got disoriented on their maps and just landed. It happens at the front. Our flyers face the same hazard. These two just happened to land and now they're our prisoners."

"No! You still don't understand. They are pulling the wool over your eyes," scoffed Stalin.

If it had ended there, it would have been a half victory, costing me nothing worse than a humiliating conversation. The more important point is that Stalin's blindness was the basis for the military campaign that followed. As a result, our troops received no reinforcement in the direction Hitler had decided on for his strike. His campaign began, and the Germans were successful.

The situation became critical, and I felt the last chance to save the day was to try again, speaking directly to Stalin. When I reached his office on the phone, he refused to speak with me. He was eating and drinking at the time. He ordered Malenkov to tell me to continue the offensive. I knew hundreds of thousands of troops would be lost.

The German offensive developed according to the plans we had captured. Stalin and the general staff sent no reinforcements. Our front was broken, and the Germans met no resistance. They took thousands of Russian soldiers prisoner.[7] The Germans moved as far as Stalingrad and Makhachkala in the North Caucasus. The Soviet Union lost the Ukraine with its industry and agriculture as well as the oil from Baku and Makhachkala. All this was thanks to Stalin's "military genius" and his docile general staff.

Over time, after huge losses, our commanders, who had been so badly prepared at the beginning of the war, acquired plenty of

7. An estimated 240,000 Soviet troops were trapped by the Germans. See Army Historical Series, Earl F. Ziemke, *Stalingrad to Berlin: The German Defeat in the East* (Washington, D.C.: Office of the Chief of Military History, U.S. Army, 1968), p. 33.

experience. In the end, those who survived the struggle defeated the Hitlerite hordes and drove them from our territory. They took Berlin and achieved the complete destruction of fascism.

Why do I go back to this period now, and concentrate so much on it? Why do I want to leave my opinions for those who will eventually be interested in this history? It's because I think the war might have taken an entirely different course if the general staff had been able to decipher Hitler's plan in May 1942, for the campaign against Kharkov.

Had we figured out correctly that the Germans' main strike of 1942 would be to the north of Kharkov, then we could have redeployed our troops and equipment to support our troops there and destroy the Germans. We had the necessary men and equipment to do that.

However, it was we who were crushed. We were pushed back across the Don River. There was no word of Timoshenko for a full three days. I had no contact at all with him and hadn't the slightest idea where he was. It was rumored that he had either surrendered to the Germans, or that something worse had happened to him. We reported to Stalin that we were unable to raise him, and that we did not know where he could be.

Only then did Stalin apparently begin to understand that Hitler had not been fooling me, but rather that he had pulled the wool over the eyes of the Soviet army's general staff — and of Stalin himself. As a result, Stalin reconsidered his negative reaction to my insistent demands that we needed to prepare ourselves along the Kharkov axis.

I feel I was rehabilitated after the campaign. Despite our defeat Stalin was forced to admit that I had been right. Of course, he did not make any announcement to that effect. No, Stalin was not nearly straightforward or honorable enough for that. He was an insidious man. I was vindicated when he called me and appointed me to the military council of the Stalingrad front.

Stalin never spoke about this whole incident after the war. He went to his death without ever mentioning it again because it was so awkward for him. Once Mikoyan mentioned it, when we had all been drinking. "Khrushchev was right when he kept insisting about that operation south of Kharkov."

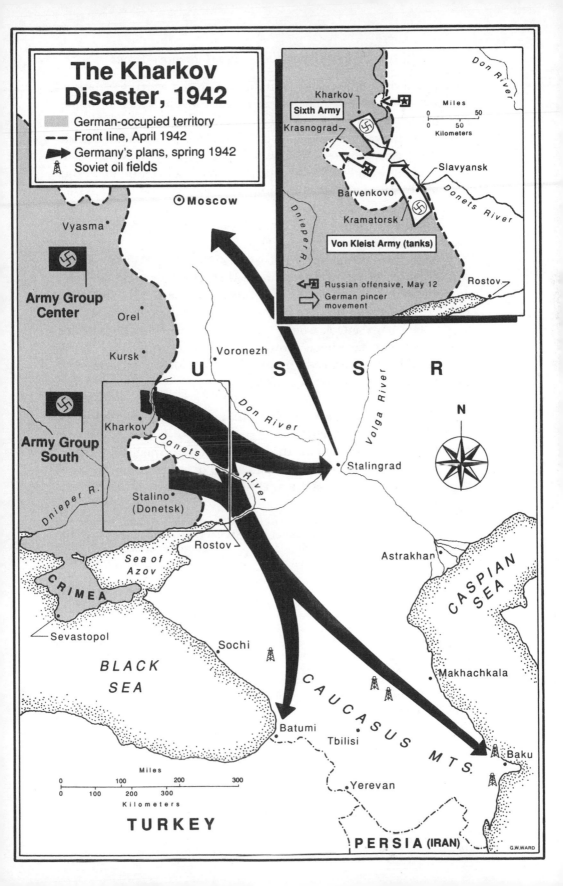

The Kharkov Disaster, 1942

- German-occupied territory
- Front line, April 1942
- Germany's plans, spring 1942
- Soviet oil fields

Sixth Army

Kharkov

Krasnograd

Slavyansk

Barvenkovo

Kramatorsk

Rostov

Von Kleist Army (tanks)

Don River

Dnieper R.

Donets River

Miles
0   50
0   50
Kilometers

Russian offensive, May 12
German pincer movement

⊙ Moscow

Vyasma

Army Group Center

Orel

Kursk

Voronezh

Don River

U S S R

Volga River

N

Kharkov

Donets

River

Army Group South

Stalino (Donetsk)

Stalingrad

Astrakhan

CASPIAN SEA

Dnieper R.

Rostov

Sea of Azov

CRIMEA

Sevastopol

BLACK SEA

Sochi

C A U C A S U S   M T S.

Makhachkala

Batumi

Tbilisi

Baku

Yerevan

Miles
0   100   200   300
0   100   200   300
Kilometers

TURKEY

PERSIA (IRAN)

G.W.WARD

Stalin flashed him a glance but did not utter a word. He couldn't very well say that I had been wrong. It was even harder for him to say that I had been right. If I had been right, then he had been wrong. Stalin was not able to admit that. Mikoyan had been a witness to my conversation with Stalin through Malenkov, when Stalin had mockingly said that "Khrushchev is poking his nose into other people's business. He is not a military man. My military advisers know better than he. I have reports from my military men, but Khrushchev says . . ." It was those military advisers who had made themselves look stupid.

To hell with them! That's not what bothers me. What troubles me is that we lost thousands of men, that we lost ground, and that we lengthened the war. I think we may have caused the war to go on an extra two years.

The Germans' attack would have been nipped in the bud and they would not have been allowed to advance further to the east. That would have mattered a great deal. The North Caucasus is our breadbasket, it's rich in minerals and oil.

Now I want to approach my memoirs from a different angle. I've been stimulated by documents that recently became available to the public. I'm referring to the war memoirs, especially those of Marshal Zhukov. Marshal Bagramyan told me that he had read Zhukov's book, but he said it was no good, unjust and distorted.[8]

8. Marshal I. K. Bagramyan (1897–1982) was a much-decorated army officer and a close World War II colleague of Khrushchev's. His own memoirs, *That Is How the War Began,* were published in 1971. Despite the official policy of not praising Khrushchev in print, Bagramyan saluted Khrushchev as an excellent wartime leader.

Marshal Georgi K. Zhukov (1896–1974) is generally acknowledged to have been the USSR's greatest commander in World War II. His immense prestige and popularity provoked a jealous and paranoid Stalin to relegate him to a series of secondary commands after the war. The war memoirs to which Khrushchev refers began to appear in the Soviet Union in June 1965 and continued through 1968. (They were published in English in 1969 by Harper & Row under the title *Marshal Zhukov's Greatest Battles.*)

After Stalin's death Zhukov became defense minister (1955–1957), and in that post he helped to put down the Antiparty Group, a loose, ad hoc coalition of old Stalinists — principally G. M. Malenkov, V. M. Molotov, and L. M. Kaganovich — which in 1957 tried to oust Khrushchev from the post of party first secretary. The group turned the Presidium against Khrushchev, but with the help of Marshal Zhukov, who airlifted the Central Committee to Moscow, Khrushchev

Bagramyan told me that "Zhukov describes how the Barvenkovo [Kharkov] operation of 1942 was evaluated and reported to the *Stavka* [general headquarters]. Zhukov says who was present and mentions Marshal Timoshenko, me, and himself; but he doesn't say anything about your presence, Nikita Sergeyevich. You, of course, were present. I was astonished that he said that he was present, while I remember perfectly that Zhukov was not there. He definitely was not there."

Why did Zhukov write that, I asked myself? It is hard to imagine that he would write that himself if he was not there. I doubt that Zhukov is capable of such a lie; so I assume that it was not Zhukov who wrote that. The book is full of such "help," which contradicts

---

was able to muster enough support to override the Presidium and turn the tables on his opponents. In return for his support against the Antiparty Group, Zhukov became a full member of the Presidium in 1957 (he had been a candidate, or nonvoting, member since the year before). Four months later he was sent to Belgrade on an official visit and returned to find himself dismissed as defense minister, divested of his posts in the party leadership, and disgraced for "violating Leninist principles concerning the administration of the armed forces." In simple language this meant Khrushchev feared that with his popularity Zhukov might oust him from power. In *Khrushchev Remembers: The Last Testament*, pp. 14–16, Khrushchev recounted the final confrontation with Zhukov during his ouster, but the text was heavily edited. The edited material is in the tapes on which *The Glasnost Tapes* is based and contains a direct confrontation that took place before Khrushchev between Zhukov and Marshal Kirill Moskalenko, commander of the Moscow military district. It reads:

"Moskalenko passionately accused Zhukov of having ulterior motives of seizing power. Then Zhukov said with all his soldier's rudeness and soldier's directness — and I believed Zhukov told the truth — 'How can you accuse me? You yourself told me many times, "Take power in your own hands. Just take it! Take power!"' When I heard that, I was stricken. How could it be? I could not imagine Moskalenko saying that to Zhukov.

"But it turns out that Moskalenko did say that. There was no reason for Zhukov to lie. And Moskalenko was not able to contradict him and deny the serious accusation of state treason hurled at him. When I told [First Deputy Minister of Defense Rodion Y.] Malinovsky about this, he on his own initiative introduced a motion to relieve Zhukov of his duties immediately. I said, 'Rodion Yakovlevich, it is hardly necessary; after all, it was Moskalenko who started it.'

"Malinovsky looked at me in such a strange way that an astonishing thought entered my mind: it was a plot, a criminal act against me. However, I still told my comrades, the members of the Presidium, 'Let us not make it an affair of state. To make it an affair of state means that we should carry out an investigation and put them on trial. Taking into consideration the role that Moskalenko played in Beria's arrest when we had to fall back on his help — and he honorably provided help — I say, let us forgive him this episode.'"

the common sense Marshal Zhukov would have expressed if he wrote and edited it himself.

The second thing Bagramyan told me was that "the book says Stalin called the front and talked with you, Nikita Sergeyevich, in Zhukov's presence. Stalin warned you that according to the information they had, there was a threat on the left flank of our front, which is in the direction of Barvenkovo and Slavyansk. But there was no such call. I was there. I know how the events developed on our front. It is sheer invention."

This invention is of no use to Zhukov. Therefore, again, I think this is not Zhukov's invention but the work of some other force to whom it would be beneficial to misrepresent the manner in which the operation was carried out. There is such a peculiar twist in this presentation.

Who are these editors? Now that we are speaking of all this, it was not Stalin who called me, but I who called Stalin when the front commander, other members of the military council, and I made the decision to halt the operation, regroup the troops, and cover our left flank, on the side of Slavyansk and Kramatorsk. That was our decision.

After we made the decision and I had left the headquarters, Comrade Bagramyan came to me, very upset, and told me, "Marshal Timoshenko talked with Moscow. Who he talked with I don't know, but he ordered me to cancel our decision and continue the operation the way it had been approved by Stalin. It means that our troops will be destroyed. The only hope is that you work it out with Stalin and convince him to cancel his decision and restore the decision we made to stop the operation and regroup our troops."

Some "wise men" now say that what matters is we beat Hitler in the end. That is true, we did beat him. But we mustn't forget the songs we sang back then: "If tomorrow there's war, today we are ready to march." That's what is important. We sang songs about our "First Officer," Klim Voroshilov, and so forth. In fact, the "First Officer" was the biggest bag of shit in the army. His lack of initiative created a situation where our troops lacked the necessary rifles and machine guns right from the war's outset. Not during its first year, from its very first day! All this must be taken into consideration and lessons must be learned.

After the victory, Stalin strutted around like a rooster, his chest puffed out and his nose sticking up in the sky. I can understand that. However, I also remember him at the beginning of the war at the high command headquarters on Myasnitskaya Street.[9] That was a different Stalin, a bag of bones in a gray tunic. I remember his asking me, "How's it going?"

"Badly," I replied. "We've got no weapons."

Stalin answered slowly, in a low voice. "Well, they talk about how smart Russians are. Look how smart we are now."

I still feel the pain of these memories. I still experience an ache for the people of Russia. Even with the insufficient arms we had, we could have organized a better resistance. Those who shield Stalin from blame are nothing but his ass-kissers. They know their responsibility.

MALENKOV and, it seems, Beria told me about a very secret step that Stalin took, probably in 1942, when the Germans already occupied the Ukraine and Byelorussia. Stalin tried to make contact with Hitler in order to reach an agreement with him yielding to Hitler territory in the Ukraine, Byelorussia, and other areas of the Russian Federation. It was pretty much the territory that the Germans had already occupied.

Stalin personally had approaches made. Beria was responsible for getting them done. Beria had some kind of connection with a banker in Bulgaria who was a German agent there for Hitler. There was also some kind of connection between the banker and our intelligence.

Our agent was sent to Bulgaria and instructed to inform the German contact that the Soviet Union was ready to enter into negotiations and that we were willing to make some territorial concessions. But there was never any answer from Hitler. Apparently he was so sure of victory that he felt the Soviet Union's days were numbered. Why should he enter into negotiations when everything was practically his anyway? Hitler was planning further offensive actions and the taking of Moscow — in a word, the destruction of all of Russia as a state.

Well, the process of feeling Hitler out on the subject failed. Of

9. It was renamed Kirov Street after Kirov's death.

course, Stalin could have explained that he had wanted to stall and gain time to amass his forces later and win back what he would have given up. But to gain time at the cost of such concessions! To lose the Ukraine, to lose Byelorussia and the western regions of the Russian Federation! That would have been substantial. I don't know how long it would have taken to win it all back later.

At the time this was going on, I heard nothing from anyone. I found out only from whispers from Beria and Malenkov. Now I can't even be sure if it was told to me while Stalin was still alive, or only after his death. But I specifically remember that such a conversation took place. Was the conversation between the three of us, or was I alone with Malenkov and did Malenkov relate it to me mentioning Beria? Actually I think Beria told it to me himself.

DURING the war when I visited Moscow I suffered. Almost every evening I would get a call from Stalin: "Come over, we'll have dinner together." The dinners were horrible; we would return home only toward morning, before breakfast, and I had to go to work. I tried to get in on time, by ten o'clock, so during my lunch break I was forced to get some rest and take a nap.

What was really terrible if you didn't grab a quick nap then was that when Stalin called you up again, you'd start to fall asleep when you were with him. It always ended badly for anyone who started to doze at Stalin's table. It might seem improbable now, but it happened. He would throw a tomato at you if you nodded off. I saw it happen myself during the war years. We would go to the dacha to talk over military matters, and after reports were over he always invited us to his quarters. Then the dinners would begin.

The dinner would end with fruit being thrown, tomatoes and the like. It got so bad that he would pelt people with forks and spoons. This exasperated me. How could he do it? Really! A man of his stature, a leader, a genuinely smart man — then he would get so drunk that he took such liberties. I am convinced that those who commanded at the front — now they are all marshals — all know about it. They had all gone through it, through the trial, so to speak.

Of course, this all took place in 1943, after Stalin had acquired a uniform and began assuring us that we would win the war. Before this he walked around like a wet hen. I don't recall that there were any dinners with drinking before 1943. He was so depressed that it was pitiful to look at him.

I remember an American delegation coming to Moscow after the war. It was headed by Secretary of State James Byrnes. I was in Moscow at the time and was present at the dinner given by Stalin in honor of Byrnes. Aneurin Bevan, the leader of the British Labor party, was also there. He was in Churchill's wartime cabinet and a man of influence. Stalin was naturally the host and toastmaster. He was very active. Stalin badly mistreated Bevan, even though Bevan was from the working class. He was a longshoreman. When Stalin made some digs and nasty remarks, which were completely out of bounds, Bevan replied: "I was the first to raise my voice for the defense of Russia, and I organized a strike of English longshore-men under the slogan 'Hands off Soviet Russia.'" That was so. He was telling the truth. What caused Stalin to behave that way? This is difficult to explain. I think he believed he could run the policy of the whole world. That's why he behaved in such an unrestrained way toward representatives of countries that were our partners.

At the same time, however, Stalin was extremely courteous to Byrnes. But there was another side to this courtesy. At the dinner there were also representatives from the American embassy. Stalin courted Byrnes and flattered him with compliments, while saying all kinds of things against Truman, the president of the United States.[10] This is absolutely inadmissible — to throw compliments in the face of Truman's representative while abusing the president. Byrnes tried to wriggle out of the situation. Of course, he didn't accept the compliments. When some of us talked it over later, we were indignant. Even Beria said: "How can he do that? How can he do that? As soon as Byrnes leaves, Truman will know everything that happened." Maybe that explains why Truman burned with such strong anti-Soviet attitudes and such an antipathy to Stalin.

10. Harry S. Truman succeeded to the presidency after Franklin D. Roosevelt's death on April 12, 1945.

4

Unfinished Business

IN my meetings with people I am sometimes asked what caused
us to create the Warsaw Pact. It was formed for the defense of
socialist countries. The Cold War was declared by Western Europe
on the Soviet Union and its socialist allies. It was Churchill who lit
that torch — he initiated that war.

Churchill was socialism's most outspoken opponent. He took
such a dislike to communism that he did everything he could to
set up barricades around the capitalist world, to organize it, and to
position it against communism in hopes of reining in the socialist
countries.

He did not just want to prevent the development of socialism;
he did all he could to destroy it. [Secretary of State John Foster]
Dulles picked up where Churchill left off. He wanted to restrict
socialism's base, to tear from the Soviet Union its socialist allies.
Naturally there were other opponents of socialism, but I wanted
to focus on these two.

The Western capitalist countries formed NATO [in 1949] as a
military organization opposed to the Soviet Union and its socialist
allies. This powerful organization brought great harm to bear on
the socialist world. We as Soviets, and as the leaders of the socialist
movement, were blockaded. Almost no Western country would
trade with us, especially the kinds of goods we needed most —
sophisticated equipment and instruments. The West just would
not give up those things and, if you ask me, continues to this day
not to trade them with us. That is especially true of the United

States. The Americans have even passed a law against trading with the Soviet Union.

At the time we started the Warsaw Pact [1955], Molotov was minister of foreign affairs. When we decided that it was necessary to create such an organization, the Presidium of the Central Committee instructed Molotov to prepare some proposals about it. When he presented them to the party leadership and the government for consideration, what kinds of improvements did Molotov's proposals need? First of all, Albania and the German Democratic Republic [East Germany] were not on the list of members.

When I saw this, I asked Molotov, "Why aren't these countries on the list?"

Molotov still lived in a Stalinist world, where war was expected to break out at any moment. Because of this, antiaircraft batteries were set up all around Moscow. These were manned around the clock. Live shells were laid out next to the guns. They were ready to be fired on the command, "Powder ready! Fire!" That is how Stalin perceived the situation. The fact is that he was afraid that the capitalist countries would attack the Soviet Union. Most of all, America.

America had a powerful air force and, most important, America had atomic bombs, while we had only just developed the mechanism and had a negligible number of finished bombs. Under Stalin we had no means of delivery. We had no long-range bombers capable of reaching the United States, nor did we have long-range rockets. All we had was short-range rockets. This situation weighed heavily on Stalin. He understood that he had to be careful not to be dragged into a war.

Shortly after Stalin died [in 1953], significant qualitative changes had occurred in those areas. But Molotov was just a shadow of Stalin when it came to military affairs and international politics. So when the leadership asked Molotov why the GDR and Albania were not on the list of members of the Warsaw Pact, he said that Albania was far away, with no common border with the USSR, and virtually inaccessible. Our only land contact with Albania was through Yugoslavia. At that time, Molotov did not consider Yugoslavia to be a socialist country but an enemy. So Albania was right next to stronger foes of socialism, which could always attack.

There was no way we could help Albania. So Molotov concluded that there was no need to include Albania in the Warsaw Pact.

"What about the GDR?" we asked. Molotov replied: "Why should we fight with the West over the GDR?"

That amazed me. I said, "Do you see, Vyacheslav Mikhailovich, if we form a military organization that some socialist countries join, but the GDR and Albania don't, then it will send a signal to our Western foes: 'You are allowed,' speaking crudely, 'to eat up Albania and the GDR. You decide when yourself.'"

That is how it would be perceived. And that would inflame the appetite of the revanchists and other Western powers that would like to tear from us Albania and, most important, the GDR. This is why that was unacceptable.

A full exchange of ideas eliminated all doubts about forming the Warsaw Pact, and there was no longer any disagreement about its composition, Molotov included. Everything else fell into place, and the GDR and Albania joined the Warsaw Pact.[1]

The structure of the Warsaw Pact, I think, is clear enough. Every member country contributed a certain number of troops. As we discussed this with the member countries, they expressed their opinion that the leader of the Warsaw Pact should be a Soviet general or marshal. Everyone understood that the Soviet Union had the world's mightiest army and most powerful industry. Also, having lost 20 million to Hitler's armies, we had the most extensive war experience. Each member country's minister of defense is a Warsaw Pact deputy commander.

I think it is important to say that in setting up the pact, we wanted to make an impression on the West. It is safe to say that the time when the West could talk with the Soviet Union and its socialist allies from a position of strength passed long ago. We formed the Warsaw Pact in response to their formation of NATO.

Those two forces oppose each other throughout the world. And we have never stopped saying that we created the Warsaw Pact because they created NATO. We have never quieted our propaganda or eased up in our fight for our ideals. Many times we have officially expressed our willingness to liquidate our Warsaw Pact if

1. In addition to East Germany and Albania, the Warsaw Pact members were Bulgaria, Hungary, Poland, Romania, Czechoslovakia, and the Soviet Union.

the West would liquidate NATO. Because of this it cannot be said that the Warsaw Pact is a preparation for war. It is a preparation for defense in case of war against socialist countries. That was our primary goal. And I still think it would be reasonable for our opponents to become our partners, and for them to eliminate NATO, and for us to dissolve the Warsaw Pact.

We then proposed equal and mutual arms reductions for NATO and the Warsaw Pact. We offered to dismantle our military bases located on the territories of third governments. The Soviet Union at that time [1955] had a base in Finland. We also had soldiers stationed in Port Arthur, China. We called them home and dismantled the bases. We wanted to show our good intentions to the West.

But the West did not follow our example. It continued to strengthen its organization and develop its military might. That forced us — as it still does — to maintain our own forces at a comparable level. We occupy class positions — the proletarians for socialist construction, and the United States in the classical position of a strong capitalist state pursuing its own goals. The United States was not just pursuing its own goals, however; it had taken on the additional duties of the world's gendarme.

While Stalin was alive he gave military questions much thought. But I believe that our greatest advances in defense have come about since he died. The main reason is that after the war, industry grew very quickly. Second, we had a better understanding of the new directions being taken in military industry. From that it follows that we could invest in the areas that would produce the most effective weapons.

We set as our goal the development of an atomic-powered military submarine fleet capable of launching both nuclear and nonnuclear missiles. We developed intercontinental missiles and strategic rockets with ranges of two and four thousand kilometers. We also developed short-range weapons carried by infantrymen that could launch either nuclear or nonnuclear missiles. Nuclear weapons were the main thing that increased our military might.

When we formed the Warsaw Pact, Western countries had a great advantage over us in their economies and their nuclear arsenals. Because of that we had to mobilize and make better estimates of our forces in the event that the enemy should attack either the

Soviet Union or our allies. Our military union was a product of the times we lived in. Things are different now. The military and economic balances have shifted to our favor. That makes it easier for us to take the offensive in the areas of disarmament and world cooperation.

AFTER the war, we had to deal with the question of what to do about Austria. Austria itself had not fought against us, but it had been part of Germany when the war with Hitler began. When the war ended, Austria was treated separately and was to have its own peace treaty with us.

There were negotiations on a peace treaty with Austria while Stalin was still alive. All the main issues were settled. The treaty was being prepared for signature with Austria. It contained a point stating that Trieste was to become part of Yugoslavia.[2] But as the draft of the treaty was being drawn up, relations with Tito and with Yugoslavia took a sharp turn for the worse. So the peace treaty with Austria was not signed while Stalin was alive. I remember Stalin saying, "We didn't sign any peace treaty. Why did we have to refuse to sign? That was a mistake, all because of Trieste. Now that issue doesn't even exist anymore."

Stalin did not want to argue for having Trieste go to Yugoslavia, because he was so embittered against Tito. He was ready to go to war against Yugoslavia, and I suspect that he was thinking about this, although I never heard any conversation mentioning military action. Stalin, however, began to send out agents and put on displays of strength as soon as the break with Tito occurred.

At that point in Stalin's life, there were no meetings of any kind in the real sense of the word, with a secretary, a protocol, proposals, exchange of ideas, formal decisions. There was none of it. Stalin behaved like Almighty God with a host of angels and archangels. He might listen to us, but the main thing was that he spoke

2. Trieste was part of the Austro-Hungarian Empire until World War I, when it was captured by the Italians. In World War II, Tito's guerrillas attacked the Germans occupying Trieste. At the end of the war Yugoslavia and Italy claimed Trieste. The United States supported the Italian claims. The Soviet Union supported Yugoslavia until Stalin broke with Tito, in 1948, and the issue was not resolved until after Stalin's death.

and we listened. He did not explain his reasoning, but passed down the word to lesser mortals. They did what they were told when he wanted it done.

This is how matters were discussed and conclusions were reached. We had gotten used to it, and no one had any complaints. It was very rare that anyone spoke his mind on any issue. Stalin might listen to you respectfully once but scream rudely at you the next time, as if to say, "Mind your own business. You haven't the slightest idea what you're talking about."

His decisions were then formalized through the Council of Ministers or through the Central Committee apparatus. International issues were formalized through Molotov and the Ministry of Foreign Affairs: a diplomatic note there, or an exhortation in the newspaper, through [the news agency] TASS.

When Stalin died we went on as before, out of inertia. Our boat just continued to float down the stream, along the same course that had been set by Stalin, even though we all sensed that things were not right.

We were burdened by the conditions that existed between Austria and the USSR. In effect, our two countries were still at war. Our relations could not develop, and we had no embassy in Austria. Our troops were in Vienna and we occupied large portions of Austrian territory.

Like Germany, Austria was divided up between the United States, England, France, and the Soviet Union. And, like Berlin, Vienna was divided into zones.

We owned things in Austria. We had factories, and we were running them. We set up management systems and established an economic network among the factories. They probably belonged to German capitalists, but we confiscated them and assumed ownership.

These factories employed several thousand people, although they were generally small and medium-sized. They were equipped with outdated equipment and therefore not very productive. If they had modern technology and equipment, that would have yielded a higher level of productivity and made sound economic sense, producing higher profits and allowing higher wages for the workers.

There was no way to remedy the situation, however. We were a socialist country that owned and operated these factories in Austria. Yet we employed Austrian citizens, who earned less than those who worked at capitalist businesses.

This constituted a fairly serious problem for us. There was no way to squeeze more production out of the equipment installed at the factories. It was too old. Competition with the capitalists was too complicated. They were experienced in management. They had gathered the best managers and scientific and technical workers. Most of the really talented specialists had left our factories for capitalist businesses. Many of them were against the socialist system.

We were faced with deliberate work stoppages, although the Austrian Communist party did everything it could to maintain production and reconcile the workers with our administration.

We began to have doubts. Did we really need to own these factories in Austria? Weren't we creating a damaging comparison between working conditions at socialist-owned enterprises and the conditions at capitalist enterprises? So why not divest ourselves of the factories and sell them back to the Austrian government?

Another issue was the presence of our troops in Austria. We were increasing our efforts on behalf of peaceful coexistence, and we were seeking the withdrawal of troops by other countries that occupied foreign territories. Yet our troops were in Austria. As our commander reported, this led to all kinds of tension with the government — that is, with the petty bureaucrats. The populace, it must be said, was fairly warm toward us. I don't remember any reports of trouble between the Austrian people and our Soviet troops, who conducted themselves the way they should. They did not interfere in internal affairs; they went about their own business and were not the object of any criticism or the cause of any kind of difficulty. Still, we understood full well that foreign troops on any country's soil are not a gift from God but a necessity of war. The war had been over for how many years, yet we had not formally ended the war.

Stalin was gone but Molotov was still around, and he had put together that policy along with Stalin. Therefore, the views of Stalin were really the views of Molotov and Stalin. Which one of them had played the first violin? No doubt Stalin. But Molotov had

played his own violin as loud as possible. Molotov, by the way,
really did play the violin. I can't assess how well, but Stalin used
to make jokes about him, often in an insulting manner. Molotov
once told us that when he was in exile in Vologda or somewhere
he played the violin in a restaurant. Drunken merchants used to
summon him and demand he play songs. They paid him well.
When Stalin was irritated with Molotov, he would say, "Those
drunken merchants you played for must have smeared mustard all
over your face!" I have to confess I was on Stalin's side. I thought
it was humiliating for a man — particularly a political activist, a
political exile — to play the violin to please drunken merchants.
He might have looked for some other way to provide for himself
materially.

I felt we needed to be done with the matter of Austria. As minister of foreign affairs, Molotov was not taking any initiative on it,
so I exchanged ideas with Anastas Ivanovich Mikoyan. I considered
him an experienced colleague and very sensible. I enjoyed discussing international issues as well as domestic problems with him.

He felt the same as I did. The time had come to quit talking
about how abnormal the situation was. We had to remove the
abnormality by concluding a treaty with Austria. Withdrawing our
troops would untie our hands to carry out our propaganda against
the United States, which had sent its troops to many countries on
many continents to carry out its aggressive, policeman-like policies
within its sphere of influence.

I then took the matter up with Molotov. "Vyacheslav Mikhailovich, I would like to ask your opinion. How do you feel about signing a peace treaty with Austria? How about negotiating a treaty
with the Austrian government?"

To my surprise, Molotov reacted sharply to my suggestion and
started to lecture me. "How can we sign a peace treaty? We have
a difference of opinion with the United States." He was referring
to Trieste.

"That's true," I said, "but we need to reach some kind of solution
and remove this obstacle. You know yourself Stalin raised the issue
before his death."

But Molotov remained stubborn and abrasive. Molotov was a
very harsh man, and when he was convinced of something he could

be quite unrestrained. The harshness came through in the intensity of his passion of being right. He knew the way something needed to be done, and there was no other way.

"Mind your own business. I'm an old politician. I have many years of experience with such matters and you have only just started down this path. I was minister of foreign affairs during wartime! I've had all kinds of meetings and conducted all sorts of negotiations on issues concerning our country. And now here you come, without consulting me, trying to force your ideas on me — ideas that are not right, that are harmful to our interests." He said all this very harshly.

I said, "Vyacheslav Mikhailovich, calm down and just listen to me for a minute. I don't understand your arguments; they're unconvincing. All I'm saying is that you need to think about concluding some kind of peace treaty."

I was the first secretary of the Central Committee at the time. So my voice, as they say, carried some weight. My position as leader of the Presidium of the Central Committee also carried some weight.

That's why I began to insist. By this time the matter of Trieste had been settled with Yugoslavia. Tito had not made any claims on the city and agreed to let it become part of Italy. The Yugoslavs had reached an agreement with Italy.[3]

But Molotov was like a windup toy. Once he was wound up and let go, his gears and wheels would turn and turn and turn until all the tension had gone out of his spring.

So we had to settle the issue against the wishes of the minister of foreign affairs. To those who will eventually pay attention to my memoirs, I guarantee the validity of what I'm saying here. As believers used to say, "I swear it by the Gospel." (We are not believers and do not acknowledge the Gospel. Even before I was a party member, I was an atheist, a nonbeliever. I say "I swear by the Gospel" only because it is popular to use such proof and arguments to enhance your credibility if someone doubts your word.)

I am stressing this because it sounds so improbable. A sane man might say, "Well, Khrushchev, it seems, has a grudge against

3. The agreement on Trieste was signed between Italy and Yugoslavia in London on October 5, 1954.

Molotov and that's why he is attributing such rubbish to him. Molotov is no fool. How could he really defend such foolishness?" It really was garbage. Unfortunately, to my disappointment that is the way it happened.

While Stalin was still alive, I had a lot of respect for Molotov. In my eyes, Molotov was a man who sometimes might even question what Stalin said. More than once he raised his voice on my behalf, or on behalf of others who were suffering momentarily from Stalin's explosive wrath.

Apparently it was no accident that in 1939, when I was in the Ukraine, Vyacheslav Mikhailovich Molotov tried mightily to convince me to become his deputy when he was named minister of foreign affairs. I tried to convince him not to do it, but he went ahead and appealed to Stalin. Stalin agreed.

My final argument was the only one that worked. I said that it did not make sense for me to leave the Ukraine since the outbreak of war was imminent. I was used to the Ukraine. The Ukraine had gotten used to me. Why bring someone new in at a time like this? If the newcomer was unfamiliar with the republic, and if the population and local leaders were not used to him, it would only create difficulties.

Stalin saw it my way and told Molotov: "Forget it. Khrushchev is right. He should stay where he is." I am relating this to demonstrate the kind of relationship we once had. It eventually turned into another kind of relationship, which I did not initiate. Our strained relations were not my fault.

We had grown accustomed to hearing Stalin call Molotov a dullard. Stalin conditioned us to think of Molotov this way. Molotov occasionally showed unbelievable stubbornness, bordering on stupidity. That's the way he was with the Austrian question.

"Well," I said, "all right. Let's bring the matter up with the Presidium of the Central Committee. We'll discuss it and take your position into account. You'll explain it yourself. We will reach a decision, because I feel we cannot drag it out any longer. It can only do us harm. And it is in no one's interest for us to continue this policy of not signing the peace treaty. It benefits neither our foreign policy nor our relations with Austria nor the interests of the Austrian people."

Then I asked Molotov, "Do you think we need to maintain our

position in Austria in order to be ready and better prepare to start a war?"

"No," he answered. "That is not what I want."

"Then what is your argument?" I asked. "The Trieste issue is gone. The only other argument can be that we are readying ourselves for war there; our troops are staying on Austrian soil so that they will be deployed close to the borders of the Western countries who were our allies but have now become our enemies."

"No," said Molotov. "That is not what I want."

"Well," I said, "if you share my opinion and do not foresee war, the most logical thing is to do away with this remnant of World War II and sign a peace treaty."

In the end we agreed that the Soviet Union needed to conclude a peace treaty with Austria. We readied the appropriate documents and began negotiations.

We informed the Austrian Communist party of our actions so that its members would not be caught by surprise. We told them that after we signed the treaty we would withdraw our troops from Austria, but only after all the other countries occupying Vienna and the rest of the country also pulled their troops out.

The Austrian Communist party leaders had no objections. They understood our position completely and told us it would strengthen them. They said they were being heavily criticized for relying too much on the presence of Soviet troops, especially in Vienna and in the Soviet-occupied sector. It was said that they were not truly an independent party of the working class, but rather just Soviet agents carrying out directives from the Soviet Union.

During the negotiations that produced the treaty, there was one episode when we had sat down to a luncheon. I was seated next to Julius Raab.[4] He was an obese man, with a large head and large face. His head was quite round. We sat there talking and I said, "You know, Mr. Raab, this is the first time in my life I have sat next to a real capitalist. I have met with the servants of capitalists, when I was a workman and we went on strike where I worked. I had the trust of my fellow workers and was included in the committee that led strikes and that conducted negotiations with the

---

4. Julius Raab was chancellor of Austria from July 1953 to April 1961.

administration. So, as they say, I have gone nose to nose — not with actual capitalists, but with their servants." This was because the capitalists that owned the businesses where I worked were high and mighty, and lived in St. Petersburg; we never laid eyes on them. "And here I am," I said, "sitting at the same table with a capitalist in the flesh, one I can touch."

He burst out laughing, and so did everyone else at the table.

He said, "Mr. Khrushchev, what do you mean! Am I really a capitalist? I am a *klein, klein* capitalist; I am a very little capitalist."

I answered, "Yes, Mr. Raab, you may be a *klein, klein* capitalist, but you are one nonetheless. You have men who work for you. And I am a working man. I could work for you." We continued the joke.

"But," said Raab, "we have just accomplished a good thing." We ended up by saying, "Let's drink to that." And so we drank to our accomplishment.

I greatly enjoyed talking to Raab's deputy.[5] He was easy to converse with. I think he was a working-class man, but very well trained. He led the Social Democrats and so was deputy chairman of the Austrian coalition government, the bourgeois government.

He also joked with us. When the two of them were arguing about something, I interjected, "I'm on Mr. Raab's side."

The other man said, "Mr. Khrushchev, do you know what *raab* means?"

"No, I don't," I answered.

"A *raab*," he said, "is a crow. In Austrian it means 'crow.'" He looked at Raab and grinned.

I said, "Ah, a crow. This old crow and I are doing a good thing together. You should join us."

We were very satisfied with the treaty.[6] I felt then, and still do, that this was a great international victory for us. We, the leaders of the Soviet Union, were very satisfied that we had attained this after Stalin's death. On the subject of the relations between the Soviet Union and the capitalist world, Stalin took every chance to instill in us the idea that we were mere kittens, calves to be led around by the rest of the world. "The West will wrap you around

5. Adolf Scherf was Raab's deputy.
6. Khrushchev neglects to mention the main Soviet concession in the negotiations. Once a peace treaty was signed the Soviet Union would abandon the right to reintroduce troops into Austria. The treaty was signed on May 15, 1955.

its finger," he would warn us. Stalin never expressed any confidence that we were worthy of representing our socialist nation, or defending its interests in the international arena.

But our nation's interests needed to be defended within limits, and along lines that did not harm other countries. We needed to proceed to create the kind of relations with other countries that would strengthen peace and the peaceful coexistence of nations with differing social and political systems.

Austria was a first step for us, a demonstration that we could conduct negotiations and conduct them well. We defended the interests of the Soviet Union and the other socialist countries and were able to force other countries — capitalist countries, that had already undertaken aggressive policies against socialist nations — to agree to our way of thinking. Austria became a neutral country.

So we celebrated a great international victory. It was the European debut for a country bumpkin, and it did us a lot of good. The bumpkin had learned a thing or two. We could orient ourselves without directives from Stalin. We had exchanged our knee pants for long trousers in international politics.

ANOTHER thorn in our side left over from the war was the absence of a peace treaty with Japan. The military situation had been resolved in our favor. Justice was restored in relation to our Soviet state, but there was no diplomatic resolution — all because of Stalin's abnormal way of thinking. If he had correctly assessed the situation as it existed right after Japanese militarism had been crushed, we would have been able to preserve our representation in Japan at a time when conditions were ripe for establishing contacts with the country's more progressive elements. Yet we failed to exploit this situation because we had isolated ourselves. We paid a heavy price for our stubbornness and stupidity.

Let me explain what I mean, because it concerns a significant period in the development of the Soviet Union and of our diplomacy. A few months after the end of the war with Germany, Roosevelt and Stalin agreed at Livadia in Yalta that we would enter the war with Japan and help the United States.[7] Our interests were

7. Livadia, two miles southwest of Yalta, is a seaside resort on the southern

in the southern part of Sakhalin Island and in the return of the Kuril Islands to the USSR. We were to occupy Port Arthur and regain our rights to the property we had and lost in Manchuria and Korea before the war of 1904–1905 — a war that had been forced on us by Japan. Russia had been defeated, and Japan imposed a degrading peace treaty on us.[8] Before World War II, Japan had always been hostile to the Soviet Union. I'd go further than that: it was insolent and demanding. Japan pursued an intolerable policy, yet we were forced to sit still for it because we were weak and Japan was strong. Besides, we understood that the problem was not with Japan alone. We were up against Japan in the east, Germany in the west. We had to play diplomatic games, maneuvering in order to secure peace, or at any rate not allow the enemy to start a war. We didn't want to face a war on two fronts, east and west. We were then too weak to wage such a war.

Then, toward the end of World War II, the moment came for our troops to cross the border from Siberia into Japanese-occupied Manchuria. I remember that at one point, when I was in Moscow, Stalin was leaning on our officers to start military actions as soon as possible. Otherwise, he warned, Japan might capitulate to the armed forces of the United States before we entered the war. Stalin had his doubts about whether the Americans would keep their word. He worried that they might take advantage of a condition in the [Yalta] agreement: the territories that Japan had seized from Russia had been promised to us — but only if we participated in the war against Japan. What if we didn't participate? What if Japan capitulated before we entered the war? The Americans might say, We don't owe you anything.

We crushed the Kwantung Army [Eastern Region (Manchurian)

---

coast of the Crimea. Before the revolution it was an imperial estate with two palaces, one of which was the site of the February 1945 Yalta Conference, attended by Roosevelt, Churchill, and Stalin.

8. The conflict of Russian and Japanese interests in Asia led to a Japanese attack on the Russian naval base of Port Arthur in Manchuria in 1904. The immediate cause of the war was the Russian refusal to withdraw from Manchuria and the expansion of concessions in Korea, which the Japanese considered their area of exploitation. The Russian navy was defeated in the Battle of Tsushima Strait in May 1905, and in the peace treaty signed in September 1905 Russia ceded to Japan the southern half of Sakhalin Island, Port Arthur, and the southern line of the Chinese Eastern Railway.

Army]. By then, the Americans had dropped their two atomic bombs, and Japan was already broken. You could say that Japan was staggering in the throes of defeat. The Japanese were looking for any way possible to get out of the war. We entered the fighting literally in its last days, liberating Manchuria, Sakhalin, and half of Korea.[9] Just look at the seizure of the Emperor Pu Yi.[10] Our plane landed in Mukden and took prisoner the emperor of Manchuria, Japan's protégé. We arrived, as the Russian saying goes, at the moment the guests were putting on their hats to leave.

If Roosevelt had still been around, things might have gone differently and turned out better for us. Roosevelt was a clever president, and he had a high regard for the Soviet Union. Stalin could do business with him. Stalin said he had good personal relations with Roosevelt, and that was probably so. Certainly Stalin's relations with Roosevelt were much better than with the other allies, such as Churchill of Great Britain. But Roosevelt was gone. Now the war was being waged by Truman. He was not a clever man. He had become president by chance. He carried out an unstinting, unbridled reactionary policy toward the Soviet Union, which was intolerable. Only later did this become graphically clear.

When Japan did capitulate, we had no representatives present at the surrender ceremony. This was not by chance. Even though we had not fought on the Japanese islands, the Americans might still have invited their ally to the ceremony and waited until we arrived. But Truman didn't want that. He seemed to be making a point of signing the surrender in our absence. This irritated us.

Then, when a committee was established to observe and supervise the capitulation of the Japanese army, our role was that of a poor relative at the wedding of a rich man. We were ignored.[11] The

9. The Soviet Union entered the war in the Far East on August 8, 1945, only six days before Japan surrendered.

10. The last Ching dynasty emperor of China, Hsuan Tung, better known as Henry Pu Yi, ascended to the throne in 1909, when he was three years old. He was forced to abdicate on February 12, 1912. In 1932, after their conquest, the Japanese established him as the puppet emperor of Manchuria and called it Manchukuo, or Manchu land. After World War II Pu Yi was imprisoned by the Chinese Communists and released after "reform through labor." In 1960 he told Field Marshal Viscount Montgomery: "I am a new man, I am the new Pu Yi. I am much happier today as a gardener than I ever was before." He died in 1967, and became the subject of Bernardo Bertolucci's film *The Last Emperor* (1987).

11. Khrushchev is most probably referring to the Allied Council for Japan, an

others didn't give any consideration to our views. In a word, they mistreated us. After the committee was disbanded, we stayed there for a long time. We didn't want to leave, claiming the right of a victorious power that had accepted the surrender from Japan. When the Americans asked us to get out, we resisted. In the end our people were literally blockaded there under intolerable, impossible living conditions. They weren't allowed to go anywhere. Nobody cared for them, and some of our people left.

All these incidents irritated not only Stalin, but all of us. We all felt indignant, yet there was nothing we could do. The United States had the upper hand. Were we to declare war on the United States because of that? No, of course not; that was unthinkable. We had no capabilities to do such a thing, and besides, wise statesmen don't declare war in such circumstances. However, relations between the USSR and the United States did not stay frozen — they kept on getting hotter and hotter.

It was really Truman who was mistreating us. This stemmed both from his character and from his mental abilities. A clever president would not have behaved so provocatively. He would not have goaded the Soviet Union.

However, we have to give the Americans some credit. When the protocol of the peace treaty with Japan was drafted, there was a place reserved for our signature. Our interests were totally taken care of there. All we had to do was sign, and everything would have fallen into place; we would have gotten everything we were promised. We would also have restored peaceful relations with Japan and been able to send representatives of our diplomatic service to Tokyo.

We should have signed. I don't know why we didn't. Perhaps it was vanity or pride. But primarily it was that Stalin had an exaggerated idea of what he could do and what his influence was on the

---

advisory body located in Tokyo, with four members: the supreme commander, General Douglas MacArthur, who was chairman and the U.S. representative; a representative each from the Soviet Union and China; and a member representing jointly the United Kingdom, Australia, New Zealand, and India. The council met every two weeks "to consult and advise" the supreme commander on the implementation of the terms of the surrender and the occupation and control. It exercised only very limited authority because in practice the occupation was essentially a U.S. operation.

United States. He took the bit in his mouth and refused to sign the treaty. I think his logic worked like this: If we signed the treaty, we would be recognizing the fact — perfectly obvious to any thinking man — that the United States had suffered the main losses from Japanese treachery and borne the principal burden in crushing Japan (although the interests of England, Holland, and other European colonial countries were also affected). Stalin didn't want to do that. There was no question that the Americans gave us the back of their hand, refusing to recognize our contribution to the extent that they should have. Still, we should have taken a sober view of events. If we compare what we contributed with what the United States contributed to the defeat of Japan, then we have to recognize that we did even less in the war against Japan than the Americans and British did to defeat Hitler's Germany. In fact, their contribution against Hitler was larger, even though they gained victory mainly through the blood of the Soviet people and the exhaustion of our resources. However, they gave us significant help by Lend-Lease. Several times I heard Stalin acknowledge this aid within the small circle of people around him. He said that if the Americans and British had not helped us with Lend-Lease — if we had had to deal with Germany one-on-one — we would not have been able to cope because we lost so much of our industry.

When the treaty was ready [1951] we were again invited to join in the signing. But we didn't. I couldn't understand why then and I can't understand now. It was Stalin who made the policy. He never asked for anybody's advice. He was too cocky, particularly after the defeat of Hitler's Germany. He imagined himself to be Kuzma Kryuchkov: he could cross any sea; he could do anything, no matter how difficult. People of the younger generation may not know this cartoon hero, who was created around World War I. His picture appeared in newspapers and magazines, running through ten Germans with one thrust of his lance. He was like Vasily Tiorkin, but much worse, of course.[12]

But now that the war was over and the main enemy was defeated, the West was mobilizing and unifying its forces against

12. Vasily Tiorkin is the hero and title of Aleksandr Tvardovsky's poem about a happy-go-lucky World War II soldier whose good humor and gaiety are curbed only by his grim duty as a defender of his motherland. Tiorkin was the Soviet GI Joe of World War II.

the Soviet Union. Therefore, when we refused to sign the Japanese surrender, forces in the West probably thought it was to their advantage. And it later turned out they were right. Just look at who benefited from the situation: it was our own fault because if we had signed we would have had an embassy there. We would have had access to Japanese public opinion and influential circles. We would have established trade relations with Japanese firms.

We missed all that. That's just what the Americans wanted; it was in their interest. They didn't want our representatives to be in other countries. In general, they wanted to isolate us. That is the policy they carried out from the first day of the Soviet state: encirclement, nonrecognition, and intervention. Now we ourselves swallowed this very bait and ended up pleasing aggressive, anti-Soviet forces in the United States, all because of our shortsightedness.

Since we had absolutely no contacts with Japan, our economy and our policy suffered. The Americans, meanwhile, not only had an embassy in Tokyo, they were masters there. They behaved brazenly. They built bases. They waged an anti-Soviet policy. They incited the Japanese. They did what the most frenzied monopolists and militarists wanted them to do. They seethed with hatred against the socialist camp, primarily against the country that first raised the Marxist-Leninist banner of the working class and achieved great successes.

After Stalin's death I spoke to Mikoyan, Bulganin, and Malenkov about it. We all agreed that we needed to find a way to sign the treaty and end the state of war with Japan. That way we could send an ambassador to Japan who would carry out proper work. But Molotov showed the same fierce stubbornness, the same obtuseness, that he did when the question of concluding a peace treaty with Austria was discussed. "We can't do it," he said. "They haven't done this, and they haven't done that. There is no way we can sign the agreement." In short, he repeated all the same arguments that Stalin had used to refuse signing the treaty the first time around.

We told him: "Comrade Molotov, you must look at what we are able to accomplish here, exactly what kind of influence we have. What's done is done; it's water under the bridge. The only thing we can do is try to fix the situation. If we can get them to let us sign the treaty, it will set things right. Strictly speaking, all the conditions affecting us laid out in the protocol have been met. Yet we are still technically at war with Japan. That's why there is no Japanese ambassador in Moscow and no Soviet ambassador in Tokyo. Who benefits from our absence in Tokyo? The Americans, that's who! The United States is in control of Japan. Our return to Tokyo would benefit the Japanese, especially the progressive people there. As soon as our embassy reopens in Tokyo, it will act like a magnet, attracting all those who are dissatisfied with Japan's current policies. These elements will begin to establish ties to our embassy, and we will begin to exert some influence on Japanese politics."

There was, naturally, great dissatisfaction in Japan, first because of Hiroshima and Nagasaki. It was the United States more than any other country that destroyed Japan. Truman's use of the atomic bomb against Japanese cities was the first atrocity of this kind in history committed against humanity. Of course, the dead can't register their dissatisfaction, but the wounded, their relatives, and the politicians — they were of a single strong mind on this issue. But they were unable to take any action because they had been weakened, and the United States had behaved quite arrogantly. American soldiers were rude and committed acts of violence against the populace. Also, the Japanese lost Okinawa to American occupation — a fact that could have been a major impetus for friendship with the Soviet Union, and for mobilizing forces against the occupiers.

I told Molotov, "The biggest favor we could do for the Americans would be stubbornly to reject contacts with Japan. That would give them a chance to exercise absolute power there and to turn Japan steadily more against the Soviet Union. We'll be making it easy for the Americans to claim that the Soviet Union illegally seized this or that piece of territory and that the Soviet Union still has some hidden intentions." Of course, not even Stalin had any such thing in mind.

I was actually on friendly terms with Molotov. I could see he was a man of some intelligence. Sometimes I enjoyed talking to him. After Beria was put out of the way, Molotov was especially well disposed toward me and said so often within our circle. At an official dinner in honor of my sixtieth birthday [in 1954], Molotov made a very warm speech about me. He particularly emphasized my role in organizing Beria's removal. I don't wish to seem immodest, but that move was made at just the right time. If we had not removed Beria when we did, both the internal and foreign policies of the Soviet Union would have taken a completely different turn. Beria was a monster, a hatchet man. He was close to taking the law into his own hands. At the time we moved against him, all his hit men were gathered in Moscow and either already had or would soon have had their assignments. After Beria's arrest these men were identified. This experience brought Molotov and me closer together. Molotov understood Beria well and knew what he was capable of. He knew that if Beria had been given the chance, our two heads would have been the first to roll. Beria needed to remove anyone in his way. A sea of blood would have been spilled — more than under Stalin.

I've digressed in order to explain my good, trusting relationship with Molotov. For many years I always addressed him politely, using either his full name, Vyacheslav Mikhailovich, or the formal form of address. When he suggested we use the familiar form with each other, I was uncomfortable at first, but I got used to it. All I'm saying here is that I really had no reason to be against him. But there were basic differences in our understanding of the simplest truths. They were readily apparent to any average person, even one unschooled in politics. Molotov was just plain thick; he was always in the dark on whatever the issue was. When I saw how difficult he was being over Japan, what kind of resistance he was putting up, I thought to myself, My God! How could this man have been responsible for our country's diplomacy under Stalin? He represented us to the world! How many years — including some of the most crucial — was he minister of foreign affairs?[13] And before the war he had been chairman of the Council of People's Commissars. A man of such limits, so closed-minded, with no understanding of the simplest things. I found it all very puzzling. I wasn't really angry. Rather, I felt pity for Molotov.

We finally did adopt a resolution to take some diplomatic steps that would allow us to establish contact with the Japanese government — and, more important, with the United States over the matter of the protocol. Our ability to sign the protocol, this

13. Molotov was foreign minister from 1939 to 1949 and from 1953 to 1956.

peace treaty with Japan, depended on the United States. Well, the United States refused to let us sign. The Japanese, of course, were also opposed to our signing. Here I'm speaking of those Japanese who advocated anti-Soviet policies. They were the ones in power at the time and were on America's side. The United States determined who would fill what posts in Japan's governmental bodies and that way exerted a decisive influence.

I remember that once we did establish an embassy in Tokyo [in 1956], a liberal prime minister, Ichiro Hatoyama, visited the Soviet Union.[14] The minister of agriculture and fisheries, Ichiro Kono, accompanied him. He was a young man and quite energetic. We discussed the possibility of the USSR's signing a peace treaty with Japan. The attitude of the prime minister was promising. He was very attentive to what we had to say and made efforts to normalize relations with the USSR. In the end he was blocked by internal political forces in Japan, but the main obstacle was the influence of the United States.

Perhaps if that man had lived longer and increased his power, public opinion would have changed, but he was elderly when he visited [in October 1956], and very ill. Soon after returning to Japan, he died. Our relations with the United States had already been strained to the breaking point. I can understand why the Americans didn't want us to have any influence in Japan. The Americans had put a lot into securing their own position there, particularly their military bases. Passions ran high immediately after the war and the United States was savoring its victory over Japan. At the same time, every move the United States made was intended to demonstrate that Japan needed U.S. protection against the Soviet threat.

About this time the Japanese raised the issue of the Soviet Union relinquishing two of the four Kuril Islands that lie right off Japan's coast.[15] There was no historical basis at all for Japan to claim that territory, since Japanese imperialists had seized the islands by

14. Hatoyama (1883–1959) was prime minister from December 1954 to 1959 and was responsible for restoring diplomatic relations with the Soviet Union.

15. There are fifty-six islands in the Kuril chain. The dispute centers on the four islands closest to Hokkaido, in northern Japan: Kunashiri, the Habomai Islands, Shikotan, and Etorofu. The islands control access from the Sea of Japan to the Sea of Okhotsk for Soviet naval vessels based in Vladivostok.

force at a time when Russia was weak and unable to defend its own territory. Nonetheless, we discussed their demand at length within the Soviet leadership and came to the conclusion that we should meet the Japanese halfway and agree to give the two small islands to Japan — but only on the condition that we sign the peace treaty and that U.S. troops no longer be stationed in Japan. Otherwise, it would have been sheer folly to relinquish the islands to Japan when the country was essentially under American occupation. We figured that the minute we gave Japan the two islands, the United States would turn them into military bases. We would have been trying to obtain one thing and would have ended up with quite another. Therefore, as we told the Japanese, any discussion about transferring the islands to Japan could only take place when the Japanese–U.S. military alliance aimed against the Soviet Union was no longer in force.

Why were we willing to yield on the issue of the islands? We felt that this concession really meant very little to the Soviet Union. The islands were deserted; they were used only by fishermen and also by our defense forces. In these days of modern military technology, the islands really have very little value for defense. With missiles that can attack at distances of a thousand kilometers, the islands have lost the significance they had in the days when shore-based artillery was the main defense. Nor have the islands ever had any economic value. As far as I know there has never been any mineral wealth discovered on them. On the other side of the equation, the friendship that we would have gained with the Japanese people would have had colossal importance.

There was another consideration, too. We wanted to strengthen the influence of that particular prime minister both at home and abroad, so that Japanese policy might develop in the direction of strengthened friendly relations with the USSR.

These were the primary arguments that guided us in trying to resolve this issue.[16] I feel today that the decision we made was the right one. Governments come and go, but the people remain. And the interests of the Japanese people are parallel to the interests of

16. There is still no peace treaty between Japan and the Soviet Union, and the islands remain the stumbling block between the two powers.

the Soviet people. If Japan becomes friendly toward the Soviet Union, it would benefit the Japanese people both economically and politically. The pact presently in effect between Japan and the United States is primarily a military one.[17] Such treaties exhaust the material resources of a country. Also, it could lead Japan into a catastrophic conflict — one more terrible than that which the Japanese people survived when they were A-bombed during World War II. If war were to break out nowadays, there is no telling how many of what kind of bombs would hit Japan, and then what would be left of Japan?

On the other hand, Japanese friendship with the USSR and the withdrawal of U.S. troops from the islands would create an opportunity to use human resources to develop our economy and to raise the standard of living of the Japanese as well. Japan would have the chance to obtain raw materials from a neighboring country that lies literally at its side — lumber, oil, gas, iron ore, coal. And something more — our knowledge of Siberia and the Soviet Far East is broadening and deepening.

I remember that when I was still in the leadership, Japan expressed an interest in our lumber. No wonder. Japan needs lumber — craves it, I'd even say. As for our part, we need a market where we can sell our lumber, and we need goods that Japan can send us. The Japanese suggested the following arrangement: they would give us equipment to process lumber and produce pulp; in exchange for the pulp, they would give us nylon cords for making tires. The conditions of the agreement were truly beneficial to each side. We would be getting some of the highest-quality technology in the world.

We were reminded of what a grave error we made in not signing the Japanese peace treaty later, when our relations with China had utterly deteriorated. [In July 1964] Mao Zedong received a delegation of Japanese industrialists — bourgeois figures of some kind. I was still working in the leadership then. During their discussions, the Japanese raised the issue of their claims against the Soviet Union, including southern Sakhalin and the Kuril Islands. And what happened? Mao Zedong supported their claims!

17. Khrushchev dictated this material in 1969.

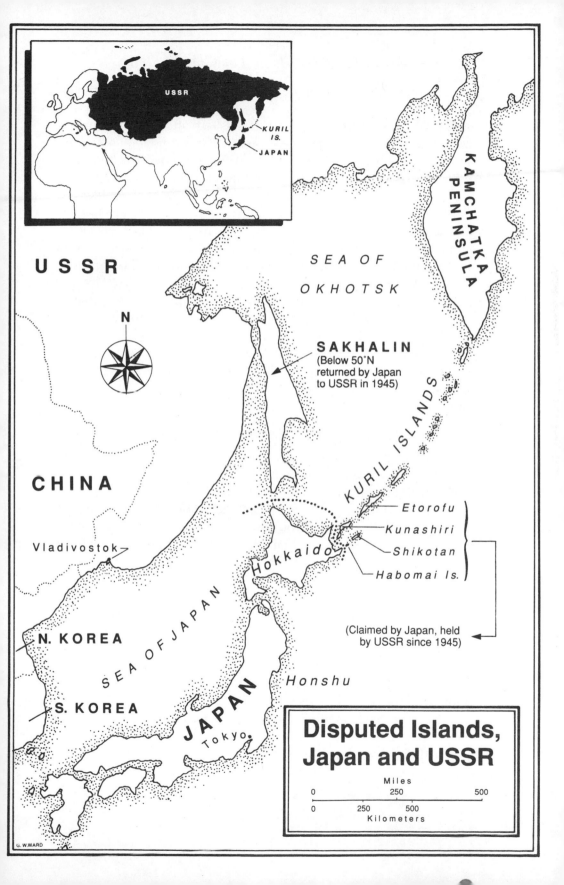

Disputed Islands, Japan and USSR

"Yes," he said. "We support you. Your claims have strength and a legal basis."

I learned this from material published after the delegation returned to Japan. The Japanese press reported how Mao Zedong was sympathetic to their "national anguish" or whatever. It was all part of an attempt on Mao's part to find an issue of mutual understanding between Japan and China, but he chose an issue that did not serve the cause of peace. But that's Mao Zedong's character. Unfortunately, he has remained true to his character even today, and is not acting to the benefit of socialism or communism. I hope that the fraternal relations we once had with China will be restored in the future, but it will take time.

In any event, the point I want to stress is that Mao was able to exploit against us the concrete results of our own errors in dealing with Japan right after the war.

I remember how we had long discussions with Japan trying to reach an agreement on air travel. The shortest route from Japan to Europe is over Soviet territory. Right at the very end of my time in office we did reach a kind of working agreement: there could be flights but, of course, they had to be our planes, under our control, and so on and so forth. The two key factors in determining our position were, first, pressure against us from the United States, and second, we were hindered by the psychological baggage and improper understanding inherited from Stalin's time.

Now, I suppose you'll say again that I blame everything on Stalin. I don't really. But you must realize that for many, many years it was drilled into us that we should not make the slightest concession to the West. We should never allow a foreigner to fly across the Soviet Union. Yet, as I was saying, the air route from Japan to Moscow is nearly the entire length of our country. If we gave foreigners the right to fly across the country, we felt that their intelligence services would turn us inside out. They would know everything. Of course, we looked at things a bit suspiciously. We condemned Stalin, but we continued to see the world through his eyes and do things according to his style and way of thinking, even though it was false, incorrect, unhealthy — I would even say sick.

Of course, we shouldn't provide imperialist intelligence agencies with a chance to spy on us. We were right as rain on that point. Nevertheless, we have to be reasonable. Not everyone is a spy.

What we need to do is make sure our counterintelligence is capable of countermeasures. Intelligence work will continue to exist as long as there are different social and political systems — as long as the world is divided the way it is today, into socialist and capitalist countries. There will always be struggle and conflict. Each system, using its intelligence forces, will strive to accomplish its own goals. That's why you need to keep your ear to the ground, as the saying goes. But my point is: that doesn't require self-isolation, which is beneficial not to us, the Soviet Union, but to the great imperialist powers, to the leaders of the capitalist world.

I'm going into some detail about all this because Japan occupies an important position in the world. It ranks third in manufacturing output, right behind the Soviet Union. Its economy is rapidly developing. So Japan is a force to be reckoned with. Japan is a fascinating country, truly fascinating. If I speak about Japanese industry and technology not only with admiration but with a touch of bitterness, it's because that country has made such huge strides forward — despite being smashed in the war, despite its lack of raw materials.

I remember how our engineers would travel to Japan and bring back models of various products. They would pass them around, and our experts' mouths would gape in wonder. I would ask, "How much did this cost?" They would answer, "Nothing, they gave it to us as a present." At this I would caution them: "If they gave it to you as a present, you can be sure it's no longer being produced." No company ever gives away models of something that is still in production. That's only logical. Competition, profit — that's all they care about. But my point is that technological knowledge is so advanced in Japan. Some say West Germany gives them competition. There's another country that was utterly destroyed in the war! These facts force us to look at the way we're organized and to think about the work our scientific research institutes do.

There is apparently some great defect in our system, for we have no fewer engineers, scientists, or mathematicians than West Germany or Japan. Statistics show that the number of scientists and technicians we produce is constantly increasing. How many master's degrees and doctorates do we have? Yet we still need to buy the best things overseas. It makes you think. More than that, it should make us analyze the situation and come up with ways to fix it. Victory will go to the system that makes the best use of the opportunities provided by science and research, by industrial design. The system with the highest productivity will win.

I speak about Japan without hiding my envy. I am saddened and envious that fifty-two years have already passed since the October Revolution. We have had great successes, and we have transformed an entire country. But we have no cause to brag about our technology and science. Our scientists know, probably better than I do, how we are being propped up by scientists from the capitalist countries.

Success in this respect is not a matter of a country being socialist or capitalist. It's not possible to say that only capitalist countries create the conditions necessary to develop science. One can't agree with that theory. We in the Soviet Union have an organizational defect of some kind, one that needs to be identified and removed. We need to free our hands so that scientific thought, which is vigorous in every corner of the world, can be developed and harnessed to serve socialist society.

Now there is some sort of agreement on the withdrawal of U.S. troops that Prime Minister Sato reached with the United States before his trip to meet President Nixon. The agreement is not very clear — it mentions something about Okinawa. What it actually means in the real world remains to be seen, and one should not be in a hurry to draw conclusions. In any case, clearly the United States is not about to get out of Japan or give up on its military pact with Japan against the Soviet Union.[18]

[MY wife] Nina Petrovna and I have an acquaintance, Anna Iosifovna. She is an unfortunate woman who did time in the camps. While she was there her husband was executed, so were her brother and her brother-in-law. Her mother and father were burned to death in a fire set by the Germans. What could be worse?

18. Khrushchev is referring to the November 1969 meeting between Prime Minister Eisaku Sato and President Richard Nixon in Washington, at which agreement was reached to return administrative control of Okinawa to Japan. This was not done until May 14, 1972, after U.S. Senate and Japanese Diet approval. The 1969 agreement, however, enabled Sato and his Liberal Democratic party to overwhelmingly win the 1970 election and prevent the opposition parties from attempting to abrogate the 1960 security treaty with the United States, which was subject to renunciation for the first time in 1970.

She told us that a friend of hers, an old woman from Lvov, had left with her family for Israel. Anna Iosifovna went to visit her old friend and see how life was there. Many Jews live well, but the elderly from the Soviet Union are homesick. The friend she was visiting said that she would like very much to come back to the Soviet Union, but her children wouldn't budge for anything. What was the main problem with the USSR as far as the children were concerned? They got tired of being called *zhids* all the time![19]

Israel is far and away better than the Arab countries, though. The Israelis live better and are more culturally enlightened. I once heard a Russian-language radio lecture on what the Israelis had done with agriculture. I listened enviously. They had gone so far in using the most modern methods of irrigation.

I personally take the side of the Arabs, but I laugh when they curse Israel. I think immediately of Peter I. When the Swedes took a chunk out of his ass outside Narva not once but twice, then he understood. He thanked the Swedes for the lessons they'd taught him and promptly destroyed Charles at Poltava.[20]

The time will come, of course. If the miserable Israelis don't begin to show some intelligence the Arabs are going to smash them. Today the Arabs have caught on and are learning some valuable lessons from Israel. The Israelis are beginning to knock some sense into them.

The people who always take the beating are the ones with no organization. Well-organized groups do not get beaten — they're the ones who do the beating. That's what it all boils down to: two and a half million organized themselves so well they were able to beat 30 million Egyptians in six days.[21] Even more than 30 million — Syria, Iraq, Jordan, all the sympathetic Arabs — 50 million.

19. *Zhid* is a derisive, anti-Semitic word for Jews in Russian, like "yid" or "kike" in English.

20. Peter I, the Great (1672–1725), was defeated by Charles XII of Sweden at Narva in 1700 and lost other battles until he defeated the Swedes at the Battle of Poltava, in July 1709. On the night of the battle Peter toasted the captured Swedish generals and said, "I drink to my teachers in the art of war."

21. Khrushchev is referring to the Six-Day War between Israel and Egypt, June 5–10, 1967.

After we established good relations with the Arab countries, it was not possible for us to establish good relations with Israel. Many times the Israeli ambassador asked me to receive him. I wanted to officially receive the Israeli ambassador but I could not do that because it would have enraged the Arabs. At that time Israel was already playing the role of the agent of American imperialism in the Near East. We didn't want to offend the Arabs, so we kept Israel at arm's length. Actually, if you are talking about this or that capitalist nation, Israel is no worse than most. It is possible to establish normal relations with Israel. I think their agriculture is organized at least as well as in Poland. Remember, Poland has no collective farms.

I have never been an anti-Semite, never. I lived in Yuzovka and worked side by side with Jews, and I had many Jewish friends. As a young boy I worked for a Jew in a factory. He was a welder, Yakov Isaakovich Kultikhov. He got two rubles a day. I got twenty kopecks a day. He was a very good man.

I have known other Jews, some of them scoundrels. Haven't I seen Russian scoundrels too? I hear Russians putting our Georgians down. I say to them, "If you were put into the land the Georgians occupy, you son of a bitch, you'd start to do a lucrative trade in bay leaf too. The only reason you're not a profiteer is that you just can't grow anything on your land."

I think we need to move now toward more relaxed methods, to increase interest in the collective farmers to produce specific kinds of crops and other food. I no longer go out to the market so I don't know very well what is there, but I hear there's no dill in the stores, for instance. What passes for dill is just some kind of weed. That's just garbage and it rots. Given the proper conditions, we could have mountains of dill.

I hold [Moshe] Dayan in high esteem as a soldier.[22] He was a good fellow. I joked that if I were premier and he were in the Soviet Union, I would appoint him minister of defense immediately. He

22. Moshe Dayan (1915–1981) was chief of staff of the Israeli army from 1953 to 1958 and defense minister from 1967 to 1974. From 1977 to 1979 Dayan was foreign minister; he played a key role in the Camp David talks that led to a peace treaty with Egypt in 1979.

was worthy of it. I've heard that he speaks Russian, but what Jew doesn't speak Russian? I sometimes listen to Radio Israel. You can hear Jerusalem beautifully. The men and women announcers are all from Odessa. Their language is beautiful and they speak fluently. It is as if the broadcast were coming from Moscow. The Jews are a nation dispersed around the entire world, so they know all languages.

They say the Arabs are fanatics, but there are different kinds of fanatics. If you pull down a fanatic's pants and whip him once or twice, he'll run off without looking back so you don't whip him again. The thing is that the Israelis are better organized and handle their weapons better.

However, I feel that the war will eventually turn against Israel. I have no doubt. It was a Pyrrhic victory. Like in our own history: The Swedes defeated Peter at Narva. Then we beat the Swedes. So the Arabs will defeat Israel, I have no doubt. I just don't know when.

Now the Israelis are drunk with victory. Their military broadcasts are very aggressive. The most logical thing for Israel would have been to defeat the Arabs in the Six-Day War and then immediately withdraw their troops to the old borders. That would have shocked the entire world! They would have won incalculable sympathy, but now . . .

If I were head of the Arab nation, I would obtain the necessary weapons and in three days finish off Israel. It is possible. They don't need Russian troops for that. The Russians can teach the Arabs. War is a science. Anyone can learn it. The Arabs have already been to school. Let me tell you about a conversation I had once with Molotov. Later Churchill also told me about it. When Molotov flew to London for the first time during the war, Churchill received him. Churchill was a smart man but exceedingly rude. He said, "Comrade Molotov! In that seat where you are sitting now I received Savinkov in 1918.[23] I talked with him about organizing the landing against you in Archangel. You should say thank you.

23. Boris V. Savinkov (1879–1925) was a writer and leader of the Social Revolutionary party who took part in the assassination of the minister of internal affairs in 1904 and fled from Russia. After the February 1917 revolution he returned to Russia and became deputy minister of war. He fought against the Bolshevik Revolution in October 1917, played a leading role in organizing counterrevolutionary forces against the Bolsheviks, and carried on negotiations with

You should thank me, because I taught you to fight. We organized an intervention and you fought well. You kicked us right out. Now you are good fighters. I gave you your schooling. I was minister of defense then."

It is the same with the Arabs. This is a learning process for them. You mustn't forget that Israel is surrounded by the Muslim world, which is sympathetic to the Arabs. There are only a handful of Israelis: three million, or perhaps two and a half. I have always maintained that Israel has no possibility of holding on to territory that it gains. Yet they do hang on to it.

What can the Arabs do? Mass themselves, as Peter did in his time, and arrange a Poltava for the Israelis.

Israel just doesn't understand its real situation. One day you are on the banks of the Suez Canal, and the next you have lost Tel Aviv. That's politics. I play no determining role in politics today. But war is war. If, for example, you take the borders in existence before the Six-Day War, well, a good runner could start out in the morning from there and be in Tel Aviv by lunchtime. That's the heart of the matter. The country can be shot full of holes. It is not at all like the Soviet Union, where the Germans took forever to get to Stalingrad and still had ten thousand kilometers to go.

Israel's politics right now are not very sound. Victory has made them light-headed, and so they cannot evaluate their position in the world soberly at all. This is dangerous — they will be beaten.

---

the British and French governments to provide aid to the White forces. He was arrested in 1924 and committed suicide in prison.

5

Comrades to the West

STALIN was convinced that after the war Germany would stage a revolution and follow the path of creating a proletarian state. Stalin wasn't the only one who incorrectly predicted this. All of us thought it would happen, because we wanted it so much. We believed a socialist revolution would be the solution to the German problem; Germany would stop being a militaristic state and a threat to others. We thought the war had created the most favorable conditions. All the working elements would come together and establish a working-class, revolutionary state with no private property. It would be possible to start building socialism.

It was against this background that Stalin supported a united Germany. He wanted to gain sympathy in Germany for Soviet policy and to make Germany a Soviet ally.

We had the same hopes for France and Italy. I remember when de Gaulle and a French delegation came to Moscow in December 1944. There was a reception, and Stalin got completely drunk. We worried that it might create a bad impression. Stalin kept hugging the French and lurching around. We were afraid they would think he was a drunkard. Actually, they would have been right, but stopping Stalin from drinking was impossible. It would mean making yourself his enemy.

Stalin later told us that he asked de Gaulle, "Are you going to arrest Maurice Thorez?" Thorez was in Moscow at the time. He was planning to return to Paris after the defeat of the Germans. Stalin didn't attach much importance to the French-Soviet treaty that was signed during de Gaulle's visit. Stalin liked to say that he was always looking farther down the road. "When Thorez arrives on the scene," he said, "then real work starts." At that time the Communist party in France was large and powerful enough to have real political influence. It also had arms caches from the war. Stalin had hopes that the Communists would lead and that a new government headed by Communists would come to power. Then de Gaulle decided to invite Thorez to join in the government of France. It was a wise move on de Gaulle's part. He was anti-Communist, but he recognized the authority of the Communist party.

There was a similar situation in Italy. Togliatti was preparing to make his own move. He was ready to start an armed insurrection. It might have occurred had it not been for the presence of American troops. Stalin restrained Togliatti. He warned that an insurrection would be crushed by American forces that were occupying Italy and France, much as the English crushed the Greek insurrection with tanks.[1]

We still had our hopes. Just as Russia came out of World War I, made the revolution, and established Soviet power, so after the catastrophe of World War II, Europe too might become Soviet. Everyone would take the path from capitalism to socialism.

However, after Potsdam, events did not develop in our favor.[2] The powerful economy of the United States prevented the devastated economies of the European countries from reaching the point of a revolutionary explosion. Things did not happen the way we expected and predicted in accordance with Marxist-Leninist theory. Unfortunately, all these countries stayed capitalist, and we were disappointed.

IN the days leading up to Stalin's death, we believed that America would invade the Soviet Union and we would go to war. Stalin trembled at this prospect. How he quivered! He was afraid of war.

1. British forces occupied Greece and put down a Communist attempt to seize power at the end of the war. In February 1947, President Truman extended economic and military aid to Greece and Turkey to prevent Communist takeovers under the Truman Doctrine of combating Communist expansion in the Mediterranean (and elsewhere). Aid was extended to Italy in 1948 to prevent a Communist victory in the elections.

2. The Potsdam Conference, in July–August 1945, was attended by Harry S.

He knew that we were weaker than the United States. We had only a handful of nuclear weapons, while America had a large arsenal of nuclear arms. Of course, in other areas — conventional forces and ground forces — we had the advantage.

Stalin never did anything that might provoke a war with the United States. He knew his weakness. This fear stayed with him from the first days of World War II, when he said: "Lenin left us a state and we turned it to shit." Our victory in the war did not stop him from trembling inside.

Stalin insisted on absolute secrecy and no discussion whatsoever about weapons. If anybody showed an interest in weapons, Stalin believed he had switched his allegiance and been recruited as an agent. Stalin would say the reason for that person's interest was his desire to inform his "real masters" — the catchphrase we used at that time for enemies. The arrests started again, and soon the prisons were overflowing. Many of those arrested were former prisoners of war who had returned home. However, they did not return to their apartments or their collective or state farms; they were sent to camps. They worked in Siberia, Kolyma, and other remote areas.

Throughout the country there were arrests and trials — for example, the Leningrad Affair, and the Jewish conspiracy trial involving prominent political figures. Mikhoels perished; so did Lozovsky.[3] Mikhoels was murdered in a plot and his killer was rewarded by Stalin. Mikhoels was buried with honors. Lozovsky, on the other hand, was put on trial on trumped-up charges, convicted, and executed. Among the other victims was Molotov's wife.[4]

Truman, Stalin, Churchill, and (after July 26) Clement Attlee, who succeeded Churchill when Britain's Conservative government was replaced by Labor.

3. Solomon A. Lozovsky was a Jewish member of the Central Committee and deputy minister of foreign affairs, well known to Western correspondents and respected by them as the official Soviet spokesman. In 1949 the secret police fabricated a story about the existence of a "pro-American Jewish conspiracy," which was followed by the arrest of leading officials and public figures of Jewish origin, including Lozovsky, a member of the Jewish Antifascist Committee, who was shot. Solomon M. Mikhoels, also a member of the antifascist committee, was the most prominent actor and director of the Yiddish theater.

4. Madame Molotova, better known as Comrade Zemchuzhina, an important figure in her own right, was for a time head of the State Cosmetic Trust, which

Thus, we started to move back to the terror of the late thirties. The arrests, the anti-Semitic policy and discrimination continued. That was the scene at the end of Stalin's life. We inherited this state of affairs.

A similar sickness affected our relations with fraternal countries. Stalin's understanding of friendship with other countries was that the Soviet Union would lead and they would follow. We have to give Stalin his due. He had a sense of purpose about how to develop the socialist system. However, we must distinguish between ends and means. Stalin's means were barbaric. He purged the leadership in all the people's democracies. He sent his "counselors" — actually informers — to those countries to determine who were the enemies of the people. Stalin waged the struggle against the enemies of the people there in the same way that he did in the Soviet Union. He had one demand: absolute subordination. If anyone dared to have his own point of view, it provoked in Stalin the suspicion that such a person was insincere and not loyal to Marxism-Leninism. It meant that such a person was just one step away from death.

It was enough for the Yugoslavs to show some disagreement with Stalin for him to accuse them of treason. He completely wrote off their contributions during the war. The Yugoslavs showed such determination and stamina during the war. No other nation in the world has ever acted so proudly. Tito should be given credit for successfully organizing resistance early in the war. He was unequaled. It is a real sin to belittle Tito and the Yugoslav contribution to defeating Germany. Because of Stalin the Yugoslavs became enemies of the Soviet Union. They became followers of capitalism. Actually, some socialist principles were not destroyed but continued to strengthen in Yugoslavia. However, since the Yugoslavs made the changes without Stalin's approval they weren't Communists. Stalin's intolerance was unbearable; it spoiled our relations. I don't know what would have happened if Stalin had lived longer.

The anti-Yugoslav campaign began in the Soviet press. Although

---

introduced perfumes and lipstick to the Soviet Union. She was sent into internal exile in 1948 and was not released until after Stalin's death, in 1953.

the accusations against the Yugoslavs were false, Stalin had high hopes they would trigger internal opposition to Tito. When his hopes were frustrated, he tried to remove Tito by other means — sending special agents there. When I worked in the Ukraine, I remember, one of my aides reported witnessing military men in civilian clothing boarding a ship in Odessa. They were heading for Yugoslavia on assignment, although perhaps they went to Yugoslavia via Bulgaria.

Stalin would not tolerate Yugoslavia's innovations and originality. Stalin believed that everything Soviet was the best in the world.

There were two international meetings on the Yugoslav question. I remember that at one meeting Gheorghe Gheorghiu-Dej, the Romanian leader, delivered the principal report. Of course, the report was prepared in Moscow by Yudin, Suslov, and Malenkov.[5] Gheorghiu-Dej just read it out loud. Everything was artificial, contrived. Personally, I had no hard feelings against Tito. Stalin by that time was old and addled. He was losing his grip on things and we were losing our respect for him.

The leadership did not really understand what Stalin had against Tito, but that did not matter because ever since Kirov's death there was no democracy in the Politburo. Stalin forced the situation with Yugoslavia close to open warfare. If we had had a common border with Yugoslavia, Stalin might have decided on military intervention.

After Stalin's death I tried to improve relations with Yugoslavia, but I faced opposition from Molotov, Voroshilov, Suslov, and Shepilov, the chief editor of *Pravda*.[6] Shepilov wrote a number of articles from the Stalinist point of view, attacking Yugoslavia. Mikoyan supported me. The only position Malenkov took was to look over his shoulder and listen to what the others were saying.

At the beginning of my talks with the Yugoslavs I tried to sell

5. Mikhail A. Suslov, the Communist party's chief ideologue, directed the campaign against Yugoslavia in 1948–1949. P. F. Yudin was a party ideological hack known for arrogance to subordinates and sycophancy to superiors. He was later ambassador to China. Malenkov was then prime minister.

6. Dimitri T. Shepilov worked under Khrushchev as a political commissar on the Ukraine front during World War II. In 1957, when he emerged supreme, Khrushchev ousted Shepilov "as the one who attached himself to" the so-called Antiparty Group.

them on the idea that Beria had been the evil genius behind Stalin. We used to put everything on Beria's back. However, neither Yezhov nor Beria invented Stalin.[7] They weren't the ones who put the ax in his hands. It was the other way around: Stalin invented Yezhov and Beria and turned them into the tools of his arbitrary rule. Who was better, Beria or Yezhov? Both were scoundrels.

I remember how at one point I had a heated argument with Popovic.[8] He told us the Yugoslav opinion of Stalin. In simple, plain language Popovic told us the truth: "Stalin was the principal killer."

What did we give to Yugoslavia? Arms. Later we sent them the bill, but the Yugoslavs responded by suggesting we write off the debt. I led our delegation to Belgrade in 1955.

There were crowds lined up in Belgrade to greet our Soviet delegation. Actually, I did not care much for the display. I sensed that there was still some displeasure and dissatisfaction with us because of years of our anti-Yugoslav campaign. I knew the technique. You put people into a specific place. Everyone is told what to shout. Everything has been orchestrated. We specialized in putting on such spectacles during the struggle with the opposition. I myself used to direct this kind of cheap theater.

During my visit we arranged for a flight from Moscow to deliver the diplomatic pouch and official papers. We designated a Tu-16 bomber as the plane to carry the pouch. There were lengthy discussions to find the proper landing field for the bomber. The bomber arrived and, after dropping the pouch, immediately returned to Moscow without refueling. We did this for the propaganda effect, and later our agents informed us that it was all properly understood by the Yugoslavs.[9]

*   *   *

7. Yezhov was named head of the secret police in September 1936, and the Great Terror, also known as the *Yezhovchina* (Yezhov's reign), accelerated. In the Ukraine, Khrushchev presided over the purges that were carried on by a Yezhov appointee, who himself perished. Yezhov was replaced by Beria in September 1938 and disappeared in 1939. In his Twentieth Party Congress speech, Khrushchev described Yezhov as a degenerate.

8. Koca Popovic, the Yugoslav foreign minister from 1953 to 1965.

9. Krushchev's unsubtle reminder was that, despite the thaw, the Soviet Union could still bomb Yugoslavia with ease.

UNDER Stalin our relations with Albania were not an issue. During the war the Albanians joined with the Yugoslavs to fight the enemy. Tito told me that the Albanians had been of enormous assistance against the Italian fascists. Tito also said they had sent Vukmanovic-Tempo, and that he had almost single-handedly organized the Labor party in Albania. [10]

When relations with Yugoslavia were at an all-time high and Tito had absolute faith in Stalin, Stalin dictated a telegram to Tito. In essence it said that the Yugoslavs should forge their future relations with Albania in such a way as to get Albania to join the Yugoslav federation.

Of course, Albania knew nothing of this. It's almost certain they were not even told. Stalin once let it be known to a small circle that a Balkan federation of socialist countries was to be formed. I think he was talking about Yugoslavia, Bulgaria, and Albania. It seems construction had already begun near Belgrade on a governmental palace for the future federation. When I was in Yugoslavia I saw the beginnings of this construction. A fair number of structures were already in evidence, but then they were later abandoned.

As it turned out, of all the socialist countries, Albania conducted the most intensely anti-Yugoslav policies. For a time we approved and promoted these sentiments. But when we began to take steps toward normalizing relations with Yugoslavia [1954], Albania's position hurt us. The Albanian Communist party received our initiative very poorly and argued that the Yugoslavs were not to be relied on, that they were not real Communists. All this was said condescendingly, with great malice and spite. Enver Hoxha's character was such that he spoke with particular vehemence, his face twitching and his jaws grinding. [11]

Finally Albania was forced to agree with us, they had no other choice. We looked at Albania's position on the issue in the same way an older brother looks at a younger brother. We felt that

10. Svetozar Vukmanovic-Tempo, a World War II partisan and close comrade of Tito's, was the outspoken head of the Yugoslav trade union organization.

11. Enver Hoxha, first secretary of the Albanian Communist party from 1948 to 1985, rose to power as a member of the Albanian wartime resistance, using arms supplied to him by the Allies and the Yugoslavs against his nationalist rivals and the Germans. Hoxha supported Mao and China in the Sino-Soviet split.

although they did not understand now, they would grow up and gain understanding; we saw nothing alarming in their position.

With respect to granting aid, our relations with Albania were not just fraternal — for fraternal relations between the socialist countries are relations on an equal footing — but more along the lines of an elder to a younger. While we granted aid to other socialist countries on a reciprocal contract basis, Albania received aid from us mainly in the form of free gifts. We were completely responsible for maintaining their army. We gave them uniforms, bread, ammunition, and weapons. All for free.

Why did we do this for Albania? I think our actions were justified. Any person with common sense would understand and approve. Albania had to be seen as a base on the Mediterranean. To put it simply, it made no difference whether we had our own troops stationed there or Albania had its troops there. But alone, Albania would only have been able to maintain a small number of troops. They only produced, perhaps, rifles.

For this reason it was beneficial for us to aid the Albanian army, to make sure its troops were sufficient to create a good impression and that they were armed with modern weapons. So they received tanks, artillery, and other arms. If the maintenance of Albania's army had come out of its own budget, Albania would have had nothing left for other necessities such as industrializing the country and restructuring the economy on a socialist base.

Later we reached an agreement with the Albanians to establish a submarine fleet there. We negotiated with them as socialist equals, just as with any other socialist country. We decided to deploy twelve submarines. This was a strong fist — twelve submarines in the Mediterranean. It would be a force for our opponents to reckon with. Our sailors went to Albania with a full complement of surface and maintenance support for the fleet, to instruct the Albanians and turn the vessels over to Albanian crews as they were gathered and trained.

This shows the respect and fondness we had for the Albanians. All our economic relations were built exclusively in their interests. Even Albanian oil was completely useless, yet we felt we had to find a use for it in our economy. We were forced into doing this because no one would buy it from them. We wanted to turn

Albania into a pearl that would be attractive to the Muslim world, especially for countries in the Middle East and Africa.

Then we offered to build a powerful radio station in Albania. Our motive was propagandistic. The radio station could have been used to broadcast our ideas, our politics, and Communist party politics in the fight for socialism.

After the Twentieth Party Congress our people in Albania told us that the political leaders and party cadres of Tirana had a stormy meeting. It lasted several days. Enver Hoxha, Mehmet Sheku, and Bequir Balluku held on to power by a thread the entire time. This was of crucial significance for the future of our relations. Enver Hoxha was scared to death by the turn of events. His triumvirate was shaken by the fact that they had nearly been ousted from their leadership posts.

Our conflict and subsequent break with Albania centered around issues of principle. [In 1961] the Albanians openly announced their opposition to us and their support of China. The Albanians, with their practice of covert and open murders, became a party that held on to power by terror and fear. They could not accept the outcome of the Twentieth Congress.

They, like the Chinese, adopted Stalin as a defense against the Communist Party of the Soviet Union. Stalin was their ideal. Stalin was a real Marxist, a true Leninist. All the rest were revisionists. This was a tragedy, of course, for the Albanian people.

When relations between our two countries became really strained, we decided to take back our submarines and the equipment and repair base that supported them. The Albanians fought this.

Three of our submarines were manned 100 percent by Albanian crews. One or two had mixed Albanian-Soviet crews. We finally managed to withdraw only eight or nine submarines. Three or four remained in Albania; we were unable to negotiate their return. When we were recalling the others, we fully expected some kind of aggressive act on the part of Albania. During the operation, our warships cruised along the Albanian coastline, in order to take some kind of action and scare the Albanians if they tried to use force to prevent our submarines from leaving.

This was our final break in relations with Albania. The Chinese had become involved in Albania, and I'm not sure the Albanians gained from it. We ceased granting Albania aid and severed all ties. There were stories that China had assured Albania of aid, and apparently they granted it. I don't know if they gave the Albanians as much as we did, because the Chinese were in a very difficult situation themselves.

BEFORE World War II, I remember, there was tension on the border with Romania and Romanian guards occasionally shot across into our territory. I even got shot at myself when I went to the border and my car got stuck in the mud. Probably the Romanian officer was right in ordering his soldiers to shoot. He believed we were staging a provocation or that we were there for the purpose of reconnaissance.

As a result of the Molotov-Ribbentrop pact the Soviet Union took Bessarabia and Bukovina and moved to the old czarist border along the Prut River.[12] Historically, the population of Bukovina was Ukrainian. That is why Bukovina was given to the USSR.

Hitler had lured Stalin into a trap, enticing him to seize the land of others while Hitler prepared for his major goal: to attack the Soviet Union and annihilate the Slavs. Many historical factors, today evaluated in different ways, came together to cause the Soviet Union to make its pact with Hitler. It was not a pact made out of logic or good sense, but rather out of necessity.

Hitler let Stalin have Bessarabia in order to secure the support of Romania in the war that followed.[13] I was in Bessarabia when our troops occupied it at the end of the war. Moldavia was then an autonomous republic that was part of the Ukraine. The capital at that time was Tiraspol, a lovely garden city on the banks of the Dniester. The issue of making Moldavia a union republic came up. It was my idea to create the union republic with the capital in

12. The area is the fertile steppe bounded by the Danube, Dniester, and Prut rivers and by the Black Sea. These lands had been Russian from 1812 until 1918, then Romanian under the name Bessarabia from 1918 until 1940; they were occupied by the Germans and their Romanian allies during World War II, and were formally restored to the Soviet Union as part of the Moldavian Republic in 1947.

13. Romania fought on the Axis side to regain Bessarabia until August 1944, when the profascist government was overthrown by a coup. Then Romania joined the Allies.

Kishinev. I put the suggestion to Stalin, and the decision was made accordingly. Now Moldavia is one of the republics of the Soviet Union, with a successful economy and developed culture.

I first met Romanians during the war and even interrogated prisoners. There were Romanian troops at Stalingrad fighting against the Soviet Union. They were poorly organized and fought badly. The Romanians probably did not know what they had been fighting for. I remember there was one artillery regiment that did not fire a single shot and intentionally surrendered rather than go on fighting. In our report from the front, the Romanians' surrender was portrayed as a major victory against the enemy!

I met Petru Groza in Sochi in 1951.[14] Nina Petrovna and I were staying in a dacha on the Black Sea. We really enjoyed the small, cozy dacha close to the water. Marshal Voroshilov lived in a luxurious dacha built in Sochi on his orders to replicate the czar's Livadia Palace, which Stalin used and where the Yalta Conference took place in 1945.

One day I got a call from Stalin urging me to come to Gagry and move into the "number-one dacha," where Stalin himself was staying. I tried to refuse politely, saying the dacha was too far from the sea and that Nina Petrovna and I liked where we were. Stalin insisted, "Why are you living in that shack?" He was so insistent that if we hadn't moved he would have taken it badly. He couldn't understand simple human reasons. I told Nina Petrovna, "We'd better go," and we did.

We did not, however, move into Stalin's main house, but stayed in a nearby guesthouse. Then Voroshilov called. I asked him, "Where are you?"

"I've moved to the dacha where you were staying," Voroshilov replied.

"Why?" I asked.

"Stalin called and told me to let Petru Groza have my house," Voroshilov said.

I understood. Stalin needed the most luxurious dacha for Petru

14. Petru Groza was a rich landowner with progressive ideas who gave up his land and headed a splinter left-wing party known as the Plowmen's Front. The Soviets directly intervened in Romania's postwar political scene to install him as premier.

Groza. That was simple enough; Stalin's thinking was more complicated. Voroshilov could have been moved directly to Stalin's dacha, but Stalin wanted to make it humiliating for him, so he sent him to a much more modest place instead. Voroshilov's pride was wounded to the quick.

AFTER the Twentieth Party Congress [in 1956] I spoke with the Romanian comrades about arrests in Romania. Gheorghiu-Dej told me that it was right to have arrested Anna Pauker and Vasile Luca.[15] There was a predominance of Jews among the leadership of the Communist parties in Eastern Europe and in the Romanian party leadership. After all those arrests the national leadership included only Romanians, with the exception of one Hungarian.[16] When our relations with Romania soured, the word Sovrom — for Soviet Romanian Society [a joint economic group] — became something like a swear word in Romania. I think that Stalin would have understood this if he had been mentally sound. After Stalin died, we immediately liquidated Sovrom on our own initiative.

After Stalin's death it was Molotov's responsibility to deal with the leaders of the fraternal Communist parties. Molotov followed Stalin's approach. He was very haughty and arrogant. His position was "Do what you are told." Dej complained to me about Molotov. Molotov was rude and harsh. When he thought that he was about to encounter opposition a characteristic tic contorted his face. It was exactly with that face that he talked to the Romanians.

IN the fifties we threw ourselves into the development of our oil and gas industries. We needed machine tools. I received reports that ours weren't anywhere near the same level as American

15. Anna Pauker, a rabbi's daughter, was foreign minister of Romania in the first postwar government. She was considered to have the most thorough grounding in Marxism-Leninism, having served in the Comintern in Moscow before and during the war. Vasile Luca, a Hungarian Jew, was a Communist organizer in the Polish Ukraine before it became part of the Soviet Union. Khrushchev met him there in 1940 when the territory was taken over by Soviet troops, following the Molotov-Ribbentrop pact in 1939. Luca spent the war years in Moscow.

16. Khrushchev means an ethnic Hungarian, part of the Hungarian minority living in Romania.

The young Khrushchev.

Khrushchev at Yuzovka.

Khrushchev in Moscow sometime after receiving his first Order of Lenin,
for work on Moscow subway, probably 1934.

Joseph Stalin in 1926.

Svetlana Alliluyeva (left) in 1932; her mother, Nadezhda Alliluyeva,
is at right. Behind Nadezhda, in military uniform, is Marshal Kliment
Voroshilov; next to him, hat in hand, is Vyacheslav Molotov.

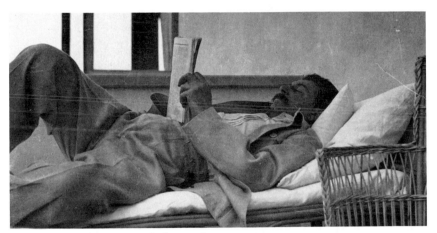

Stalin reading a newspaper.

Khrushchev voting, probably at Seventeenth
Party Congress, 1934.

Stalin (second from right) with the leadership on the Lenin Mausoleum in the 1930s.

Khrushchev and Leonid Brezhnev in 1942, when they were both in the Red Army as political commissars.

Khrushchev in 1943.

Khrushchev with troops in 1943, after the liberation of Kharkov.

Khrushchev rafting with Ukrainian officials
outside Kiev after the war.

Left to right: President Harry S. Truman, Secretary
of State James Byrnes, and Foreign Minister
Molotov at Potsdam Conference, 1945.

Mao Zedong and Khrushchev in China, 1954; Anastas Mikoyan
is on the right.

Khrushchev and Antonín Novotný in Hradčany Castle
in Prague, early 1960s.

Khrushchev and Wladyslaw Gomulka after Gomulka
came to power in Poland.

Khrushchev and Brezhnev in 1962.

Fidel Castro showing Khrushchev and Brezhnev
a Polaroid picture he took.

Khrushchev in his final days, walking to the river near his dacha
at Petrovo-Dalneye.

machine tools. Then out of the blue the Romanians came up with machine tools. The Romanians! Beating us, the Soviet Union! I asked Dej, "How can it be?"

He just laughed and said, "We had some engineer, or some capitalist, working in the American oil industry — a Romanian. He helped us steal American blueprints. That's how we produced them," he said. So the machine tools were Romanian, but the plans were American. We wanted to buy the plans from him, but that didn't work out. Then I said to Dej, "Just give them to us," and he replied, "Take them." Of course, that doesn't mean we got them right away. For Romanians, there's a huge difference between offering something and actually handing it over!

I give the Romanians credit. They are very clever. Good for them. They quickly began to develop their economy, industry, and collective farms. The Romanians were culturally less developed than the other socialist countries, yet they managed to lift themselves up by their bootstraps.

WHEN Yugoslavia and Romania agreed [in the early 1960s] to build a power station on the Danube River, the Bulgarians demanded a share of the output. The Romanians believed Moscow was behind the Bulgarian claim. This was not so, and I had a very difficult talk with Gheorghiu-Dej trying to convince him that there was no conspiracy between the Soviet Union and Bulgaria. We sent a delegation to Romania to clear tensions. In the delegation were myself, Aleksei Kosygin, Mikhail Lesechko, and from the Central Committee, Yuri Andropov.[17]

There are other examples of how supporting cooperative relations with fraternal countries creates problems. The Soviet Union imports tomatoes from Bulgaria, but they are garbage. I can taste

17. Kosygin was chairman of Gosplan, the State Planning Commission, from 1959 to 1960, when he became Khrushchev's chief deputy on the Council of Ministers. Lesechko was one of Khrushchev's economic experts for socialist bloc countries. Andropov, in those days, was a Central Committee secretary dealing with Soviet bloc affairs. Andropov became head of the Committee for State Security (KGB) in May 1967 and held that position until May 1982, when he was named a secretary of the Central Committee. He became general secretary of the Communist party and leader of the Soviet Union from November 1982 to his death, in February 1984.

the poor quality when Nina Petrovna buys them. Why do I say they are lousy? I grew up eating Bulgarian tomatoes, and they were really something back then. The Bulgarians saw to it that they came to market fresh, but now we get something else, from a "fraternal" country. The Bulgarians have gotten used to the fact that Russians will eat any old shit, if you'll excuse the expression. They pick the tomatoes when they're still hard and green, then store them. When they ship them to us, they turn ripe on the way. The result is garbage.

The Bulgarians also export tomatoes to West Germany, but what a difference in the fruit! I'm sure that the West Germans wouldn't buy the ones we get. Why? Because there's competition in that market, while we are compelled to buy from our fraternal Bulgarians. They've got nothing else with which to repay their debt to us. And who suffers? The consumer. The one who has to eat these tomatoes — that's who suffers.

The Bulgarians don't eat the tomatoes they send us — you won't find garbage like that in their markets. They eat tomatoes picked one day and sold the next morning. They have wonderful tomatoes right there. The Bulgarians are the best gardeners in the world, I know.

My point here is that there are a lot of problems left to solve among the socialist countries. I'm talking about legitimate concerns. If they are not addressed, they could lead to serious rifts within the socialist community. More than anyone else, I'd say, the Soviet Union suffers. They all look on the Soviet Union as one big feeding trough. I know because I've dealt with them all.

After Gheorghiu-Dej's death [in 1965] we preserved the outward appearance of the same comradely politeness in our relations, but it began to feel artificial. I think Comrade Maurer was to blame for that.[18]

Romania wanted to have autonomy for its armed forces. It wanted to be independent from the other Warsaw Pact countries. We realized this for the first time when Romania refused to buy arms from Czechoslovakia in accordance with the pact's procure-

18. Ion Gheorghe Maurer was Romania's chief of government from 1961 to 1974. From 1958 to 1961 Maurer was chairman of the Romanian Presidium, until he was replaced by Dej in 1961.

ment plans. There were other facts reported to me by Marshal Grechko.[19] Molotov felt this was a tragedy, but the Romanians had the right to make decisions on their own in such matters.

IN 1956 Comrade Bierut died. There was a special plenum of the Polish Central Committee.[20] I did not attend the plenum because we didn't want the Soviet Union to be accused of interference in the internal affairs of the Polish Communist party. The meeting was stormy and many of those who spoke expressed disaffection with the Soviet Union. Tensions rose, and we grew concerned.

They chose Comrade Ochab as the first secretary of the Central Committee of the Polish Communist party. I personally had very good relations with Ochab and respected him. He was an old Communist. He was of working-class origin and, as we say, graduated from the school of Polish prison.

Bierut's wife was of Jewish nationality, but she was a good comrade. Again the question of favoritism in appointments for Jews arose in the party leadership. We in the Soviet leadership were for removing the party secretary responsible for personnel, but he was too powerful and kept his position.[21] We opposed him because everywhere only Jews were in positions of influence and there was no place for Poles. If a Jew who occupies a high place in the party structure promotes only Jews, he will do more harm than any anti-Semite, because such actions stir up ethnic enmity and conflicts.

19. Marshal Andrei Antonovich Grechko (1903–1976) served with Khrushchev in the Ukraine during World War II; he was commander of Soviet troops in Germany from 1953 to 1957 and later first deputy minister of defense and commander of the Warsaw Pact (1960–1967). He became Soviet defense minister in 1967 and served until his death.

20. Boleslaw Bierut, first secretary of the Polish Workers Party, the Polish Communist party, died in Moscow on March 12, 1956, after attending the Twentieth Party Congress. Bierut was a symbol of the old Stalinist puppet government placed in power in Warsaw at the end of World War II. Khrushchev attended Bierut's funeral in Warsaw and stayed for a week "heavily canvassing the candidature of Edward Ochab for First Secretary, and on 21 March Ochab was duly elected." See Nicholas Bethell, *Gomulka, His Poland, His Communism* (New York: Holt, Rinehart and Winston, 1969), p. 201.

21. Roman Zambrowski was head of the personnel section of the Polish Central Committee. He had been in Moscow during the war and reentered Poland with the Red Army as part of the "Lublin Committee," formed by Stalin to act as the first puppet government after the war.

When I discussed our policy of exposing Stalin's crimes with the Polish leadership, they were reluctant to conduct a similar campaign in Poland. Nor was Comrade Ochab in a hurry to release Gomulka from prison.[22]

"Why are you keeping Comrade Gomulka in prison?" I asked him. "Once, when I put the same question to Comrade Bierut he answered me, 'I do not know myself why he is there or what crimes he is accused of.'"

So, I said to Ochab, "maybe you could think about it and free him."

He told me it was not possible.

Not only was Gomulka in prison, but so were Spychalski, Loga-Sowinski, and Kliszko.[23] Many people were in prison.

Then Comrade Ochab went to China. On the way back he stopped in Moscow and I had a talk with him. By that time Comrade Gomulka was out of prison. I suggested to Comrade Ochab, "What would you say if Comrade Gomulka came to the Soviet Union for a rest in the Crimea, on the Black Sea, or in the Caucasus?"

He mumbled something and quickly left for Warsaw. It did not relieve my concerns. Then we learned about developments in Warsaw [in October 1956]: the Soviet Union was being reviled with abusive language and the government was close to being overthrown. The people rising to the top were those whose mood was anti-Soviet. This might threaten our lines of communication and access to Germany through Poland. Therefore, we decided to take certain measures to maintain contact with our troops in the German Democratic Republic.[24]

22. Wladyslaw Gomulka was secretary general of the Polish Communist party in 1945 when Khrushchev was sent to Warsaw by Stalin to restore municipal services, especially water and sewerage. Gomulka was a Khrushchev favorite, but Stalin distrusted him and had him removed from the leadership in 1949 and jailed in 1951. Gomulka had actually been released from jail at the end of 1954, but the fact was not announced officially until April 7, 1956.

23. Marian Spychalski, Zenon Kliszko, and Ignacy Loga-Sowinski were removed from the leadership in late 1949 and arrested in July 1951.

24. Riots in Poland during the summer against the increase in food prices spread, and by October 1956 a full-scale workers' revolt was threatened. Marshal Konstantin K. Rokossovsky, a Polish-born Soviet army commander who had been

We decided to send a delegation to Poland and have a talk with the Polish leadership. They recommended that we not come. Their reluctance to meet with us heightened our concern even more. So we decided to go there in a large delegation. I was the head. There were Mikoyan, Bulganin, Molotov, Kaganovich, Marshal Konev, and others.[25]

We landed at the airport and were met by Ochab and Gomulka. The meeting was cool. You could see great concern on the face of Ochab. We began speaking harshly in raised voices. Ochab boiled up even more and said with anger, "Why are you blaming me? I'm not the Central Committee secretary anymore. Ask them."[26] He pointed to Gomulka and the others.

The situation in Poland grew even more difficult. We did not know what to do. We were more afraid than ever that a leadership would arise that would be anti-Soviet. We did not want the relations to return to what they had been before the war, when Poland had a bourgeois leadership.

During our talks in Warsaw, Gomulka made an anxious but sincere declaration: "Poland needs friendship with the Soviet Union more than the Soviet Union needs friendship with Poland. Can it be that we failed to understand our situation? Without the Soviet Union we cannot maintain our borders with the West. We are dealing with our internal problems, but our relations with the Soviet Union will remain unchanged. We will still be friends and allies." He said all this with such intensity and such sincerity that I believed his words. When we met alone, I said to our delegation, "I think there is no reason not to believe Comrade Gomulka."

We explained that the reason our troops were on the move to

---

appointed the Polish minister of defense, warned the Kremlin leadership that the Polish army was hostile and would fight against a Soviet invasion.

25. Mikoyan was first deputy chairman of the Council of Ministers. Nikolai Bulganin was prime minister. Molotov was foreign minister. Kaganovich was a senior Politburo member. Marshal Ivan S. Konev (1897–1973) was the Warsaw Pact commander, 1955–1960, and first deputy defense minister. He was commander in chief of Soviet ground forces in 1955–1956.

26. Khrushchev arrived in the middle of the Eighth Plenum of the Central Committee of the Polish Communist party. At the first session Gomulka, Zenon Kliszko, Marian Spychalski, and Ignacy Loga-Sowinski were added to the Central Committee.

Warsaw was in conjunction with maneuvers that would be taking place. Nobody believed this false explanation, but everybody was pleased by the fact that an explanation was given.[27]

WITH Poland in particular, I always tried to be sympathetic to flare-ups of anti-Soviet sentiment. Sympathetic in the sense that you have to remember history and that czarist Russia was a party to Poland's being carved up among the Germans, the Austrians, and the Russians. That left its stamp on the Polish soul.

Yet I, as a Russian, must express the following. I worked with Poles at a machine-building plant and in coal mines. We had the same views regarding our legal and material rights, that is, honest wages. To the capitalist boss we were simply a work force. He did not inquire whether I was a Russian, a Pole, or a German. It was an issue of class and not of nationality.

Some Polish land and some Polish people were under the boot of the Russian czar. We were also oppressed by our czars, by our landowners, and by our capitalists. That's why we overthrew our government. We turned all the historical foundations upside down; we did away with both feudal landownership and capitalism.

We were united in the struggle. We joined forces with the Poles and other people. Our October Revolution bears witness to this. How many Latvians took part in the government after the revolution! How many Poles! And the position the Poles occupied under Lenin! What position did Felix Dzerzhinsky occupy, and what kind of respect does he enjoy today?[28] This all speaks of the fraternal relationship of the Soviet Union to our allies and brothers, the Polish people.

In connection with Gomulka's imprisonment, I cannot agree that Stalin was responsible. I knew for a fact, I heard it from Stalin, that he did not order Gomulka's arrest; on the contrary, he even voiced doubts about the arrest. He trusted Gomulka.

After Gomulka was restored to power, relations between our two

27. Khrushchev accepted Gomulka's plea and decided against sending Soviet troops into Warsaw.
28. Felix E. Dzerzhinsky (1877–1926) was the founder of the Soviet secret police, originally known as the CHEKA, Russian initials for Extraordinary Commission to Combat Counterrevolution and Sabotage. His statue dominates Dzerzhinsky Square, where the headquarters of the KGB are located.

countries improved. Anti-Soviet slander began to die out, and for this Gomulka needs to be recognized. He was in a very good position; you might say, he had suffered. He had been in prison several years and people said it was at Stalin's request, although I categorically deny that in this case. It was easy for Gomulka to say, "I also was in prison, and I know it was wrong." After that, he could speak about the need to strengthen our friendship and say that Poles got more out of the relationship than Russians. Anti-Soviet sentiment finally fell silent. I say fell silent because it was not actually eliminated.

According to information I received in 1968 [after the invasion of Czechoslovakia], anti-Soviet sentiment flared up again as a result of a performance in a Warsaw theater. The play was about the struggle of Poles who had risen up against the occupation by czarist troops.[29] When it occurred, the progressive Russian intelligentsia stood on the side of those Poles who rose up, but in 1968 the anti-Russian words heard in the theater were perceived by the audience as relating to the contemporary situation.

These sentiments were strong and widespread. I don't know how deep they ran, but they were vocal, and the stability of the society was seriously hurt in 1968. I am not judging harshly, because there are Poles today who want to fan anti-Russian, anti-Soviet feelings. These are people who do not take the socialist position. They use any means to mobilize a struggle against the building of socialism in Poland. If you play the Russian card in a nationalistic way, it works. As they say, all's fair in love and war. We need to understand the situation.

We cannot stop the anti-Soviet slander campaign with a wave of the hand. We need time to win people's trust and to make those who have strayed realize the error of their ways. We want them to realize that we are a friend of the Polish people, and that our friendship could really achieve peace and Poland's safety. If Poland relied on our friendship she could preserve what she had gained in the West when the Germans were destroyed.

Poland gained very rich territory and natural resources. Historically these lands belonged to the Polish state, but that was a long

29. Khrushchev is referring to the play *Forefathers' Eve*, by poet Adam Mickiewicz (1798–1855), considered to be the Pushkin of Poland.

time ago. The reality of the situation was that only as a result of the destruction of the Germans by our troops did the Poles obtain these territories. If the Germans had gone one-on-one against the Poles, there would have been no chance of the Poles' hanging on to the territory. They would have had to have given it up under pressure, or as a result of the war the Germans would have launched against them.

Certainly the Poles would have been defeated. That was the opinion then, [again after World War II,] and that, I think, is the way it is now. That has been deeply ingrained in the consciousness and understanding not only of Communists but of the Polish intelligentsia as well.

One day we were talking and Gomulka said, "You know what our intelligentsia fears most of all? The Germans. And the Germans will become a threat to the Poles if our friendly relations with the Soviet Union are ruined."

Politically aware individuals in Poland have this idea in their heads. On the one hand they were dissatisfied with what we did, but on the other hand they understood that our relationship had to be fixed and made friendly again, and not destroyed. These people understood that the Poles should rely on friendly relations with the Soviet Union in order to maintain the borders they had received as a result of our crushing the German army.

I think that in my time we did not gain much materially from our friendship with the Poles. Instead, our friendship strengthened our mutual interests in international politics and in the fight for peace and in opposing the forces of capitalism, militarism, and war. Ideally, neither country should suffer materially from the relationship. If the expenditures of one or the other country to defend our mutual interests are analyzed carefully, there is no doubt that the Soviet Union is making the biggest material contribution of all the socialist countries within the Warsaw Pact.

One only need calculate the cost of maintaining our missiles — they are all on our territory. Calculate how much we spend on the nuclear explosives we produce. Calculate the overall cost of maintaining a huge army. All the socialist countries rely on our army in the fight for peace. Expenditures for this army are far from proportional. If expenses were divided per capita among all the socialist countries, it would become clear how many times more than our share we, the Soviet people, are contributing. This is not just for weapons. To take an accountant's view, we are carrying a heavy burden by maintaining our troops abroad. Now I am retired and have no influence on events, but as a citizen and former political figure, I feel it to be unfair.

The Polish comrades had no basis to accuse the Soviet Union and its people of enjoying benefits created by the labors of the Polish people. Nor can they argue that some of our policies hurt the Poles while benefiting us. No, on the contrary. I once told Comrade Gomulka that we needed to withdraw all our troops from Poland. Poland was already a powerful, strong nation. It had a well-equipped army. I told him we wanted to stop getting our eyes poked out for maintaining Soviet troops on Polish soil and supposedly forcing the Polish people to follow our wake in international and domestic policies. If we withdrew our army, the Polish leaders and the Polish people would feel that they were following the socialist path out of conviction, for the benefits it provides, and not out of coercion by the Soviet Union. This is true even today.

To my surprise and amazement, Comrade Gomulka objected sharply and argued the case for having our troops remain in Poland. I was surprised because I still carried in my memory how the Poles had vilified us in 1956. The Soviet Union really got it then, especially the army. There was even a demand that Rokossovsky be recalled. Gomulka said then, "You must understand that under present circumstances there is no trust in Comrade Rokossovsky. So it would be better if he returned to the Soviet Union." He came back, and here he received a medal and a hero's welcome. We valued highly the service Comrade Rokossovsky gave in the war. He was of Polish descent himself, and a Communist, a good, honest fighting man. He possessed all the qualities of a modern progressive man and a modern military figure. Of course, no one [in Poland] trusted him. Although he was a Pole, he was not a Polish Pole, but a Soviet Pole. Everyone thought he would conduct policy in Poland with the interests of the Soviet Union in mind.

I began to rack my brain trying to figure out why Gomulka

objected to our withdrawing our troops. From the point of view of Soviet strategy and the strategy of the socialist countries, there was nothing to justify the presence of our troops in Poland. They cost us a lot to maintain there. My military advisers had told me that each military division stationed in Poland or Hungary cost twice as much to maintain as the same division on Soviet territory.

Then, I understood. If our troops are stationed in some other country, that government receives a lot of additional income. Gomulka said, "It's politics, after all, and you can't measure politics in quantitative expenditures." This is true, but nevertheless it was we who were doing the spending.

By comparison, when our enemies' troops are stationed in West Germany, well, West Germany pays for at least a large portion of their maintenance. There was a lot of debate on the topic, complete with pressure from the United States. Germany took on some or maybe all of the cost of maintaining the troops of its NATO allies located on its soil.

People aren't generally aware of this, but after the war, East Germany paid us reparations in the form of contributions to maintain our soldiers stationed there. In fact, they were paying more than it really cost to keep our troops in East Germany. When I found this out, I was surprised. We wanted East Germany to make its standard of living competitive with West Germany's. We lowered the amount. By that time East Germany had already made reparations. Later we just started absorbing the cost of maintaining the troops ourselves, and had to make payments to East Germany.

The Poles liked that idea and also started to take us to the cleaners, profiting because our troops were stationed in Poland in Poland's own interest. That's a fact.

Who ever has any extra money to spend on defense? I say, no one, that's who. It's something you are forced into. For example, when the Warsaw Pact was debating how to divide up responsibilities for strengthening defense, it was decided that Romania should be responsible for obtaining a specified number of tanks. They were also to build some kind of ships on the Black Sea. They kept dragging their feet. My minister reported that they weren't going to live up to their part of the bargain. Then the Czechs told me that they had built tanks for the Romanians, but that the Romanians had no money to buy them. The Romanians never bought the tanks, and they never built those ships. Why not? Because they knew that the Soviet Union would defend them anyway.

IN 1956 there were events in Hungary similar to those that occurred in Poland. Now we had two Communist parties with an unsatisfactory situation in the leadership. In Hungary, many people had been arrested, not on Rákosi's initiative, but on the initiative of Stalin, through the advisers he placed there. I won't say that the rebellion was organized by Imre Nagy, but he became its leader. There was an element of spontaneity in the uprising.[30] It didn't happen all at once. First there were stormy rallies, mainly of young people. They were directed mostly against Rákosi, and then later against the party.

This was to be expected. Once a movement like this gets started the leadership loses the ability to influence the masses. Other forces that were hostile to Marxist-Leninist teachings and in favor of a return to capitalism replaced the old Hungarian Communist party.

The people did not support such a movement. Not at all. If the people had supported it, it would never have been as easy as it was to deal with the uprising.

That's why we needed to lure people away from the side of Imre Nagy. Some Hungarian comrades understood the need and tried to appeal to the masses with a broad-based platform. They felt that many of those who had sided with Nagy were actually honest people who were still in favor of socialism in Hungary and friendship with the Soviet Union.

In this respect Enro Gero took the most active part.[31] He was

30. On October 23, 1956, more than 200,000 demonstrators marched through Budapest demanding freedom and the return of Imre Nagy as prime minister. Nagy had been named prime minister after Stalin's death, in 1953, but was ousted in February 1955 after a power struggle with Mátyás Rákosi, the Stalinist general secretary of the Hungarian Communist party. Nagy was admired because he tried to end concentration camps in Hungary and institute reforms. His effort to establish a government during the October uprising failed. Khrushchev's memory of the Hungarian rebellion remained fixed on the unlikely idea that there was a counterrevolution taking place which had to be put down. Grudgingly, he acknowledged that there was a popular uprising against Stalinist-dominated party rule, but he insisted that, except in Budapest, there was support for the Soviet use of troops and Soviet domination of Hungary.

31. In July 1956 Enro Gero, Hungary's economic czar, replaced the Stalinist

involved with Hungary's Gosplan (State Planning Commission), and he was a good comrade and Communist. He and Comrade Kádár produced documents with appeals to the working class, to the peasants, to the intelligentsia, and to all the Hungarian people to ensure that everyone had a correct understanding of the need to overthrow Imre Nagy's government and restore the order that had existed before.[32]

When we were debating whether or not to use military force against the counterrevolution in Hungary, neither Anastas Ivanovich Mikoyan nor Suslov was present at the meeting. They were in Hungary. Then, just as Malenkov, Molotov, and I were getting ready to fly to a meeting with our Polish comrades on the Soviet-Polish border, Anastas Ivanovich and Suslov flew in — at night, as I recall.

Anastas Ivanovich's apartment and mine were on the same floor. He found out through his secretary that we were getting ready to leave. I don't know how his secretary knew this; we had tried to keep our departure a secret. Mikoyan called and asked to meet with me. When he came over I was already dressed to go to the airport. I told him about our decision [to use force in Hungary].

Anastas Ivanovich started to object. He said that armed intervention was not right and that it would undermine the reputation of our government and party. He said that we should not use force and that, in a word, he was dead set against the whole thing.

I said, "What can I tell you? The decision has already been made. I agree with it."

Mikoyan protested that he and Suslov had not been present.

I answered, "You were not even in the city, so we couldn't bring you in on the meeting."

"I demand another meeting," said Mikoyan.

"But the decision has been made and the timetable has been established," I replied. "That would have to be changed in order for us to meet again. Our whole plan would be ruined. I can't do it. I have to catch a flight with Molotov and Malenkov, just as the

party secretary Mátyás Rákosi, who was deposed at a Hungarian Central Committee meeting presided over by Mikoyan, who was acting on orders from Khrushchev and the Politburo.

32. János Kádár was freed from jail in July 1953 and became the party secretary of a large Budapest industrial district.

Presidium decided. I personally still think we made the right decision, and that you're wrong."

Anastas Ivanovich by this time was quite agitated. He even threatened to do something to himself as a sign of protest — I don't want to use his ominous words — something about that he would end it all.

"That would be very stupid on your part," I told him. "I believe you are a rational man. I know that in the end, if you think about it, you will see the necessity for our decision."

On that note we parted.

I have always been on good terms with Anastas Ivanovich as a comrade. We would always talk things through and even argue quite a bit. In this instance I was saddened that he took the position he did. Not only could I not sympathize with his view, I was categorically opposed to it.

We sent in our troops. The Temporary Revolutionary Government of Hungary was installed in Uzhgorod [in the Soviet Ukraine]. The new government addressed the Hungarian people by radio, calling on the people for support.[33]

Marshal Konev reported to us before the time scheduled in the operations plan that Hungary's airports had been occupied by our troops without any resistance at all. All the cities except Budapest had been taken, and the temporary government was in control. Of

---

33. The fighting began on October 23, 1956. When at first it appeared to Khrushchev that the newly formed Nagy government in Budapest would remain in power, the Temporary Revolutionary Government of Hungary, so called, was set up by the Russians on Soviet soil near the Czech-Hungarian border. It was a puppet organization, made up of remnants of the old Hungarian Communist party, which had completely disintegrated. János Kádár had actually joined the Nagy government and appeared publicly in support of it, together with Ferenc Munnich, who for a few days was Nagy's minister of the interior. These two men suddenly disappeared without warning on November 2, deserted Nagy at the moment of crisis, and turned up in the Soviet camp at Uzhgorod. Two days later Kádár made his famous broadcast, allegedly from eastern Hungary, claiming that he had formed a new government and appealing to the Soviets to send in troops to crush the revolt. Together with Munnich he returned to Budapest in the wake of the Soviet troops and, backed by Soviet tanks, he established the new regime. Munnich, as defense minister and minister of the interior, was responsible for the harshly repressive measures that brought Hungary back into line. Kádár remained as head of Hungary until he was forced to resign in 1988. He tried to live down his treacherous and quisling past by introducing a degree of economic reform in Hungary.

course, our troops had lent support, but in all these cities the temporary Hungarian government had named officials who took over by themselves.

Budapest put up quite a bit of resistance. There were some officers of the Hungarian army against us. The rebels' artillery pieces were taken up to the tops of buildings and fired down on streets. The resistance could have been put down earlier, but more destructive methods would have been required. That was not in our best interests, because it would have meant a longer period of unrest and more casualties.

It was all over in three days. The peasantry, by and large, was not affected by the work disruptions organized by Imre Nagy. In some cities and industrial centers, as well as in the coal-producing centers, there was some wavering. In each of these places there was a unit of Communists who took a firm position against the restoration of capitalism in Hungary.

It is necessary to fend off attacks from those who would say that this was a revolt against socialism, against Marxist-Leninist teachings. No! It is only the enemies of socialism who frame the issues this way, and they are not right to do so. The subsequent course of events bore out our point of view. We were right in believing that the majority of the population was in favor of friendship with the Soviet Union, and in favor of building socialism in Hungary.

The new government began to function. The situation began to stabilize. The party itself was renamed the Socialist Workers party.

The Hungarian press said the [pro-Nagy] counterrevolution was a revolution. How could people be called on to rally around a government and a leadership headed by Comrades Kádár, Munnich, and others if the uprising against Rákosi had been a revolution?[34] If that's so, what should the government that now exists be called? As the Russian saying goes, people were lost amidst three pine trees.

Comrade Malenkov was there because we felt there should be some point of contact between the new leadership and our army. General [M. I.] Kazakov was in command of the troops. He

34. Munnich, who joined the Soviet side with Kádár, was later prime minister under Kádár. Khrushchev's argument was an attempt to rationalize the use of force with a dubious dialectical formulation.

seemed to be a good man, who understood the task before him, who did his work among the troops vigorously and maintained order in the country. For all intents and purposes there was no Hungarian army, and our army took upon itself the function of maintaining order. Our army set up a covering force against Austria to halt the use of this counterrevolution by hostile forces against socialist Hungary.[35]

I called Malenkov and said, "Do you have any idea what the Hungarian papers are saying about what happened?"

He answered, "Yes, I am following it carefully."

"How can you allow it to go on and not explain to our Hungarian comrades that there can be no normalization in Hungary with explanations like those appearing in the newspapers?" I asked Malenkov. "If it was a revolution against Rákosi, then what do you call the actions taken against Imre Nagy? It's an enormous contradiction!"

Malenkov answered, "Well, what can I say? I tell them, but they disagree. They just disagree."

I told Malenkov, "It is a fundamental issue. And if they disagree, it is clear that they simply don't understand, even though it is very simple. There is no way to reconcile with their views. You must not have been active or insistent enough."

"That's not true," said Malenkov, "I have done all I could. I have talked with their leaders, and they just don't agree."

I understood that Rákosi had fouled his own nest so badly that every voice raised against him was considered to be the voice of the revolution. This was a tragedy, a great misfortune for Hungary.

I said, "Dear comrades, please understand that you are defeating your own purposes. How can you rally people to your cause if you represent yourselves as people who have overtaken a revolutionary government? If you follow the logic of your slogans, that this was a revolution, then what kind of government are you? This throws the people, the workers, and the Communists mixed signals.

"You need," I said, "to give your people the right orientation. You need to tell them that this [Nagy's movement] was a counter-

35. Khrushchev's way of saying a blocking force was positioned against American or NATO support for the Hungarian freedom fighters, which never materialized.

revolution. If it was not, then how could we have used weapons? What were the slogans of this uprising? It was carried out under antisocialist slogans. Imre Nagy has essentially been transformed into a cover for blatantly counterrevolutionary Hungarians. This is the interpretation we are already seeing from Hungarian emigrants living abroad. You need to understand this so you can explain to people and organize them under your leadership."

After this, the events that had transpired were portrayed in a different way. People learned that a new revolutionary government had come to power, and that it was waging war against holdovers from the counterrevolutionary movement of Imre Nagy, and against the corruption of the party line that had occurred under Rákosi. Imre Nagy was tried and found guilty. He paid for the casualties that resulted from his putsch.[36]

A consequence of this was that our relations with Yugoslavia again cooled. I very much regretted this, but there was nothing I could do. The Yugoslavs had apparently come to their own conclusions. I do not accuse them of trying to restore capitalism in Hungary. No, that would be foolish. They only wanted Rákosi's leadership to be removed so that a new leadership, whatever it might be, would establish amicable relations with the leaders of the Yugoslav Communist party.[37]

The Yugoslavs realized that the counterrevolutionary, reactionary, and bourgeois forces had their own agenda — to liquidate any progressive movement not based on capitalism. This was already something that concerned Yugoslavia because it was a socialist state. Developments in Hungary contradicted the views and convictions of the Yugoslav Communist party. Therefore, when we

36. Nagy and members of his government took refuge in the Yugoslav embassy to avoid arrest and stayed there for two weeks until Kádár promised them safe passage to return to their homes. As they were leaving on a bus from the Yugoslav embassy, Nagy and the others were kidnapped by the Soviets and taken to Romania. They were held incommunicado there for two years and then returned to Budapest, where Nagy was tried secretly and hanged with three others in the spring of 1958. In June 1989 Nagy's remains were exhumed from an unmarked grave and reburied. He was rehabilitated and honored as a hero of Hungary.

37. The proper name for the Yugoslav Communist party is the League of Communists.

notified Comrade Tito that we wanted to undertake a particular action against the counterrevolution that was raging in Hungary, he said right away, without hesitation — and this surprised me — "That's right. You must do it. But do it yourself. Don't involve any other socialist countries."

WE have no border disputes with Hungary. In the Transcarpathian region [of the Soviet Union] we have about 120,000 Hungarians, but János Kádár has no claim on them. Why? Because the Hungarians took advantage of their position when the Transcarpathian Ukraine was part of the Austro-Hungarian state. The Hungarians, the ruling majority at the time, forced the Ukrainians off their land into the more mountainous areas and took over the best land in Tisza. That's the way the Hungarians did it. They took the best land, the floodplains, just like Israel is doing today in Jordan, ruining the Arabs and settling in their lands. The Hungarians are a harsh people, very harsh. That's why, if Kádár takes it into his head to ask for that land, he won't find any support in his favor.

The Hungarians' biggest conflict is with the Romanians, over Transylvania. When I talked with the Romanians they practically frothed at the mouth proving to me how the province belonged to them. The Hungarians say, How can it belong to Romania? Since when? Transylvania has always been Hungarian. The culture was Hungarian, the language was Hungarian. Now the Romanians have taken strong measures to turn the place upside down, as they say, to root out everything that remains of the Hungarians. But the Hungarian people are still there. I don't know how many, but quite a good number.[38]

There are more Hungarians in Romania than anywhere else. I can't be exactly sure of the number, because there aren't any official numbers anymore. You won't find such information in any handbooks, and I probably got the figure of 2 million from Kádár.

The big conflict is between Yugoslavia and Albania. There are more Albanians in Yugoslavia than in Albania. I don't know how that came about, but Enver Hoxha is very apprehensive. He is

---

38. There are an estimated 2.5 million ethnic Hungarians in Romania.

afraid that the Albanians in Yugoslavia are not loyal to Albania. They see an Albania without him. They are better off in Yugoslavia. Tito is a better politician and more intelligent.

I first met Czechs in 1915 when I worked in the electric power station of the Pastukhov mines [near Yuzovka in the Donbass]. They were prisoners of war from Austria-Hungary, but they lived like other workers and had no special restrictions placed on them. They were intellectuals. I learned about the Slavophile movement from them and for the first time heard the names of the Czech statesmen Tomáš Masaryk and his son, Jan Garrigue Masaryk.[39] Since then I have had the image of kind Czechs, people who call themselves our Slavic brothers. They do not want to fight against us because they are fellow Slavs. Their feelings of brotherhood with us do not come from class consciousness.

The next time I met with a representative of the Czech people was in 1935 when I was serving as secretary of the Moscow city party organization. I was a delegate to the Comintern Congress. At the Central Committee's suggestion, the Moscow party organization held a reception and luncheon for the Comintern Congress members. As the host I met the delegates and representatives from the Communist parties of the other socialist countries. That's when I first became acquainted with Klement Gottwald.[40] He came up and introduced himself. He was a young man of medium height who was really sloshed, but like everyone else that day he was under control out of respect for the host organization, the Moscow Party Committee. There was a woman with Gottwald. At the time, I didn't know she was his wife. She was also tipsy, and made an

39. The Slavophiles were a nineteenth-century philosophical and political movement that emphasized the national individuality of Russia, idealized the Russian past, and opposed westernization. The leading Slavophile thinker, Ivan Kireyevsky, held that logic is not the sole function of the intellect. He stressed the linking of intuition and instinct in seeking to define Russia's contribution to the world spirit of civilization. Slavophile ideas merged with Pan-Slavism in the 1860s. Tomáš Masaryk (1850–1937), who wrote on Pan-Slavism, was the father of Czechoslovakia, and his son, Jan Garrigue Masaryk (1886–1948), was foreign minister from 1940 until his death by defenestration in 1948.

40. Klement Gottwald was Czechoslovakia's prime minister from 1946 to 1948 and president from the Communist takeover in 1948 until his death in 1953, shortly after he attended Stalin's funeral in Moscow.

odd impression on us. We lived like monks in those days, as far as clothes and other things went. Yet here she was wearing a gold ring and gold earrings. To our way of thinking, she looked like an extravagant woman who had fallen under petit bourgeois influence.

Over time I got to know Comrade Gottwald. The Czechoslovakian Communist party was among the strongest in Europe and had a good proletarian character. For this reason the reputation of the Czechoslovakian Communist party was very high and Gottwald, as its leader, had a great deal of authority and commanded much respect.

Three years later, in 1938, I was transferred to the Ukraine. I was a member of the military council of the Kiev military district. The first victim of World War II was Czechoslovakia.

We had a treaty with the Czechs stating that we would come to their aid and give them military assistance if they ever needed it. However, there was a clause in the treaty stating that we would offer aid only if France also provided military assistance. The French and British ended up betraying the Czechoslovakian republic, and Hitler, without a single battle, added Czechoslovakia to his territory.

We also talked to the Poles about aiding Czechoslovakia, but they refused to permit our troops to pass through their territory. What was worse, the Poles refused to participate in any kind of joint effort against the aggression that was rising against Poland from Germany. On the contrary, there was an exchange of pleasantries between the Polish and the German governments. The Polish foreign minister, Józef Beck, went to Berlin on Poland's behalf and a fascist leader came to Poland from Berlin. That's how the two countries demonstrated their friendship.

Everything was worked out to the final details. That was German fascism's tactics: to solve its problems and make its moves one at a time.

After the war began we had no contact with the Czechs. I was told that some of our citizens were in Prague right after it was taken by the Germans. They said the Czechs were sluggish and worn out, like autumn flies. They could not raise their eyes. It was as if the people were in mourning.

The Czech ambassador to the Soviet Union at the time was a

Social Democrat named Fierlinger.[41] He became a Communist. He understood the necessity of strengthening friendship with the Soviet Union. I considered him to be an honest and decent man.

Stalin, in conversations with us, said he distrusted the ambassador. What did he base this on? The basis was simple, and very convincing to Stalin: Fierlinger's wife was French. I only met him later, after Stalin's death, when I was in Czechoslovakia. We never had any doubt about Comrade Fierlinger or about his wife. She never gave us cause for suspicion, politically speaking. But she was under a cloud while Stalin was alive. I don't know why Stalin spared her or why Fierlinger himself was not compromised. I have no idea what became of him as a result of the recent events that have taken place in Czechoslovakia.[42]

I met Gottwald again when he visited Moscow after the war. He and I developed a good relationship. Stalin, too, was well disposed toward Gottwald. Then something happened in 1948, after the victory of the Czech proletariat and the overthrow of the reactionary leadership.[43] Stalin was vacationing in the Crimea, and Gottwald and his wife came for a visit. I didn't know that Gottwald was there, but one day Stalin phoned me and asked if I couldn't come down to the Crimea.

"When do you want me?" I asked.

"As soon as you can get here," said Stalin. "Gottwald is here and says he can't get along without you. He absolutely demands that you come."

It was Stalin's way of joking. "Very well," I said. "I will be pleased to meet with Comrade Gottwald."

The next day I flew to Yalta. Stalin was staying in the Livadia

41. Zdenek Fierlinger was the Czechoslovak minister to the Soviet Union in 1939 and defended the Hitler-Stalin pact. A Social Democrat, he was a Soviet stooge who was known by the nickname Quislinger, after Quisling, the Norwegian collaborator with the Nazis. Fierlinger consistently sided with the Soviet government and the Czech Communists against the Czech democratic movement led by Dr. Edvard Beneš. See Josef Korbel, *The Communist Subversion of Czechoslovakia, 1938–1948* (Princeton, N.J.: Princeton University Press, 1959), pp. 4, 99, 120.

42. Khrushchev's reference to the "recent events" is the Soviet invasion of Czechoslovakia on August 20, 1968. Fierlinger was honored in 1970 with the Soviet Memorial Award after his long career had ended. He died on May 2, 1976.

43. Khrushchev is referring to the forceful seizure of power by the Communists in 1948.

Palace. Gottwald was staying there too, and so did I, when I arrived. It was a large complex that included an enormous outbuilding that had been added by the czar. It was known as the Retinue's House, and it had housed the czar's staff and servants when he vacationed in Yalta.

We met over meals. The table conversation was relaxed and wide-ranging. By that time Stalin could not resist forcing liquor on people to get them drunk. This is what he did with Gottwald, who already had a fondness for drink. Stalin didn't have to work very hard at getting him drunk. Actually, Gottwald had to be restrained from drinking because it was affecting his health. Gottwald's wife was a robust woman who knew her husband's weakness and, as I already said, liked to drink herself. Often, when Stalin was pouring drinks, she gladly stood in for Gottwald.

"Allow me, Comrade Stalin," she said, "to drink in my husband's place. I will drink for both of us."

Gottwald still ended up drinking more than he should have. He had obviously been weakened from alcohol and became drunk fairly easily.

I remember the following conversation. Gottwald asked, "Comrade Stalin, why are your people stealing our technical secrets? They steal everything they can. We can see what's happening. It offends and insults us. We have no secrets from you. If you need our new technology or advanced designs, just say so and we'll give them to you ourselves. It would be much better. Not only do we not want to keep secrets from you, but we are fully prepared to become part of the Soviet Union. I am asking you, Comrade Stalin — let's sign a treaty adding Czechoslovakia to the Soviet Union."

Stalin stopped him right there. He didn't acknowledge that we were stealing secrets, even though it was a fact. Stalin became indignant when he heard this, but the stealing continued. By then it was already a habit. It's like with gypsies: if you ask a gypsy what he'd do if he were king, he'll answer, "Steal a couple of horses and run away." How's that for a kingly wish! What more does a gypsy need?

Stalin tried to gloss over the issue, saying, "Well, anything is possible." He categorically rejected the idea of Czechoslovakia joining the Soviet Union. I think he was right to do that.

At that time Stalin's broom reached into many socialist countries that had been liberated after the destruction of Hitlerite Germany. The leadership of the Polish Communist party had been destroyed by Stalin before the war began. After the war a new leadership was created, but I think Stalin felt it was too new for him to trust. No one inside the Soviet Union or out had Stalin's trust. Stalin looked into everyone's eyes, searching for the smallest sign that the person was not loyal to him.

Only the Czechs were an island. There was no treason there, no betrayal or subversive activity within the Czechoslovak Communist party. Stalin naturally put pressure on Gottwald. "Your secret service probably doesn't do its work very well; you probably can't spot your own enemies," he often said.

Gottwald answered, "Comrade Stalin, our party has no traitors. I will tell you why. First, our party was very strong before the war in capitalist Czechoslovakia. Second, our party was legal and everything was open. Our enemies had no need to infiltrate it with agents. We had public meetings, and all our work was in the open. Both our friends and our enemies knew each step that we took."

Stalin was aggravated by such talk. Inside our own circle, behind Gottwald's back, Stalin called him "a blind man, a pussycat. Gottwald, what does he know? He argues that there are no enemies inside his party. That cannot be!" For Stalin, of course, it was axiomatic that there were enemies of the people everywhere. Gottwald felt that the Czechoslovak party itself could deal with them. He saw it as a class struggle, which in Czechoslovakia would lead to the ultimate victory of the working class, and the creation of a Communist society.

Stalin offered Gottwald our Chekist advisers. He said they were experienced and could help the Czechs. I don't know how Gottwald felt about this offer, but he accepted. Gottwald had to agree, because if he rejected the offer Stalin would take it as a sign of Gottwald's complete untrustworthiness.

Other socialist countries already had Chekist advisers: Romania, Bulgaria, Hungary, Poland, the GDR. In these countries the elimination of cadres had already begun. People were branded as traitors. They were the same cadres who had just moved into top leadership positions, or they were people who had distinguished themselves in battle. In other words, they had already undergone a kind of natural selection, so to speak. Wherever our advisers were sent, many such individuals went to their deaths as traitors. Czechoslovakia was the only exception.

As soon as our advisers arrived in Czechoslovakia, we started to get material on individual leaders. I say "we" but that's not really accurate. There was no internal party democracy at all; there was only the cult of Stalin. All information like that went exclusively to Stalin. We were only given "background material," that is, information that Stalin sent around to all the Politburo members with his decisions already attached.

Then material started to come in on Rudolf Slansky and other leaders of the Czech Communist party.[44] They turned him into an enemy of the people. I don't know how long it took, but not long, once Stalin got negative material on him. Stalin was triumphant because he had been proven right. He said he had sensed Slansky's real nature all along. Gottwald, who had assured Stalin that he had no enemies within the party leadership, really had turned out to be a pussycat, and a blind man who could not see what his enemies were doing right under his nose. Gottwald, as they say, threw in the towel.

How did I feel about Slansky's arrest? I can say now that I don't remember having any doubts about it at the time. I had no opinion of my own.

If Slansky, the general secretary of the Czechoslovak Communist party, was really an enemy of the people, then what could be said about the leaders picked by the Czech Central Committee? Naturally, Slansky had influenced their selection. People who were Slansky's favorites were rounded up. It followed that they had to be enemies of the people as well. The meat grinder began to turn, destroying cadres the same way it had in the Soviet Union since 1935 and the way it continued after the war. It worked with a different intensity, but it never stopped.

I remember another talk between Stalin and Gottwald. Stalin asked Gottwald if the Soviet Union should move its troops into Czechoslovakia. What reason was there for the movement of troops? I cannot say, because Stalin at that time would not let anyone stick their nose into an issue unless he pushed it in that direc-

44. Rudolf Slansky was Communist party secretary from 1945 until his arrest in November 1951.

tion. The reason could have been that the Cold War was beginning to gain momentum. Truman was still president at the time, and Stalin feared war with America.

Gottwald answered, "Anything, but not that. Under no circumstances, except if our borders are violated. It would poison the well and create impossible difficulties for our Communist party. Now we have good relations between Czechs and Slovaks. Soviet troops in Czechoslovakia would mean the loss of our independence, which we fought for against the Germans and Austrians."

Stalin only probed Gottwald because he was not ready to make a decision. He was not influenced by Gottwald's plea. I think it was only reasonable that we did not move troops into Czechoslovakia. Compared with other countries, the warmest and the most brotherly feeling toward us came from the Czechoslovaks.

Gottwald died shortly after Stalin, in 1953. He was succeeded by Antonín Zápotocký, a former Social Democrat. Zápotocký was a tested person, and we respected him.[45] Molotov was responsible for dealing with party officials abroad because he had been close to Stalin and foreign affairs were his responsibility.

I remember that on my visit to Czechoslovakia [in 1954] I met with Antonín Novotný. He made an excellent impression on me.[46] He had lived life with a solitary purpose — to advance the cause of the Czechoslovak Communist party. Although we had doubts about some of those purged by the Czechs, we did not interfere because it was internal party business. However, we made our opinion known.

During that visit I also visited a foundry with Molotov. A worker

45. Antonín Zápotocký died in 1957 and was succeeded as president by Antonín Novotný, who also retained the position of party secretary, so that he was, in effect, dictator of Czechoslovakia.

46. During World War II Novotný spent four years in the Nazi concentration camp at Mauthausen in Austria. He established a bad reputation there based on his performance as a *kapo*, or trustee, winning privileges for himself and his friends at the expense of less fortunate prisoners and using his special position to break his enemies. Novotný's swift rise after the war was largely due to the part he played in helping to unmask the alleged conspiracy of his colleague Slansky and others, which led to charges of treason and to trials and executions in the manner of the Soviet treason trials of the 1930s. Novotný ruled in the Stalinist manner until the spring of 1968, when he was forced to resign. After the Soviet invasion in August 1968 he was not returned to power.

ran up with a jar full of beer and gave it to me. I joked with him: "In our country this would be drinking on the job." Then I tasted the beer and embraced the worker. The Czechs had a very good attitude toward us, fostered by the Soviet liberation of Czechoslovakia from the Germans. This was especially so in Prague.

Two years later, after the Twentieth Party Congress, I had a conversation with Novotný that made me quite depressed.

Although we now openly discussed Stalin's abuses of power at the congress, we still trembled before the memory of his power and were unable to condemn fully the atrocities he had perpetrated. We still could not speak with our own voices. We were still, to some extent, trying to whitewash Stalin. There's a Russian proverb, "You can't wash a black dog white." Our behavior flew in the face of common sense. I understand this today, but I didn't then. We wanted to go easy on Stalin, even in death. We used to blame the devil, and say what had happened was the devil's work. First Yezhov, then Yagoda was the devil, later Beria.

There was no logic in this, because Beria came on the scene only after the meat grinder had done most of its work. Beria was mainly responsible for the cleanup that followed. He only continued the work that Stalin, aided by Yezhov and Yagoda, had started, if you can call the annihilation of human beings work.

I told Novotný there had been a great internal struggle over giving a report on Stalin's crimes to the congress. The main opponents of the idea were Molotov, Kaganovich, and Voroshilov, the same Voroshilov who was later given a hero's funeral and in whose honor a city was named. He was responsible for killing people in Voroshilovgrad [now Lugansk, in the Ukraine]. How many people died because of that man?

Soviet citizens must have the right to call things by their own names. We still haven't the courage for that. Crimes cannot be forgiven, especially crimes as heinous as those committed by Stalin and his closest aides, Molotov, Kaganovich, and Voroshilov. We must not forgive them. To do so would mean to give our blessing to new criminals for new crimes. In discussions with party representatives of all the other socialist countries, we said they also had to take a critical look and correct mistakes that had been made. We were completely sure that the cases there had been faked too, and that innocent people, honest Communists, loyal to the revolution, and loyal to the cause of Marxism-Leninism, had suffered. They had become the victims of ruthless excess.

When I expressed these ideas to Novotný, I was struck by his reaction. He seemed very nervous. He flinched and said, "No, Comrade Khrushchi" — that's what he called me, Comrade Khrushchi — "no, that's not the way it was with us. We did everything according to the letter of the law. We had grounds for the arrests and the harsh sentences."

"Comrade Novotný," I said, "I don't want to argue with you. We're making this recommendation on the basis of our own experience. Like you, we believed everything was done according to the law, that all our arrests and executions were well grounded, that those convicted were truly enemies of the people. Now, after our lawyers have looked at the evidence, it seems that there was not nearly enough to arrest anyone in the first place."

"No," insisted Novotný. "It was different with us. We —"

"Look," I said, "you executed Slansky, the general secretary of the Czechoslovak Communist party."

I remember all too well Stalin trying to persuade Gottwald that he also must have enemies of the people. Gottwald answered that they had no such enemies. I remember how quickly Stalin's Chekist advisers found the enemies of the people by using the methods of Beria and Yezhov. Those methods are easy to implement as soon as there is an order. Stalin issued the order. We should speak about Stalin's methods.

Let me remind you how Kaganovich called me up once and said, "Try to find it . . . The document must be destroyed." It was a scrap of paper that Stalin had written to the effect that those who were arrested needed to be beaten. The reasoning was that since we were beaten in prison [before the revolution] we must be merciless with our enemies, otherwise they would never confess.

"And we," Kaganovich told me, "signed everything." Then I searched the secret files in the whole secretariat for that document. We never found it. Apparently Stalin had destroyed the document. I calmed Kaganovich down and convinced him that it no longer existed.

I was a member of the Politburo, but I had never laid eyes on the document. Stalin was the one to decide who would vote for

which document, and who would not. I only found out about it
from Kaganovich after Stalin died.

I repeat this in passing in order to more convincingly portray
the situation as it was. It explains why I had doubts about Novotný's categorical statement that there was legal proof that actual
crimes had really been committed.

"Comrade Novotný," I said, "I recognize this is an internal matter for you to settle. Why do we give you this advice? Because you
should keep in mind that if there was no basis for the executions,
then questions will arise after a period of time. Documents will
come to light. If insufficient evidence is found, things will turn
against you and against the leadership. If you want truth to
reign — and I'm sure you do — then it is much better for you to
take the initiative now. The people will demand an accounting."

The Czechs refused. Czechoslovakia stuck to its Stalinist position. Novotný did not understand his responsibility. He failed to
understand the necessity of having a pure political and human
conscience.

Now it is a matter of record how everything turned out — just
the way I predicted it would. There was no other way for it to
happen. I am very sorry that Comrade Novotný did not heed my
advice when he could have.

THE West is ahead of us in many things — in the production of
equipment, automobiles, and consumer goods. The best proof of
this is how some of our own Soviet citizens love fancy goods or any
kind of innovation. They hang around foreign delegations and tour-
ists and con them out of these kinds of items or simply buy them
outright. In our market we cannot hope to compete. It's too bad;
it's shameful, but it is a fact that can't be denied.

In the papers and on the radio they say that Czechoslovakia has
produced a machine with the Soviet Union's help. If anything is
developed or produced by Czechoslovakia it is always with the
"help" of the Soviet Union. You rarely hear that we do something
with the help of our Czech friends. Why is that? Everyone knows
the Czechs are excellent engineers, economists, and scientists.
They were able to produce the best weapons faster than anyone
else. We have often enjoyed the fruit of their intelligence and hard
work.

So why must we come across as so arrogant all the time? We hurt our friends; we take advantage of their weak spots without even stopping to think about it. It is such a typical old-fashioned merchant's attitude: If you are rich and strong, you can do anything you want. We never give any thought that we may be stepping on our dance partner's sore corns. We think it's their fault because they didn't move their foot in time. They should have followed our lead more quickly.

I want to say that even though we were often clumsy in our relationship with the other socialist countries, at least we were sincere. We never used this friendship to pursue any selfish goals. When I was in power, after Stalin's death, we never once acted in our interests first; we did everything we could to develop their economies.

Czechoslovakia occasionally found it necessary to sell a particular machine on the capitalist market in order to earn hard currency for consumer goods that were unavailable in the socialist market. I heard some harsh words about this: "Those businessmen, those traders. They won't sell to us, but they'll sell abroad." I often heard this sentiment from the Romanians.

I tried to explain that the Czechs weren't motivated by animosity toward any particular country, but by the conditions under which Czechoslovakia found itself living. We needed to understand that without an outlet into the capitalist market, Czechoslovakia could not meet its own needs.

I said we needed to treat Czechoslovakia with care, not to force it into trading only with the socialist bloc. At present we are still not able to satisfy all the Czechoslovak people's demands.

We still need more understanding and less jealousy toward the Czechoslovak leaders. So Czechoslovakia enjoys a higher standard of living than the Soviet Union or other countries. That's just the way it worked out historically. We need to conduct our policies in a way that avoids lowering their standard of living by consuming all of their resources. We should try to do just the opposite: By developing our own economy, we could aid the further development of the Czechoslovak economy. By raising the standard of living for our own citizens, we will help all the people of the socialist bloc.

On the radio these days I often hear irresponsible statements about Czechoslovakia. Honestly, I don't understand how we could reach this state of affairs in our relations with Czechoslovakia. The situation is critical. Before this our relationship with the people was so warm, so open and honest. How could this have happened? I don't really understand it even today. I am firmly convinced that the Czech people are committed to building socialism, that they support the Communist Party of Czechoslovakia, and that they are our closest allies and most loyal partners in the struggle to build socialism.

I simply can't agree that the Czechs have succumbed to imperialist propaganda, that they want to change the course of their society and return to capitalist means of production. I don't believe it. I certainly don't want to believe it. It contradicts all my understanding of progressive Marxist-Leninist teachings.

Obviously, the bad feeling runs deep and has affected the wide masses. There is no other explanation for the fact that when our troops invaded Czechoslovakia [in 1968], there were instances when they were fired upon and sustained casualties.

I personally have heard of instances where coffins were brought home and funeral services were conducted in secret. I can only imagine the suffering of those who lost their loved ones in the invasion of Czechoslovakia. [47]

It makes me feel terrible when I see sporting events on television that are held in Czechoslovakia. At a ski jumping contest there was a rally of several thousand people. An official speaker opened the competition. His speech was stamped from a mold that should have been thrown away years ago. He began by bowing, figuratively speaking, to the political leaders. This is unnecessary and artificial. It's a holdover from Stalinist times. The same thing goes on in our country too. We wanted to change things, but now it seems we didn't take enough serious steps to make a clean break with the past. We ourselves were guilty of this false vanity. It flat-

47. There were no public announcements of Soviet casualties after the invasion, but word-of-mouth gossip in Moscow and other cities soon revealed that Soviet troops had been killed fighting against Czech resistance to the invasion, what the Soviet press called "German revanchism," or the revival of fascism, in Czechoslovakia.

tered our pride that we as leaders were remembered at people's birth, at their death, at any important event.

Well that's what happened at the rally I saw on television. They began with Husak.[48] The mention of Husak's name was followed by pitiful applause. It was obvious that the people who had gathered there did not have the slightest respect for Husak's name and could not react properly. Husak is orthodox. That's what I know from the press. When the speaker got to General Svoboda, the crowd reacted more amiably. This meant that Svoboda was more respected and acknowledged in Czechoslovakia than Husak.[49]

This is terrible. It is bad that Husak, whom we and the other socialist countries recognized and supported, is so poorly thought of in his own country.

I don't think that this was an expression of anti-Soviet sentiment within Czechoslovakia. I don't think the people at the rally were against the socialist form of economy, or opponents of Marxist-Leninist thought. I'm convinced that would be impossible. It was something else. But what? This needs to be investigated. We need to think about this, and make the correct determination.

It was a mistake to send our troops into Czechoslovakia. Now the wise and logical thing is to take them back out. If not today then tomorrow, but the sooner the better. This is the only way we can regain the good graces of the Czech people, and make them truly our friends.

Of course, we could keep our troops there and use force to suppress any possibility of armed action. I don't think that anything like that will happen. The presence of a great many Soviet troops in Czechoslovakia is perceived as a sign of disrespect on our part for the sovereignty of their government.

48. Gustav Husak was the hard-line choice of Leonid Brezhnev to replace Alexander Dubček, who was ousted after the Soviet invasion of Czechoslovakia in August 1968. Husak remained in power until the fall of the Czech Communist party in 1989.

49. General Ludvík Svoboda became president of Czechoslovakia after Novotný's fall in 1968 and put up gallant resistance to Soviet bullying. Khrushchev first met Svoboda during World War II when he led a Czech battalion against the Germans. After the war Svoboda was the pro-Communist minister of defense under Beneš and played an active part in the overthrow of parliamentary democracy in Czechoslovakia. He joined the Communist party in 1948 but was regarded with deep suspicion by Stalin, who had him demoted. After Stalin's death Khrushchev helped to rehabilitate him.

All this makes me think of what that wise man Comrade Gottwald said. He knew and understood the sentiments of both the Czechs and the Slovaks. During discussions about the possibility of sending our troops into Czechoslovakia, he tried to explain to Stalin why we should not send them. He insisted that it would do great harm to the friendship enjoyed by the two countries. Many years have since passed, but Gottwald's warning rings true today.

I think time will heal the wounds and the matter will cease to be an issue. The Czech people, in the end, will fall into step with the people of the other socialist countries, and especially with the Soviet people. Our people and our party are the true friends of the Czechoslovak Communist party and the Czechoslovak people. It is beneficial for us to work together. Our goals are the same — to be side by side in the fight for socialism and communism. I think all will turn out well in the end.

6

Comrades to the East

S TALIN spoiled our relations with China. He had a deep distrust of Mao, and in general he was insensitive to the Chinese.

We gave China arms and some economic help. It was the right thing to do. Our help consisted of steel mills and factories for producing automobiles, tractors, and armaments. We gave China credits and provided the blueprints and all the technical assistance. This aid was given on a friendly basis without repayment. We sent them military instructors to help with all kinds of weapons: pilots, artillery experts, machine gunners, and so on. This was useful because arming and strengthening China meant strengthening the socialist camp and securing our eastern borders.[1]

Yet in many areas of our economic relations we had thrust ourselves into China like colonizers. It was Stalin who provided the impetus for China's poor attitude toward the Soviet Union. When Chiang Kai-shek was very weak and could not control the province of Sinkiang, we organized joint ventures with his government for exploiting the natural resources in Sinkiang, where the population is predominantly Uighur.[2] We developed good relations there and

1. Stalin first aided Chiang Kai-shek in the 1920s and then after a break resumed aid in the 1930s when Japan threatened China. After World War II Stalin supported Mao Zedong's Communists against the Chiang-led Nationalists. Mao's forces prevailed, and in October 1949, the People's Republic of China was proclaimed. Economic aid under Khrushchev began after his visit to China in 1954. By August 1960, Sino-Soviet relations had deteriorated to the point that Khrushchev ordered the withdrawal of Soviet technicians in China, and in 1962 technical aid ceased.

2. Sinkiang Uighur (Xinjiang Uygur), in the extreme northwest of China, is

conducted mining operations. When the war ended and the Communist party of China emerged victorious, Mao Zedong became impatient and alarmed at what we might do in Sinkiang. Mikoyan was sent there to direct our operations, and through Mikoyan it was announced that we would not leave Sinkiang. We were not claiming Sinkiang or trying to steal it from China, but we proposed that Mao's China join us in creating joint ventures to mine the riches that lay there. When Stalin learned that there were diamonds and gold in China, he demanded precise information about where they were located.

Naturally we supplied the capital and the technology, and the work force came from the local population of Sinkiang. All the production went to the Soviet Union. Communist China had already won, and we still tried to weasel our way in, like colonizers. This was an affront to the Chinese and was something Mao Zedong could not tolerate.

For me China was an independent country with its own traditions and a rich culture. How long had Communists in China struggled against the reactionary forces, only to win and then suddenly find out that their country was supposed to bow to the Soviet Union and give us everything we wanted? It is the business of the people's democracies to decide how to dispose of their own natural resources, even if we offer to pay for them. To try to dictate to them is insulting. Stalin's demands for concessions from China were intolerable. He created the basis for an anti-Soviet and anti-Russian mood in China. I thought it was nothing less than treachery when Stalin coveted all the raw materials and exportable goods in North Korea and China and tried to have them delivered to the Soviet Union rather than sold for hard currency abroad. Each country must have its own hard currency in order to have access to the markets of the capitalist world. After all, the Soviet Union cannot provide everything. We ourselves couldn't produce enough domestically and were forced to look for ways of acquiring hard

---

the home of Uighurs, a Turkic people dominant in Mongolia and eastern Turkestan from the eighth to the twelfth centuries. Sinkiang, which borders on Soviet Central Asia, is the site of China's nuclear weapons production and a potential area for oil and mineral exploitation. In the 1930s Chiang did not have the power to control the vast territory so far from Beijing.

currency — either through the extraction of gold or through the export of other goods to the West. Similar needs will always exist in all socialist countries.

We have to develop a policy that takes into account the interests of other countries, even though the Soviet Union, through its leverage, can force them to act contrary to their own interests. Stalin was deaf to this. He did not understand — and did not want to understand. Stalin developed relations within the socialist camp on the model of capitalist relations. That is unacceptable. Besides, others must not copy the experience of the USSR. Each country must develop economically and spiritually in its own way.

After the defeat of Hitler, Stalin believed that he was in the same position as Alexander I after the defeat of Napoleon — that he could dictate the rules for all of Europe.[3] Stalin even started believing that he could dictate new rules to the whole world. Part of his mistake was to exaggerate our capabilities and ride roughshod over the interests of our friends. This insulted them and planted the seeds for the animosity that was later directed against Stalin and the Soviet Union. By the time the animosity was apparent, Stalin no longer had the capacity for restraint. His whim had to be satisfied without question.

FOR many years we insisted that the initiative for starting the Korean War came from South Korea. Some say there is no need to correct this version of events, because it would be of advantage only to our enemies. I'm telling the truth now for the sake of history: it was the initiative of Comrade Kim Il Sung, and it was supported by Stalin and many others — in fact, by everybody.[4]

3. Czar Alexander I of Russia visited Paris in 1814 after the defeat of Napoleon to discuss the fate of the reconquered territories. This resulted in the Congress of Vienna, from September 1814 to June 1915. The congress handed over the Grand Duchy of Warsaw to Russia with the czar as king of Poland. Alexander granted the Poles a liberal constitution. He allowed them to retain Polish as the official language and maintain their own institutions, including a separate army.

4. When Korea was divided into two sectors at the end of World War II, Moscow-trained Kim Il Sung (born Kim Sung Chu in 1912) was placed in charge of the Soviet-occupied north. The Soviets had allowed Kim safe haven during the early 1940s, when he led guerrillas fighting for independence from Japan. In 1948 Kim was installed as head of the Democratic People's Republic of Korea (North

You may ask why. We sympathized with the North Koreans. We are Communists, and we wished the best to the people of Korea. We wanted to see the people of South Korea overthrow capitalism and establish the power of the people just as it had been established in North Korea. It was not Stalin's initiative, but he supported Kim Il Sung. Although I blame Stalin for all the crimes he committed, on this I am with him. If I had had to make the decision, I would also have given my consent to Kim. This was a question of the internal affairs of Korea. It was only natural that the people of Korea were fighting then, and are still fighting, to become a unified, socialist Korea.

When Kim Il Sung came to Moscow in 1949, I was present. He brought with him concrete plans for an attack. I did not participate in all the detailed discussions that took place. Probably they had talks with the general staff. I only learned of the final decisions when we all got together with Stalin in his nearby dacha.

A dinner was given there in honor of Kim and his delegation. At the table we talked mainly of a decision already made: Kim would move forward, and he was absolutely certain of success. The people would support him. The people expected this to happen. He had strong connections and everything was ready. He had no doubts of success.

Now that so much time has passed, I think that what Kim Il Sung reported then was correct. He knew the situation in South Korea well, and he probably had established a really large network of Communist cells in South Korea. He knew the mood of the people of South Korea. They were dissatisfied with Syngman Rhee.[5] This is quite natural. Syngman Rhee was corrupt, a straw man of American imperialism. The people wanted to be the master of their fate and of their own country.

Kim got what Stalin considered necessary to give him. I suspect Kim probably asked for much more. The date was agreed upon

---

Korea); he established a totalitarian state which he hopes to pass on to his eldest son, Kim Jong Il, the heir apparent.

5. Syngman Rhee (1875–1965) was an American-educated, widely respected Korean nationalist who became the first president of the Republic of Korea (South Korea), in 1948. An extremist in his views, Rhee gradually lost popularity as his government faced charges of corruption. He was forced out of office in 1960.

when Kim Il Sung would start his actions to unify Korea. The war began [on June 25, 1950].

I was present when Stalin summoned Bulganin, the people's commissar for defense at that time, and gave orders to recall all our advisers from the North Korean divisions. This made me uneasy. I think he did that because he was afraid that one of our officers would be taken prisoner and it would provide an opportunity for the United States to accuse us of participating in the war. Maybe it was prudent not to provide the grounds for accusing us. But on the other hand it weakened the North Korean army, because they lacked qualified cadres knowledgeable in military tactics. The removal of our advisers decreased North Korean combat capability and operational readiness.

The North Koreans were very successful at the beginning of the war and quickly advanced to the South, occupied Seoul, and continued the offensive. We were already anticipating with pleasure the completion of the operation and the victory of truth, the victory of the people, the victory of the working class and peasantry not only of North Korea but of the whole Korean people.

However, at the final stage, when the only thing left was to throw the South Koreans from their last line of defense [near Pusan], Kim was short of strength. I cannot say much about Pusan's population and strategic position, but I do not believe that it was a fortress. Kim Il Sung simply lost his breath. During his offensive he suffered losses in manpower and equipment — tanks. He lacked a little for the final push. I think that one more tank corps would have been enough for him to break through and the war would have ended. There would not have been such a tumor on the body of Korea as the imperialist state of South Korea.

In assessing the successes and failures of Kim Il Sung, I think our advisers, when they planned this operation, probably did not take everything into account and did not give everything needed. For this, of course, I think Stalin was to blame. Kim didn't need much more on top of what had already been given. We, of course, could have provided the tanks for another tank corps, which I think would have been enough.

But Kim was on his own. His army was retreating and losing its ability to resist. Our ambassador reported that Kim was in a desperate mood. He was crying and kept repeating that "there is no way out. The Americans are sure to come and occupy North Korea." Kim said he would move into the mountains and resume the same kind of guerrilla war he carried on against the Japanese when they occupied North Korea. What was Stalin's reaction? Here I was a witness. Stalin said, "So what? If Kim Il Sung fails, we are not going to participate with our troops. Let it be. Let the Americans now be our neighbors in the Far East." Such was his inner reconciliation. Stalin already believed that it was inevitable.

At that moment the Chinese suddenly spoke up. They suggested we meet and discuss the situation that had developed in Korea. To deal with these issues Zhou Enlai came from China as Mao Zedong's representative.

Stalin at that time was somewhere in the South, at Sochi or Gagry. Zhou Enlai met with Stalin there. When Stalin returned to Moscow he told us about the talks and shared his impressions with us. The Chinese said they had mobilized a reserve army at the border with North Korea. They offered to introduce this large army, some 500,000 troops, and provide help to North Korea.

I do not know whether the Chinese tried to set any conditions for their participation in the war, but if so, Stalin didn't accept them. I heard Stalin say we would not take part in this war. Stalin backed Kim Il Sung and gave him help, but he lacked understanding of the situation. He showed cowardice. He was afraid of the United States. Stalin had his nose to the ground. He developed fear, literally fear, of the United States.

The Chinese saved the situation. This brought honor to Mao Zedong. The Chinese Communist party made large sacrifices and put forward a large army. This army shed its blood in order to save North Korea. But ending the war was another matter, and we made our contribution to that when Stalin died.

STALIN was often bewildered by Mao. I too found Mao's logic hard to follow. When we met in China, Mao drew me into a conversation about the balance of forces between imperialism and socialism. He figured that the combined population of China and the

Soviet Union would allow us together to form incomparably more divisions than NATO.

"Look at the balance," Mao said. "What is there to be afraid of?"

This line of thinking corresponded to his view that the loss of 300 million people — half China's population — would be no tragedy.[6] For him, the main issue was not peaceful coexistence but how to prepare for war and to defeat our enemies in a war — even if it meant great losses to our socialist countries.

I said to Comrade Mao Zedong, "There is no question about our military resources. However, you have to keep in mind some other things. Such calculations would make more sense if wars were still fought by hand-to-hand combat or with side arms and cold steel, as in the old days. The one who had more clubs and spears would have the advantage. When the machine gun appeared, the balance of forces changed in favor of the better-equipped army. And when aircraft and tanks appeared, victory belonged not to the side with a larger population, but to the one with better industry and the ability to build better weapons. Now we're in the age of the nuclear missile. These weapons are great equalizers. One bomb sweeps away several divisions. To put it crudely, divisions are just so much dead meat. Therefore, our approach to war must be different. We shouldn't assess the balance of forces by measuring population. We must develop our nuclear industry and our missile industry so that our country will never be taken by surprise."

Mao replied, "No, I think you are mistaken. The balance of forces according to population is decisive."

There was no way to resolve this issue. We chose not to continue the argument. Going round and round wouldn't have accomplished anything.

It was just at that time that tensions started rising between China and the United States.[7]

6. When Khrushchev first visited China, in 1954, China's population was estimated at 600 million people. In 1990 it is estimated at 1.1 billion people.

7. Khrushchev is referring to tension that first flared up in 1954 when the Chinese Communists claimed and began shelling Quemoy and Matsu, islands off the coast of China that were still held by the Nationalists on Taiwan. After a period of shelling in 1954, the firing ceased, but on August 23, 1958 (shortly after another Khrushchev visit to China), the bombardment resumed. The Taiwan Strait crisis ended with Mao backing down in October 1958 after the United States supported

Mao Zedong told me, "If the imperialists attack China, don't get involved. We'll fight on our own. Our country is very large and we have many people. The enemy will bog down, and we will defeat him ourselves. It's very important to preserve the Soviet Union. If the Soviet Union is preserved and can further develop as a socialist country, then everything will fall into place. China will be able to restore its economy later, with Soviet help. Therefore, we should not place the Soviet Union in the position of risking war with the imperialist camp. China will deal with its enemy by itself."

See how he turned the argument around. This is very important. He tried to make it look as though he was ready for self-sacrifice, ready to preserve the power of the Soviet Union as the first country, the most powerful socialist country.

"We look at it differently," I said. "If each country relies too much on its own capabilities it will encourage aggression by our enemies, and they will defeat us one by one."

"That is not right," said Mao Zedong, and we were left with our own opinions.

On another military matter he also had a view I couldn't accept: "If there is an attack on the Soviet Union, I would recommend that you not offer resistance."

I was immediately on my guard: The imperialist states attack the Soviet Union, and we must not offer resistance? How could that be? What were we supposed to do?

Mao Zedong explained: "Retreat for a year, or two or three. Force your enemy to stretch out his lines of communications. That will weaken him. Then, with our combined strength, we will go for the enemy together and smash him."

I said, "Comrade Mao, I don't know what to say. What you are saying is out of the question. Can you imagine us retreating for a year? Would the war go on for a year? Think about what can happen in a year!"

Mao answered, "But in World War II you retreated to Stalingrad for two years. Why can't you retreat for three years now? If you

---

the Nationalists and Khrushchev failed to back Mao. See Donald S. Zagoria, *The Sino-Soviet Conflict, 1956–1961* (Princeton, N.J.: Princeton University Press, 1962), pp. 200–221.

retreat to the Urals, China is nearby. We'll use our resources and territory to help you smash the enemy."

I said, "Comrade Mao, we see things differently. We believe in immediate retaliation, with all the weapons at our disposal. Our ability to do that is what deters our enemy. We can keep him from committing aggression in the first place."

"No," said Mao, "I don't think that's right."

Later, I often wondered how to argue against such reasoning. Mao is a clever man. How could he think this way? Could it have been a provocation? I can't believe Mao would try something so stupid with us. Could he really have believed that what he was saying made military sense?

I repeat this account of what happened with my hand on my heart. I guarantee the accuracy of Mao's comments and my answers, without any exaggeration or distortion of his words. God forbid! We have enough concerns in our relations with China without my burdening them further.

When I met with Mao Zedong, he spoke unflatteringly of Stalin's role during China's fight against Japan. He cited letters from Stalin to Chiang Kai-shek and to Mao himself. He said that the Comintern carried out all kinds of sabotage against the Chinese Communist party, and blamed this on Stalin. Here Mao is correct. The Comintern did everything Stalin told it to. Mao said, "What did the Comintern advise us to do? To try to establish contacts with Chiang Kai-shek and not pick a fight with him so as to unite our efforts against Japan." Mao was especially critical of this advice, which I believe was in fact what the Comintern recommended. Actually, the advice had a certain logic, because the main danger was Japan; Mao's forces had to be coordinated with Chiang's. To coordinate forces does not mean merging them. They should remain separate but work together toward the extermination of the invader rather than fighting each other. Still, Mao believed that Stalin caused great harm to the Chinese revolution, and restrained the revolutionary forces in China.

There were many incidents which showed that China didn't trust us. An important one occurred when the Chinese carried out their operation against Chiang Kai-shek and the offshore islands of Quemoy and Matsu. Chiang's air force had American equipment, and some of the missiles launched from his fighters against China's aircraft failed to explode and fell to earth. Some were in good condition. Our advisers reported this to us. We were naturally interested in new American military weapons, particularly missiles. Here were the Americans sending samples to us via China! We asked China to send us one of these missiles so we could study it and make use of the American technology in the common interest of the socialist countries.

The Chinese didn't reply. After some time we reminded them of our request. There was still no answer. We were astonished. How could this be? Not only were we giving everything to China — all our military secrets, all our blueprints, plans for technology, and samples — but we supplied the Chinese army with our weapons. When we started insisting, they said, "We only have one, and we are studying it ourselves. We will share what we find with you."

We couldn't go along with that. We knew the missile was a piece of sophisticated technology, and the Chinese simply weren't able to cope with it, or even to learn how to use it. Because we had missiles like this in our arsenal already, we thought we were better prepared to appreciate if the Americans had something new, some interesting improvement that we might borrow.

We again approached China to give us the missile for study, and again we were refused. This was offensive and insulting to us. Anybody in our place would have felt pain. We held no secrets back from China. We gave them everything. We helped them with equipment and advisers, designers, engineers, construction workers. We treated them like brothers, virtually sharing our last crust of bread, as Russian peasants say. Yet when they got a trophy they refused to share it. However, they did give us a report about it, and we passed the information along to our experts.

Around that time we were supposed to hand over some military equipment to the Chinese. They pressed us to give it to them faster. We instructed our technicians in charge of delivery to say that we did not see why we should hurry to fulfill the order if the Chinese couldn't find it in themselves to give us the missile. Shortly afterward, China agreed to let our experts examine the weapon, and it was sent to a research institute in Moscow.

It was unwise of them to try to keep the missile from us. It left a bitter taste in my mouth and it had a sobering effect on us. The Chinese were following a Russian saying: "Friendship is fine, but let's keep our money separately."

WE started preparing for an international meeting in 1957. Everybody agreed that Moscow would be the best place to meet.[8] The Chinese delegation was headed by Mao Zedong. He was accompanied by Deng Xiaoping, Kang Sheng, and Sun Yat-sen's widow, Soong Ch'ing-ling.[9] She was considered a progressive person. She conducted herself well and behaved in a comradely way.

The Yugoslav delegation was headed by Rankovic, and his attitude toward us was good.[10] The Yugoslavs raised the possibility of changing some resolutions. We said no. The Yugoslavs said in that case they would not sign the document. We actively courted the Yugoslav delegation; we tried to talk them into signing. They dug in their heels. I even began to wonder whether they had found fault with the statement for no other reason than to have an excuse not to sign it. Maybe they were afraid of losing their position of leadership among those countries that had staked out a special position between the imperialist, capitalist states on the one hand and the fraternal Communist countries on the other. I couldn't see any other reason for them not to sign this document.

The Chinese told us, "If the Yugoslavs don't want to sign, that's their business. Let the rest of us sign on our own." So we signed it with-

8. Khrushchev is referring to the meeting of leaders of Communist parties in power, from November 6 to 20, 1957, celebrating the fortieth anniversary of the October Revolution. The delegations, with the exception of Yugoslavia, signed a declaration that reaffirmed the Soviet Union's leading role in the Communist world.

9. Madame Sun Yat-sen was the widow of modern China's founding father. Her brother, T. V. Soong, was one of Chiang Kai-shek's key men, and her sister was Chiang's wife. Deng was then general secretary of the Central Committee of the Communist party of China. Kang Sheng, an intelligence and security official, was a Politburo member who specialized in liaison with foreign Communist parties.

10. Aleksandr Rankovic was Yugoslavia's top policeman from 1946 to 1953, when he headed the Ministry of Internal Affairs and worked closely with the Soviet secret police. He was close to Tito and from 1960 to 1963 was vice president of Yugoslavia. Tito ousted Rankovic in 1966 for abusing his position by reportedly bugging Tito's apartment.

out the Yugoslavs, in order not to create further tensions with them.

Much later, when our relations with Yugoslavia improved, I learned from some of their people that when they talked with Mao Zedong, he said, "If you don't sign, it won't be a tragedy. Our masters may be upset, but they'll calm down."

This means that behind our backs China was already encouraging the Yugoslavs not to join in signing the document. China gave a reassuring nudge to the Yugoslavs in that direction.

I remember when Czechoslovakia was seriously hurt by Chinese policies. Czechoslovakia took orders from the Chinese for the production of some custom goods. China's effort to become industrialized placed a heavy load of orders on Czechoslovakia's industry. The Czechoslovaks valued this business highly.

Then Mao Zedong came up with his campaign to "Let a hundred flowers bloom." That was the first signal. It got worse. His next idea was the "Great Leap Forward" into communism.[11]

It was patently clear to us that Mao Zedong had started down a wrong path that would lead to the collapse of his economy and, consequently, the failure of his policies. We did all we could to influence the Chinese and stop them before it was too late, but Mao thought he was God. Karl Marx and Lenin were both in their graves, and Mao thought he had no equal on earth. He was at the apex of creation. Everyone had to listen to what he said and follow only his example, for only he spoke the truth. Finally we could no longer refrain from expressing our opposition, and when our discord spilled over into a public argument in the press, China suddenly canceled all its orders from Czechoslovakia. Comrade Novotný reported this to me. He flew quickly to Moscow to consult on what to do.

The Czechoslovak economy went into a collapse. The Czechs

11. The official slogan for the 1957 campaign was "Let the Hundred Flowers All Bloom; Let the Hundred Schools Contend with and Emulate Each Other." For three months criticisms were openly voiced, then the crackdown began against "rightists" who had spoken out. Some 300,000 "rightists" confessed and were sentenced to labor camps, were made to work on farms, or were demoted or discharged from their organizations. The Great Leap Forward, from 1958 to 1960, failed totally in its attempt to industrialize China with backyard steel furnaces.

were unable to unload what had been ordered, and of course they weren't paid for what had already been delivered. Their whole production process had been destroyed [in 1960–1961, when Sino-Soviet relations worsened].

We examined the situation and charged our own Gosplan and Gosplan of Czechoslovakia with the task of sifting through, item by item, all the orders China had placed with Czechoslovakia. The goal was to identify everything Czechoslovakia would be unable to sell to the West, and purchase it ourselves for our domestic use.

We ended up with quite a lot. We bought machinery and whole production lines that were complete and ready to operate. We also took some that were only partially completed. Included in the Czechoslovak production were some unique items that we could never make use of, nor were the Czechs able to sell them to the West because of their special nature. They had been made according to detailed Chinese specifications.

Mao Zedong's policies really hurt the Czechoslovak economy and didn't make economic sense to us either. I think this was precisely Mao's purpose for canceling his orders. It was no way for a true partner to behave, not at all. It was a hostile act more characteristic of an enemy than a friend.

For Mao Zedong there are no laws, no lasting agreements, no word of honor. There is nothing to stop him from deciding to unleash some vindictive policy with full force against any particular country. All's fair in war. That was China's attitude toward socialist Czechoslovakia.

I remember Ho Chi Minh coming to Moscow to ask for material help, arms and other kinds of assistance, for the Vietnamese struggle against the French occupiers.[12] Stalin didn't believe the Vietnamese could prevail, so he treated Ho insultingly. There was none of the sincerity I wished Stalin would have shown to a Communist

12. Ho Chi Minh (1890–1969), whose name (which he chose for himself) means the Enlightened One in Vietnamese, became president of Vietnam on August 29, 1945. Khrushchev is probably referring to Ho's visit to Moscow early in 1950, when Ho was seeking critical support in the Vietnamese struggle against the French. The war ended with the fall of the French base at Dienbienphu in May 1954. The mausoleum in Hanoi containing Ho's embalmed body is a replica of Lenin's tomb in Moscow.

like Ho. After all, Stalin was the leader of the world Communist movement. Under the most difficult conditions, Ho had organized the Communist movement in his country and led his people in revolt. For years he had successfully spearheaded the struggle for the freedom of his motherland. You had to revere this man, really go down on your knees before him in gratitude for his selfless contributions to the Communist cause, to which he gave all his strength and abilities.

On the second or third day after Ho's arrival we met alone with Stalin. His attitude toward Ho was offensive, infuriating. Yet perhaps I shouldn't say that, because neither I nor anyone else did anything about it except talk about it afterward.

At one meeting, Ho took one of our magazines, *The USSR Under Construction,* out of his briefcase and asked Stalin to autograph it. In France everyone chases after autographs, and Ho evidently was not immune to this habit. He liked the idea of returning to Vietnam and showing everyone the magazine with Stalin's signature on it. Stalin reacted in his typically sick, distrusting way. He considered everybody a spy or a traitor. He autographed the magazine but then gave the Chekists an assignment: he told them that he had carelessly signed the cover of the magazine, which therefore had to be confiscated. The Chekists were good at leaving no stone unturned, so the magazine was recovered. Later, Stalin used to joke: "He is still looking for that magazine, but he can't find it." I can easily imagine how Ho Chi Minh felt when he opened his suitcase and found the magazine with Stalin's precious signature missing. It must have poisoned his soul. What a way to treat a man who had such sincerity and Communist incorruptibility.

During one of the talks with Ho we made a decision to recognize the Republic of Vietnam. Later, Stalin often said he regretted the move. "We were too hasty," he said. "It's too early for recognition." Stalin did not believe in the possibility of victory for Ho's movement. However, the recognition could not be retracted. I also remember another disappointing, offensive incident. After Ho arrived, Stalin told us that Ho wanted very much to have his visit announced in Moscow and be officially received as the president of Vietnam. Stalin told us that he had refused this request, telling Ho, "The right time for that has passed. You have already come to

Moscow incognito, so there is no possibility of announcing your arrival."

So Ho proposed that Stalin give him an airplane, prepare a welcome, and Ho would then land and be received according to his rank as head of state.

Stalin roared with laughter: "Just imagine what Ho wanted. I told him no!"

In still another case, Ho Chi Minh requested that we send Vietnam quinine because the people there suffer terribly from malaria. Quinine was supposed to be the best medicine, and we had already started producing it in large quantities. Stalin showed his generosity by saying: "Send him half a ton."

Do you know how much half a ton is? You know how much good it would do for people who, with their bodies, paved the road to the victory of the Communist cause over foreign invaders? We felt indignant. Wasn't he ashamed? It wasn't just stinginess. Stalin did not believe in the possibility of victory for Vietnam.

For years there has been a struggle between pro-Soviet and pro-Chinese forces within the leadership of Vietnam. Looking at the way things are going now, I fear that Vietnam will end up treating the USSR the same way China did and drive out all our people except for a few diplomats. I think China won't release Vietnam from its paws, because the pro-Chinese forces there are very strong.

When our relations with China became spoiled, Vietnam at first wavered, but Ho Chi Minh maintained a rather good, friendly attitude toward our party, people, and state. Over time, however, Le Duan became more prominent.[13] When I held the leading position in the Communist party and government, we received reports from Vietnam that Comrade Ho Chi Minh had been moved aside from the leadership. He was alleged to have a special attachment to the Communist Party of the Soviet Union, which made him outmoded. He was supposedly unable to assess realistically the role the Chinese Communist party could play in Vietnam. Ho was

13. Le Duan was secretary general of the Lao Dong, or Workers party, the Communist party of Vietnam. He was appointed in 1960, at the height of the pro-Soviet phase, but later appeared to be pro-Chinese. Like Ho, he was primarily pro-Vietnamese, trying to tread a path between the Soviet Union and China. He died on July 10, 1986.

indeed pushed aside and for a long time afterward did not participate in important decisions of the Vietnamese Communist movement. Of course, he was still an icon in the eyes of the Communist party of Vietnam and for the Vietnamese people, so the overwhelming majority of the Vietnamese people knew nothing about his real situation. Probably in Ho's last days, when the struggle between Vietnam and the American aggressors reached a particularly brutal level, even the pro-Chinese elements understood the necessity of friendship with the Soviet Union. Therefore, Ho's position was probably again strengthened.

Why do I bring this up? Now that Comrade Ho has died, I am afraid that this pro-Chinese virus may reemerge. Now that the first light of victory over American imperialism is dawning, this would be a bad memorial for Ho Chi Minh, our dear, unforgettable friend and comrade in the struggle for the cause of communism, this apostle of the Communist movement. To complete the victorious struggle of the Vietnamese people, who are shedding their blood and sacrificing their lives in the interests of communism, the leaders of Vietnam need to show more understanding.

There are two documents that make it possible to predict future developments. One is the so-called testament of Ho Chi Minh, and the other is the speech of Le Duan.

Of course, I don't know if the document called the testament really is Ho Chi Minh's. If Ho did write it, maybe it is not the complete text or was edited and corrected after his death. Maybe it was the result of Zhou Enlai's visit immediately after his death. Only excerpts of the testament were published, not the original. Unfortunately, in politics such deviations are known.[14]

Why do I have all these doubts? Because knowing Comrade Ho Chi Minh and his attitude to the Soviet Union I am somewhat astonished that he does not mention our country or our Communist party by name in his testament. In an abstract way, Ho Chi Minh directs an appeal for unity to the people of the world and all the Communist parties. Ho Chi Minh was a clever man, and he understood that such a vague appeal could not contribute to the closing of ranks among Communist parties.

---

14. Ho died in September 1969, and his testament was read publicly at his funeral.

So I think that Ho was under pressure when this document was being prepared. It is written in a pro-Chinese spirit. I do not want to say that somebody was standing over his shoulder telling him what to write. He might have been orienting what he wrote in a way to meet Vietnam's immediate needs.

You may come back at me and say that China isn't named in the testament either. That's the point: neither the Soviet Union nor China is named, yet it is the help of the Soviet Union — great, selfless help, reflecting the sympathy that the peoples of the Soviet Union have always felt — that has been decisive in the modern war Vietnam is fighting against the United States, a rich, strong, technologically equipped, and aggressive state. The arms Vietnam needs can only be obtained from the USSR. Even today, China cannot supply Vietnam's needs.

If we analyze the testament in this light, we can say it corresponds to the saying "Pray to God, but do not anger the Devil." Neither the Soviet Union nor China is mentioned. This is in the interests of China, because it gives short shrift to the Soviet contribution.

I also read carefully the speech of Le Duan at Ho's funeral. It too was prepared in the spirit of the testament. The fact that he cites Vietnam's special wartime circumstances as an explanation for its policy is more in the interest of China than of Vietnam. I am absolutely convinced of that. For Le Duan, Vietnam's friendship with us is one of necessity, forced by the war. As soon as the war ends successfully, the mask will be ripped off and Le Duan will appear with his true face. It will be not just pro-Chinese, but a Chinese face!

With Ho dead, I want the day of victory to come as soon as possible. I want justice to triumph for the Vietnamese people in their heroic struggle for independence. Afterward I think we will have to endure bitter developments between our people and our parties. The hands of Le Duan will be untied to carry out an anti-Soviet policy, and a great loss will be inflicted on the Communist movement.[15]

*   *   *

15. After Ho's death, when this was dictated by Khrushchev, Soviet prime minister Aleksei Kosygin and Premier Zhou Enlai met in Beijing airport. Kosygin was returning from Ho's funeral. No positive results came from the meeting, and

TODAY Mao is doing the same things in China that Stalin did in the Soviet Union. He gained strength in his victory over Chiang Kai-shek and the defeat of the counterrevolution. Once he was established, he started getting rid of those who helped him achieve this goal. Mao couldn't brand his opponents "enemies of the people" the way Stalin did, because that had already been exposed at the Twentieth and Twenty-second Party Congresses. Mao himself strongly approved the report of those congresses. So he had to invent a new version — the Cultural Revolution.[16]

The Great Leap Forward and the creation of communes caused a great decline in China's industry and agriculture, leading literally to famine. It was necessary for Mao to recognize his mistakes. But that was no more possible for him than for Stalin. Stalin's worst mistakes were made during collectivization, which violated Lenin's principle of voluntary participation in the organization of collective farms. Stalin made his speech "Dizzy with Success." It was an astonishing act of treachery.[17] This slogan, "Dizzy with Success," found its way into literature and history. The "success" that supposedly made us so dizzy was actually a huge failure. He should have called failure by its own name and then corrected it, but Stalin couldn't do that. He put the blame on the local cadres, who fell on their faces and then lost their heads.

Like Mao, Stalin covered up his mistakes by saying that he was fighting for the revolution, for the party, for socialism — or against the enemies of the people. Were they really enemies of the peo-

border skirmishes between Soviet and Chinese troops broke out into major clashes in late 1969 and 1970. Khrushchev's fear of a Vietnamese shift toward China was not realized. Instead, Vietnam signed a treaty of friendship and cooperation with the Soviet Union on November 3, 1978. In return for economic and military aid the Vietnamese permitted the Soviet Union to use the former American base at Cam Ranh Bay. In February 1979, some eighty-five thousand Chinese troops crossed over the Sino-Vietnamese border into Vietnam. Beijing called the invasion a "counterattack in self-defense" against "the Vietnamese aggressors." The so-called punitive measures lasted for twenty-seven days before the Chinese withdrew and left a trail of destruction in a thirty-mile area south of the eastern sector of the Sino-Vietnamese border. It was a far cry from the days of the Vietnam War, when China and Vietnam said their relations were as close as "lips and teeth."

16. The Great Proletarian Cultural Revolution was officially launched in 1966, almost two years after Khrushchev's downfall.

17. Stalin's speech was delivered on March 2, 1930, and laid the blame for the excesses of collectivization on overzealous party activists.

ple? Of course not. Now these people have been rehabilitated, although the truth is that their names have not been fully restored with the respect required by history and Communist justice.

I used to listen to Chinese radio broadcasts. Finally I stopped, because it was simply disgusting to listen. The broadcasts were monotonous repetitions of Mao's sayings — that, and praise for Mao, like a prayer. Unfortunately, we followed the same path at the time of Stalin. We kept repeating at party and other meetings: "Comrade Stalin is our Beloved Father." People can say, on the basis of many of my speeches, that I also joined in this praise for Stalin. Yes, unfortunately, I was not an exception. I feel all the more sickened now that everything has been exposed.

We were punished by allowing ourselves to be deluded. That makes it all the more repulsive to me now to be a witness to how it is being repeated nearly in the same form — not for Stalin, who is dead, but for Mao Zedong.

I believe that the Chinese Communist party will find within itself the strength to conquer this sickness. Of course, the main control mechanism is culture, intraparty democracy, the cultural and moral level of party members and of the people in general. Only that makes it possible to defend against tyranny and abuses of power like Stalin's, against which our great Lenin warned us.

7

On the Brink: Berlin and Cuba

I have been to East Germany on many occasions. I have traveled widely, to industrial enterprises, rural areas, and state farms. I confess I was pleasantly surprised by what I experienced. The first time I visited Berlin I rode in a car with Comrade Ulbricht from the airport into the city.[1] Many, many people had been assembled, or came out on their own, to line the streets. I had expected the worst, because there had been so much blood spilled between our two peoples. I felt that the Germans wouldn't be able to come to terms with that, nor would they be able to forget. Of course, Hitler was the culprit, and he was no longer in the picture. But the country and the people had endured terrible suffering. Every family had lost someone.

Therefore, I expected some kind of demonstration — not open hostility, but silent, cold stares. Instead, I was struck by how cordial and sincere they were. True, among the people with open, smiling faces I did see some sharp looks from under furrowed brows, but they were few.

This was a relief. I felt that relations between our countries could resolve themselves and that they might develop into friendship between the people of the Soviet Union and the German people of the GDR.

I remember one meeting at a chemical plant. When the official

---

1. Walter Ulbricht (1893–1973), East German Communist leader who spent World War II in the Soviet Union as head of the Moscow-based political department of the German Communist party in exile. Stalin established him as the East German party boss after the war.

talks had concluded, an open discussion ensued. The Germans took advantage of the opportunity to ask questions about our policies. After all, we were still the occupiers. Someone asked about the prospects for unification and the creation of a unified German nation. There was a very strong trend in favor of national unity for the German people at that time [1958], and there were people who raised the issue without considering the social and political circumstances.

West Germany already existed with a capitalist system in place. East Germany, on the other hand, had chosen to build socialism. Whenever the question of unification was brought up, the issue of the social systems was usually omitted, or at least soft-pedaled. The primary concern was always the nationality issue — it was always about creating a state, a unified German state.

I took the opportunity to explain that unification of Germany was the main goal. It was a sound objective. It was only a question of the basis on which unification would be carried out. If it could be accomplished within a socialist framework, then not only would there be no objection, but we would do everything we could to accomplish unification as quickly as possible.

However, Western ideologists and the leaders of West Germany opposed this view and would push for capitalist unification. So it was necessary to seriously weigh who would lose what if unification occurred.

I remember that at the meeting there were women, office workers, and some teachers. They did not work at the plant but were from the city. What I said annoyed them. Apparently they were not particularly attached to building socialism and feared that the separation of Germany would last forever. They had friends and relatives in West Germany and were afraid that a time would come when they would no longer be allowed to see each other, or even communicate. This made them sad.

However, the significant majority of those present understood what I said. They were primarily the more politically active, so it was not entirely surprising that they supported me. Their way of thinking was close to our own. They stood firm on the issue: if Germany was not unified as a single socialist state, then it was better to continue to live under existing conditions and strive to build their own socialist state.

The German comrades have, in my mind, done very well with collectivization in the GDR. Collectivization under German conditions is a very delicate political operation. German agriculture is so advanced that it is hard to change the mind of the German peasant and lead him into cooperative management. It is hard to convince him to relinquish personal control and convert to a socialist system of management. Despite this obstacle, and despite the national idiosyncrasies of German agriculture, the German comrades have done splendidly. This is especially apparent if you compare their collectivization with, for example, that of the Soviet Union, where kulaks [rich peasants] were exiled and arrested and other administrative pressures were used. There was no place to exile German kulaks and they decided not to send them anywhere. The German peasants went onto the collective farms, and the collective farms began to do well. There was, though, a period when German efforts at agricultural collectivization faltered.

WHEN the two German republics were being formed, West Berlin became a stumbling block and destroyed relations among former allies as well as between the East and the West. The West began to step up subversive efforts inside the GDR, using West Berlin as a base. This was fairly easy for the West to do because Germans were used against Germans. The usual problems of language, of a strange culture, and of outward appearance of agents did not exist as the West looked for agents to send into the East. Besides, there used to be unrestricted travel and communication between the two sides. The borders were open borders. Of course, this meant that the German Democratic Republic also had the opportunity to send agents against the Federal Republic of Germany, but the Western countries took the most advantage of the situation.

Therefore, the issue of how to combat Western influence arose. The best and most logical way to fight it was to try to win the minds of the people by using culture and policies to create better living conditions. That way people would really have the opportunity to exercise free choice.

However, given the conditions that developed in the two German states, there was no real freedom of choice to speak of. That is because West Germany was richer, with more industrial potential, more natural resources, and more production capacity. It was hard for East Germany to compete.

Moreover, West Germany was supported by the United States' industrial and financial might. The GDR was fighting not only against the opportunities that existed within West Germany, but also against the added material incentives of the United States.

The West's goal was to turn West Berlin into what it called a mirror of Western life, a showcase for the capitalist world, in order to attract the people of East Berlin into resisting the steps toward socialism being taken in the GDR. These tactics might have seemed perfectly acceptable: let each person make up his or her own mind. There was no contradiction in this. It was a war for people's minds, not an armed conflict.

In fact, we Communists also wage a war for people's minds all over the world when we demonstrate the advantages of the socialist system of production and when we talk about how socialism is a more democratic system that gives more opportunity to the people. Socialism makes better use of the resources accumulated by the people and provides better distribution of riches among the people.

Yet if you looked at the situation that way, the picture was not quite right. The GDR's natural resources and its production capabilities were significantly less than those of West Germany. West Germany had the support of the United States, a rich country that you could say had robbed the entire world and grown fat off the first and second world wars. Thanks to more than one war, the United States had expanded its production capabilities. The Soviet Union, by contrast, had suffered more than any other country in the war and had a greater need than any other for the basic necessities: food, clothing, and housing. The Soviet Union's cities and towns, its technology, its machine-building factories and steel mills, and its housing had all been destroyed.

The Soviet Union never had a chance to compete fairly, to pit its material resources against those of the West. While the Soviet Union bled during World War II, the United States prospered and developed its power.[2]

2. Beginning in 1947, the U.S.-sponsored Marshall Plan spent $17 billion for European economic recovery over four years. The plan was rejected by Stalin, preventing the Soviet Union and East European countries from participating.

For this reason, after the war the Americans had accumulated enormous military resources, including clothing and rations. When they reduced the size of their own armed forces they threw their surpluses to West Berlin and to West Germany. In this way the competition was uneven from the very start.

The historical role of Marxist-Leninist teachings and the opportunities these teachings afford the working people of all countries are understood only by the most forward-looking segment of society, the most advanced portion of the working class and intelligentsia. Unfortunately, at a certain stage, ideological issues are decided by the stomach, that is, by seeing who can provide the most for the people's daily needs. Therefore, the attraction of one or the other system is literally decided by the shop windows, by the price of goods, and by wages. In these areas, of course, we had no chance of competing with the West, especially in West Berlin, where capitalism gave handouts to sharply contrast the material wealth of West Berlin with the living conditions in East Berlin.

Also, dividing a single people, making them live under different sociopolitical conditions, created enormous difficulties. West Germany had the chance to make itself more appealing, especially to professionals such as engineers, doctors, teachers, and highly skilled workers. This category of people was particularly attracted to move to the West. Naturally, workers tended to follow their employers.

Conditions steadily worsened in the GDR. Stalin never actually discussed issues like these with anyone else. When access to West Berlin was cut off, the purpose was more or less clear. We wanted to exert pressure on the West to create a unified Berlin in a German Democratic Republic with closed borders. This led to a very tense situation. The West mobilized all its enormous material and technological forces and began to supply Berlin by an airlift, as it was called.[3] They flew in every necessity to support industry and provide consumer goods. There was no limit to this, because West Berlin had its own airfields. Each sector — French, English,

3. The Berlin blockade began in June of 1948, when the Soviet Union deliberately paralyzed rail and road traffic in its effort to force West Berlin to become part of East Germany. From then until September 1949 the Allies supplied the city of West Berlin (population 2.5 million) by means of a massive airlift.

and American — had its own airfield, and those powers made full use of them on the basis of the Potsdam accord.

The airlift intensified the crisis. Military conflict was not impossible. That is why our army was put on alert and our troops were maintained in such high numbers after the war. Moscow was surrounded by batteries of antiaircraft weapons, on alert, fully manned, and supplied with ample ammunition. At a moment's notice they were ready to respond to a command to fire at an airborne enemy. I say this to illustrate the state of inflamed tension between East and West.

Suddenly Stalin became quite uneasy that Turkey was planning an attack against Bulgaria. Bulgarian leaders were called in urgently, and military advisers reported on what measures needed to be taken to strengthen the borders.

Stalin was unsure of himself in all this. He wasn't convinced that if a conflict were to break out, we would be able to meet the challenge. So the issue was not an offensive or an attack of some kind against the West, but rather of defensive operations to protect the Soviet Union if it was attacked. This is why Bulgaria's borders with Turkey and Greece were fortified.

By this time another sort of war was raging, over the airwaves and in the press. Here neither side spared any expense or effort. Suddenly Stalin decided to test the feasibility of negotiations to end the conflict over West Berlin. The West agreed, and negotiations were conducted. An agreement was signed and the blockade was liquidated.[4] Relations seemed headed toward normalization.

Then, after Stalin's death, when we returned to the issue of West Berlin, it became clear that the conditions specified in the agreement on West Berlin were worse for us than the Potsdam agreements. The West had been able to exploit the tension and force

4. At a meeting of the Council of Foreign Ministers in May 1949 the Berlin blockade was lifted (though the airlift continued for several more months). The West recognized the West German government, with its capital in Bonn. The Soviets established an East German government, with its capital in East Berlin. West Berlin's status was restored to its status before the blockade. It wasn't until September 1971 that the status of Berlin was finally resolved and a legal basis established for civilian access to West Berlin from West Germany. The Soviet Union guaranteed Western access to the city and the West German presence in the city was curtailed but not eliminated. The Soviet Union acknowledged the continued four-power responsibility over the whole of Berlin.

through conditions that were more favorable to itself than for East Germany.

We had to face these difficulties after Stalin died in 1953. Many places in the GDR were hit by unrest if not actual revolt. There was trouble in Berlin and in many provincial towns as well. Throngs of people went out into the streets. We were forced to move tanks into Berlin, but actual tank troops were not used and no weapons were fired.[5] It was gratifying and revealing that the government relied not just on armed forces, but also on the political parties, which had the trust of the people. A certain portion of the population fought against socialism, drawing support from Western propaganda, but the efforts of these people failed.

I remember that on one of my trips to Berlin, Comrade Ulbricht proposed, "Let's invite people from West Berlin and hold discussions with them." There were no borders at the time, and so there was really no difficulty involved. In the evening, I remember, about a hundred people gathered. There was coffee and beer. Usually when the Germans gathered like this, they smoked in an informal, uninhibited atmosphere. There were leaders from the labor movement and workers. A lot of the guests from West Berlin were Social Democrats.

The discussion developed, and I felt they were acknowledging the progressive origins of the German Democratic Republic. The Social Democrats spoke and made the point that the GDR was paving the way for all Germans — a new socialist path. They spoke passionately in favor of the GDR and socialism.

I remember an elderly woman who said, "I have been a Social Democrat for many years, and I am glad that I have lived to see the time when our dreams and ideas are being realized on German soil — in the German Democratic Republic. Socialism is being built, and we Germans, although we live now in West Berlin, will devote all our efforts to successfully develop socialism in the GDR."

5. In the spring and early summer of 1953, East German workers rebelled against a 10 percent increase in their production quotas, and a wave of strikes swept the country. Some 300,000 workers were involved in a general uprising and took over whole towns before the uprising was crushed with the help of Soviet tanks.

Another time, I remember, I headed a Soviet delegation to the Leipzig fair. I admit we had learned to conduct rallies well, but it is still significant that there were words spoken at this event in praise of the progressive role of the Soviet Union established under Lenin's leadership.

About this time, Comrade Ulbricht proposed another meeting with Social Democrats and politically independent workers from West Germany. It was at a large club or public hall. Everything was well organized and there was simultaneous interpretation provided. No matter where a speaker spoke from, there was simultaneous translation available through headphones. The workers and the Social Democrats spoke in support of the German Democratic Republic. I was very pleased. I suspected that there were probably opponents of socialism in Germany present at the meeting, but if so, they did not speak. The atmosphere was certainly open enough. I expected them to share their thoughts, but I did not hear any negative speeches.

Still, I understood that while the audience was on the side of socialism in the GDR, and that socialism had support in West Germany, the majority of West Germans then favored capitalism and still favor it today.

This is where we run into difficulties. Look at the small membership of the Communist party in West Germany. Even now, when it is legal to vote Communist, the Communist party receives a tiny number of votes in the elections. This shows that capitalism still holds the minds of the people and is quite capable of fooling them into following its path.

By 1961 an unstable situation had been created in the GDR. At the time, there was an economic boom in West Germany. West Germany needed workers badly and lured them from Italy, Spain, Turkey, Yugoslavia, and other countries. Numbers of the intelligentsia, students and people with higher education, left the GDR because West Germany paid office workers more than they were paid in the GDR and other socialist countries. The question of whether this or that system is progressive ought to be decided in political terms. However, many people decide it in the pit of their stomach. They don't consider tomorrow's gains but only today's income — and today West German industry pays you more.

Walter Ulbricht even asked us to help by providing a labor force. This was a difficult issue to face. We didn't want to give them unskilled workers. Why? Because we didn't want our workers to clean their toilets. I had to tell Comrade Ulbricht: "Imagine how a Soviet worker would feel. He won the war and now he has to clean your toilets. It will not only be humiliating — it will produce an explosive reaction in our people. We cannot do this. Find a way out yourself."

What could he do? He had to appeal for stronger discipline; but they still kept on running away because qualified workers could find better conditions in West Germany.[6]

I spoke to Pervukhin, our ambassador in Germany, about the establishment of border control.[7] He gave me a map of West Berlin. The map was very poor. I asked Pervukhin to share the idea with Ulbricht and also to ask Marshal Yakubovsky to send me a new map.[8] Yakubovsky was the commander in Berlin who developed the actual plan. We discussed the idea and the map that Yakubovsky had drawn.

Ulbricht beamed with pleasure. "This is the solution! This will help. I am for this."

I told Pervukhin, "Tell nobody about this. Keep it secret."

Unanimously, we decided to execute the plan as soon as possible. We called a closed meeting, with party secretaries and members of the Council of Ministers attending.[9]

If we had decided to have a military confrontation, the question would quickly have been resolved in our favor. We had superiority in the number of armed forces in Berlin, and we had a considerable advantage. But this would have been only the starting point. It

---

6. By July of 1961, more than ten thousand people a week were leaving East Germany for the West.

7. Mikhail G. Pervukhin, ambassador to the German Democratic Republic from 1958 to 1962. The phrase "establishment of border control" refers to construction of the Berlin Wall.

8. Marshal Ivan I. Yakubovsky, commander in chief, Soviet occupation forces in Germany.

9. Construction of the Berlin Wall began at 2:00 A.M. on Sunday, August 13, 1961. Dismantling of the wall began in November 1989, followed soon after by the fall of the East German Communist government.

would have meant shooting on some scale, large or small. War might have broken out.

The U.S. garrison in West Berlin was weak, and we could quickly have suppressed their resistance, but nobody knows for how long and how it all would have ended. We didn't want a military conflict. There was no necessity for one. We only wanted to conduct a surgical operation.

I was haunted by the knowledge that the Americans could not stomach having Castro's Cuba right next to them. They would do something. They had the strength, and they had the means. As they say, might makes right. Later, when there was nothing left of Fidel's Cuba and a new Batista was installed to speak to the world in the name of Cuba, there would be plenty of time to decide who was right and who was wrong.[10] Our aim was to strengthen and to reinforce Cuba. But how were we supposed to do that? With diplomatic notes and TASS statements? That doesn't work when the heat is on during an armed military conflict.

It was against this background that the idea arose of placing our missile units in Cuba. The development of the operation was assigned to Comrade Malinovsky [the defense minister], and only a narrow circle of people was given access to the plan. We made an inventory of our resources and came to the conclusion that we could send forty-two missiles, each with a warhead of one megaton.[11] The range of most of the missiles was 2,000 kilometers, but four or five missiles had a range of 4,000 kilometers.[12] We looked at a map and selected the launch sites. Then we picked targets to inflict the maximum damage. We saw that our weapons could inspire terror.

We decided to send a few thousand men to guard the missiles. We also brought the latest antiaircraft weapons — surface-to-air missiles (SAMs) — coastal defense missiles, and tank units to

---

10. Fulgencio Batista was overthrown by Fidel Castro in 1959 and forced into exile.

11. One megaton is the equivalent of one million tons of TNT.

12. The missiles were the SS-4 (range 1,500–1,800 kilometers, or 900–1,080 miles), with the NATO designation Sandal, and the SS-5, NATO designation Skean (estimated range 3,500 kilometers, or 2,100 miles).

defend against an invasion. All in all, it was several tens of thousands of troops. We needed to establish a headquarters, and Malinovsky recommended General Pliyev as the commander.[13] We sent our military delegation to Cuba with the task of informing Fidel about our proposals and to get his consent.

Castro gave his approval. The whole thing cost us a lot, but we thought it would be justified if we could maintain the new social order in Cuba.

We wanted to do it secretly. Our security organs had to determine whether it was possible to keep it secret, taking into consideration that American planes overflew Cuban territory all the time. The security people assured us that it was possible. They said the palm trees there would keep our missiles from being seen from the air. We installed the missiles above ground because underground sites would have required too much time to build. We wanted to hurry because we expected there was not much time before the Americans repeated their invasion. When they returned they would invade with forces that Castro could not withstand.

The security people turned out to be wrong. The Americans quickly caught us. They figured out that we were installing missiles. They also noted that we had increased the number of our ships arriving in Cuba. There was a big uproar and all sorts of demands to remove the Soviet "threat" from Cuba.

Any reasonable person has to understand that we never pursued aggressive goals. We always wanted peaceful coexistence and noninterference in the internal affairs of others. Our preference was for talks around a table and for all countries to remove their troops from others' territory. Our only goal in placing the missiles in Cuba was to prevent any encroachment on Cuban sovereignty and to assure the capability of the Cuban people to be the masters of their own country.

The invasion of Cuba [at the Bay of Pigs in 1961] was the work of aggressive American forces. Nobody believes that the invasion was paid for by the counterrevolutionary Cubans. No, it was supported by the aggressive forces of the United States and the tax-

13. General Issa Aleksandrovich Pliyev (1903–1979) was a cavalry officer whom Khrushchev knew during World War II. He was commander of the North Caucasian military district before being chosen to go to Cuba and given the rank of general of the army in 1962.

payers, who were not told about it. They were defeated. We knew that American monopolists would not rest until they crushed the revolutionary forces and ruled again in Cuba. The only way out was to put in missiles with nuclear warheads, and, if such a situation arose again, to threaten the United States. After installing the missiles we, together with the Castro government, intended to announce their presence in a loud voice. There was no sense in keeping the missiles secret, because they were not meant for attack. The missiles were the means for deterring those who would attack Cuba.

We were still in the stage of transporting and assembling the materials when we were exposed [in mid-October 1962]. Construction was not yet completed. The warheads were not yet there. It was very complicated for us to send over the nuclear warheads. When we shipped the missiles they went without their warheads, because transporting nuclear warheads requires special conditions. That's what the nuclear specialists told us.

We were very worried. Just as we were reaching the final crowning stage, our plan was discovered. We were afraid that the U.S. Navy might do something rash, like stopping our ships and blowing our cover. When we had begun shipping the nuclear warheads we thought about sending submarines to accompany the ships. The subs would be able to travel underwater, unseen. We were quite vulnerable in Cuba, militarily speaking. Our navy then was not what it is today. We did not yet have, I don't think, any nuclear submarines. Anyway, 11,000 kilometers is a serious distance. In addition, the underwater approach to Cuba would have been difficult for our submarines. We received reports that there were hundreds of inlets, underwater reefs, and shallows that posed hazards for submarine navigation. So we eventually gave up the idea. We even decided that the ships we sent would fly our flag, and that the flag would guarantee our immunity. The Americans were always careful to observe such immunity. So our ships went to Cuba right through an armada of the American fleet. The Americans didn't touch them and didn't check them. In October we had nearly completed the transportation operation. The nuclear warheads were dispatched while the atmosphere was red-hot. Every hour I expected they would capture our ships, but they didn't. We installed the forty-two missiles.

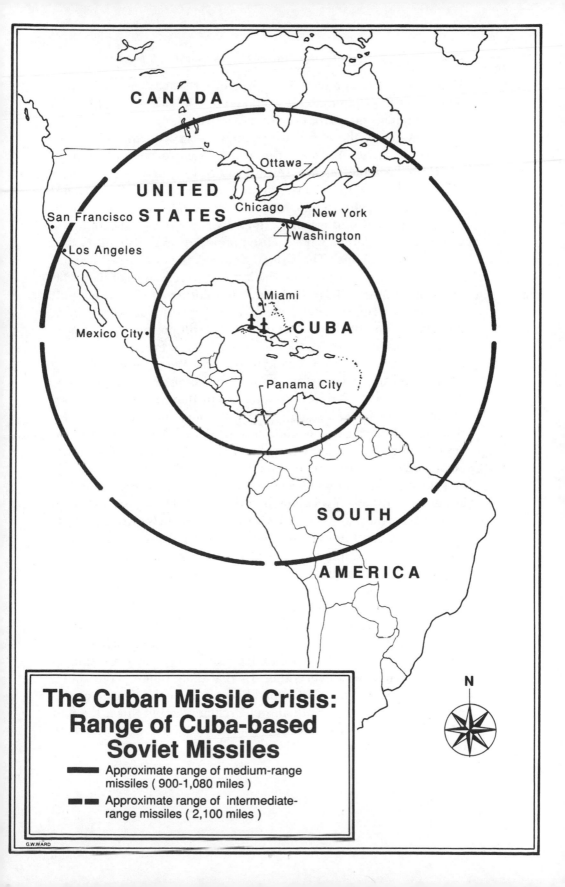

The Cuban Missile Crisis: Range of Cuba-based Soviet Missiles

— Approximate range of medium-range missiles (900-1,080 miles)

- - - Approximate range of intermediate-range missiles (2,100 miles)

CANADA

UNITED STATES

San Francisco

Los Angeles

Ottawa

Chicago

New York

Washington

Miami

CUBA

Mexico City

Panama City

SOUTH

AMERICA

N

G.W.WARD

We could have delivered a powerful strike against the United States, but the United States would no doubt have responded with a counterattack equal to, or even greater than, ours.

In spite of all the noise, we pushed ahead with the operation. [Foreign Minister] Andrei Andreyevich Gromyko was in New York at a United Nations session. It was a difficult moment; storm clouds were gathering. Gromyko was invited by [Secretary of State Dean] Rusk to Washington. Our position was neither to confirm nor to deny the presence of missiles. In answer to a direct question, we would deny. Later we were accused of perfidy and dishonesty, but who was accusing us? The United States, which encircled us with its military bases, ought to be the last one to accuse us of that. Did the Americans ever take the trouble to inform us before they built their bases? Unfortunately, we're in a kind of war where even though you do not shoot each other, you still position weapons as close as possible to each other in order to open fire in case of conflict. We were not inventing anything new. We were just copying the methods used against us by our adversaries when they encircled us with bases. There were missiles in Italy and Turkey, to say nothing about Great Britain, West Germany, and other countries that were NATO allies of the United States. All those missiles, aircraft, surface vessels, and submarines, all the military means possessed by America, were aimed at the Soviet Union.

They reproached us and accused us of dishonesty. All our honest attempts to establish relations based on mutual respect had been rejected or ignored. Who can reproach us for being treacherous? Which trust are they talking about? For so many years I made many honest attempts to come to an agreement about trust and establish good, friendly relations. Yet all efforts were rejected and ignored. Therefore, we had both a legal and a moral right to make an agreement with Cuba.

Gromyko told me that when Rusk invited him to dinner Rusk drank a lot. Gromyko later said, "I never saw him in such a state. He was not himself." Rusk told Gromyko, "We know everything." They really did know everything. By that time, photographs showing the position of the missiles had been published. "You are accustomed to living with our missiles encircling you, but this is the first time that we face such a threat. That's why we are in such a state of shock and cannot overcome it," Rusk said.

Gromyko answered like a gypsy who was caught stealing a horse: "It's not me and it's not my horse. I don't know anything." It is the usual practice used by all governments when they have something to hide. Even when they are finally exposed, they are still reluctant to acknowledge the truth.[14]

Gromyko is very moderate in his use of alcohol, and you cannot ply him with liquor. I believe he was sober at the time, and I always trusted his words. I commend this quality in a minister. After several drinks, Rusk told him, "We will see this through to the end. Tell Khrushchev we wish we could prevent this from occurring, but anything may happen." In a word, he exerted pressure, but the pressure was not threatening. He appealed to us to do something that would avoid confrontation, but he set the condition that we must remove the missiles. Otherwise, a situation might develop in which the president might lose control and there would be such pressure on him that he would be forced to make a decision against his own will, with ominous consequences for both our countries.[15]

Gromyko reported on all this to the government and the leadership. We listened to him but went on with the operation. What made the Americans think they had such a unilateral right? After all, America used our neighbors' territory to station its rockets. Now that we were doing the same, they were threatening us with war. It angered us and we agreed that we would continue to pursue this policy.

I told my comrades, "We achieved our goal. Maybe the Americans have learned their lesson. Now they have the time to think it over and weigh the consequences." If the Americans attacked

14. Khrushchev is most probably referring to an informal meeting between Rusk and Gromyko, not to the formal dinner given by Rusk for Gromyko on October 18, 1962, at the State Department. The afternoon of the dinner, Gromyko had seen President John F. Kennedy in the White House and repeated the Soviet line that the missiles in Cuba were only antiaircraft weapons incapable of reaching targets in the United States. Rusk's biographer, Thomas J. Schoenbaum, says that at the dinner Rusk deliberately steered clear of any discussion with Gromyko about Cuba. See *Waging Peace and War* (New York: Simon & Schuster, 1988), p. 312.

15. Schoenbaum explains that "although Rusk was sometimes a heavy drinker he was always in control and often used such moments to clarify a deadlocked situation."

Cuba, forty of our rockets would have inflicted a significant blow on them. The two nuclear weapons the United States used against Japan were toys by comparison.

Our comrades in the United States met with people who had power and capital. It was a difficult time for the Americans. Yuri Zhukov told me that someone told him, "If against our will the war starts I invite you to my bomb shelter."[16] There was a great war psychosis, but we didn't want war. We only wanted to stop the hand of the aggressor from attacking Cuba.

Kennedy was a clever president. I still regard him with great respect. Of course, he could start a war and the advantage would be on the American side. He understood that in spite of the American advantages, great casualties would be inflicted on the United States. America would bring down fire upon itself. The missiles that had already been installed would strike New York, Washington, D.C., and other administrative and industrial centers. If there was war, casualties would be inflicted on the Soviet Union as well. But my point is, for the United States it would be a different war — different from World War I and World War II, when the Americans didn't even hear a rifle fired in anger. Americans don't know what an exploding bomb or artillery shell really means. They have fought in foreign lands, but here they were asking for fire on their own heads, and what a fire — from thermonuclear bombs! That was exactly what we were trying to achieve: to rouse America and its leadership to realize that they were at the brink of war.

We received a telegram from our ambassador in Cuba, who was on close terms with Castro.[17] He said he had just met with Castro. He told us in great detail that Castro informed him he had reliable information that the Americans were preparing within a certain number of hours to strike Cuba. "We have incontrovertible information," said Castro. In addition, our own intelligence informed

16. Georgi A. Zhukov was a hard-line political columnist for *Pravda* and often accompanied Khrushchev on his trips abroad.

17. Aleksandr I. Alekseyev, the Soviet ambassador to Cuba in 1962, was a KGB officer who previously served as chief of the Latin American department of the KGB's First Chief Directorate. He arrived in Cuba as a journalist before the revolution and assisted Castro, thus developing strong ties with him. Khrushchev says, "Fidel and Raul Castro, particularly, saw that he was not simply a journalist, but was representing a certain agency."

us that such an action was being prepared and that an invasion would probably be unavoidable unless we came to an agreement with the president.

Concerning our intelligence agents, who had informed us about the invasion, it might have been possible that this information was planted for them to find. The American intelligence agents knew our agents. I think there are tacit exchanges of this kind, where each agency tosses out ideas to the other when one side would like to make sure the other receives something important.

Castro suggested that in order to prevent our nuclear missiles from being destroyed, we should launch a preemptive strike against the United States. He concluded that an attack was unavoidable and that this attack had to be preempted. In other words, we needed to immediately deliver a nuclear missile strike against the United States. When we read this I, and all the others, looked at each other, and it became clear to us that Fidel totally failed to understand our purpose. Only then did I realize that our friend Castro, whom I respect for his honesty and directness, had failed to understand us correctly. We had installed the missiles not for the purpose of attacking the United States, but to keep the United States from attacking Cuba. What does it mean to make a preemptive strike? We could deliver the first blow, but there would immediately be a counterblow — both against Cuba and against our own country. We started thinking. If Castro had reliable information, how could we prevent the United States from taking action? We received a message from the president through our ambassador. It was somewhere between threat and prayer — he both demanded and begged. He still insisted on the condition that we remove the missiles, nuclear warheads, and bombers.

We had given some old but perfectly good twin-engine Il-28 jet bombers to Cuba. We were removing them from production, but we still believed they could play a role in Cuba. They could reach American shores.

Malinovsky was present when we agreed on the following: We would remove the rockets and warheads if the president would publicly give assurances, in his own name and the name of his allies, that their armed forces would not invade Cuba. We believed that Kennedy could incite one of the Latin American countries under U.S. influence to attack Cuba. What difference does it make who attacks? They could accumulate a relatively big force to out-number the armed forces of Fidel Castro.

We sent that message and the talks continued. Robert Kennedy was the basic intermediary. I have to say that he showed a great deal of fortitude and he sincerely helped to prevent a conflict.

President Kennedy gave us an assurance, although not exactly the one we wanted. He did so in a loud voice, saying there would be no invasion. In the talks and exchange of messages that followed, the United States pressed us to let them inspect the sites. We told them that this was the business of the Cuban government. They addressed themselves to Castro, but he did not give his consent.

He was a young and hotheaded man, so he thought we were retreating and capitulating. He did not understand our action was necessary to prevent a military confrontation. He also thought that America would not keep its word. Once we had removed the missiles, the Americans would invade Cuba. He was very angry with us, but we accepted this with understanding. We believed this came from his being young and inexperienced as a statesman. Remember, he was deceived many times and he had the right not to believe the word of the president. So we did not take offense.

At one point, Castro ordered our antiaircraft officers to shoot down a U-2 reconnaissance plane.[18] There was another uproar. This time we feared that America's patience would be exhausted and war would break out. We ordered Pliyev to obey only orders from Moscow. However, in the case of an invasion our troops should coordinate with the Cuban forces and be subordinate to Castro.

We felt sorrow and pain to hear Castro's words of disappointment in our Cuban policy. Everything we did was in the interest of Cuba. We had no interests of our own there. Our only goal was for the Cuban people to become the masters of their own natural resources and to help Cuba embark on the path of building scientific socialism.

We felt obliged to send Mikoyan to Cuba. I suggested he go because communicating through letters would be futile. I know Mikoyan's character. He knew Fidel and had already been to Cuba.

---

18. Major Rudolf Anderson, Jr., the pilot of the U-2, was killed when his plane was shot down on October 27, 1962.

He is irreplaceable for such missions. He has the special ability to repeat the general line over and over again without giving an inch and without losing his temper. There may be a break in the talks, but when they resume he'll pick up the argument again without missing a beat.

We started removing our missiles. The Americans' appetite increased while they were eating. They said that since the Cubans would not let them inspect the missile sites, the Russians should allow them to inspect the ships. We made this concession as a result of the entreaties by Robert Kennedy. Kennedy said, "If you do not meet us halfway on this, the military will force President Kennedy to take an action that he himself would not like to take." So we permitted the overflight inspection of our ships by American planes.

We had some doubts of our own. What if the president did not keep his word? However, I had already met Kennedy [in Vienna in 1961] and thought he was not capable of such treachery. I was right.

We also removed our Il-28 bombers. There was no logic in keeping them there. There were MiG-21s there as well, and they had the same range. They were even faster and carried the same bomb load, but there were no similar demands from the Americans concerning them. Also, we had coastal defense missiles. So we could still strike a powerful blow at the vital centers of America.

President Kennedy told us through his brother that in exchange he would remove missiles from Turkey. He said, "If this leaks into the press, I will deny it. I give my word I will do this, but this promise should not be made public." He also said that he would remove the missiles from Italy, and he did that.

This agreement was primarily of moral significance and had no practical consequences. All those missiles were obsolete and America did not need them. The Americans would have removed them even if there were no conflict between us. It showed that Kennedy was a clever and flexible man. America's enormous power could have gone to his head, particularly if you take into account how close Cuba is to the United States and the advantage the United States had in the number of nuclear weapons by comparison to the Soviet Union. Kennedy recognized that the time had passed when you could solve conflicts with the USSR by military means. He explained to the American public that the USSR was equal to the United States in its capacity for military confrontation.

I had to explain this to journalists many times. They used to say that the power of America forced Khrushchev to back down. The Chinese used the same argument. We have to weigh the gains against the losses. We removed our missiles in exchange for the American promise not to invade Cuba. The aim of American aggressors was to destroy Cuba. Our aim was to preserve Cuba. Today Cuba exists. So who won? It cost us nothing more than the round-trip expenses for transporting the rockets to Cuba and back. The Americans, of course, also won. The only losers were the forces of aggression. I am proud that we were not afraid — that we showed fortitude and foresight and prevented the American imperialists from another invasion of Cuba.

President Kennedy did the right thing. He was a smart president in that he understood and tried to ease the tensions between the Soviet Union and the United States. Before Kennedy became president, American propaganda popularized the idea that the United States was ahead of the Soviet Union and the rest of the socialist countries in military strength, so it could have its own way. Thanks to President Kennedy the United States began to weigh its words more carefully and take into account the Soviet Union's military strength. America began to understand that if it could not be friends with the Soviet Union, at least it should not incite conflict. For us, that was a big victory.

If in the future we can strive for world cooperation and keep military strength at reasonable levels, we should be able to avoid war. As long as there are both capitalist and socialist countries in the world, and as long as the world is divided into two antagonistic camps, there can be no absolute guarantee of peace. But we can keep the aggressor at bay if he understands that he can lose if he starts a war. That has a sobering effect on him.

The Caribbean crisis was a classic example of this. We found a reasonable way out and eliminated the conflict on our own terms. President Kennedy gave us his assurance that the United States would not invade Cuba either directly or through proxies. When President Kennedy was killed, I was worried about how events would develop. However, President Johnson, through channels, confirmed his willingness to uphold Kennedy's promises. So far the United States has kept its promise, even under the Johnson administration.

We assessed President Johnson to be a reactionary and an inflexible politician, but he turned out to be a clever man. To tell the truth, he got sucked in up to his neck in the Vietnam War, but that was his personal stupidity. Perhaps Kennedy would have been equally stupid. I'm not in a position to judge that now. Anyway, we and Cuba achieved our goal, and I'm pleased that Cuba is developing successfully.

It was pleasant for me to talk with Castro when the fire had died down. During my talk with Fidel we discussed the economic development of his country, and I agreed with the line he decided to take on improving the economy. It is most important to make this new socialist country appealing to the populations of other Latin American countries and let them see the practical accomplishments of the Cuban revolution.

I talked with him later too, after he had already been to the Soviet Union twice and was in a different frame of mind. Our meeting was exceptionally warm and allowed for a good exchange of opinions in light of the fact that the events were a thing of the past. We discussed the past from hindsight and conducted an analysis of the events in a calm atmosphere. I saw that he still did not understand.

I told him again that we had not pursued our goal with the idea of starting a war. If the United States had invaded Cuba, of course, Castro would never have been able to withstand the attack with just his own armed forces. I have in mind not a poorly organized, poorly armed, and poorly run detachment like before [i.e., the Bay of Pigs], but rather a strong force, one the United States was capable of mustering, or that we could create, if we needed to organize such an invasion.

Of course, Cuba would not have withstood such a force. I told Fidel this later. I actually asked our minister of defense, "What do you think? Knowing the arms, the numbers, and the strength of Cuba's armed forces, how long would it take the United States to deal with Cuba's forces and crush them?" Malinovsky thought and then answered, "Something on the order of two days." When I told this to Fidel, he was bitter and tried to prove to me that Malinovsky was mistaken, that it was a faulty evaluation. "We wouldn't let that happen," said Fidel.

"Well," I said, "that's what Malinovsky says, and I agree with Malinovsky. I think he's right."

I didn't tell Castro that Kennedy promised to remove missiles from Turkey and Italy, since that agreement was just between the two of us. Kennedy asked me to keep it secret. He believed that if it became known to the American public it might bring unpleasant consequences.

When we met I told Castro it was a good thing he did not let the Americans enter Cuba to inspect whether the missiles had been removed. "If you had let them come they would have considered you to be a coward. It is one thing to accuse us, and me personally, of being cowards. We are a large country and every reasonable man would know better. But you are a small country, and therefore I think you did the right thing.

"But why did you fail to take advantage of the offer of [United Nations secretary general] U Thant and not let him come? He would have come to talk with you. You would go out and see how the missiles were being taken away. Then you would have had the United Nations on your side. U Thant would share your position and would support you within the limits of his position; but you lumped him together with the American imperialists. I think you made a mistake."

Castro replied, "Yes, in that I agree with you. I was overwrought. I was in such a state that I could not take into account the arguments you are making now."

To tell the truth, I have to say that if the Americans had started a war at that time we were not prepared to adequately attack the United States. In that case, we would have been forced to start a war in Europe. Then, of course, a world war would have begun.

He still believed that we had installed the missiles not so much in the interests of Cuba, but primarily in the military interests of the Soviet Union and the whole socialist camp. In other words, he thought we wanted to use the territory of Cuba as a base close to the United States so that we could install missiles there and hit the United States with these missiles.

I told Castro, "There is another aspect to this business. You wanted to start a war with the United States. If the war had begun we would somehow have survived, but Cuba no doubt would have ceased to exist. It would have been crushed into powder. Yet you suggested a nuclear strike!"

"No. I did not suggest that," replied Castro.

"How can you say that?" I asked Fidel.

The interpreter added, "Fidel, Fidel, you yourself told me that."

"No!" insisted Castro.

Then we checked the documents. It was fortunate that Fidel did not tell us this orally, but sent us a message. The interpreter read the document and asked, "How shall I translate this? Here is the word 'war,' here is the word 'blow.'"

Fidel was embarrassed. At that time he was a very hot-tempered person. We understood that he failed to think through the obvious consequences of a proposal that placed the planet on the brink of extinction. The experience taught him a good lesson, and he later began to consider his behavior more thoroughly.

8

The Intelligentsia: Scientists and Writers

NOWADAYS it is no longer a secret to our adversaries or to our own people what kind of fuel is used in Soviet and American missiles, but it used to be. We fueled our missiles with a mixture of oxygen and an acid, while the Americans used hydrogen. Hydrogen — although scientists have different opinions — has a higher calorific value than oxygen. Therefore, it would appear that hydrogen is better. However, our technology was developed around the use of oxygen. Probably it is still the same. At any rate, in my time, when I was in charge of the state, that's how it was.

One day I suggested the idea of developing a missile that could be launched on short notice. The idea reached Yangel.[1] Anyway, after some time Comrade D. F. Ustinov [minister of defense industries] reported to me that Yangel had taken it upon himself to design such a missile. It could sit on a launch pad with the trigger unlocked. It would use an acid as a fuel. Yangel at that time had not risen to a high position. He was not known to the same extent as Korolyov.[2]

I latched on to Yangel's offer. This was exactly what we needed

1. Academician Mikhail Kuzmich Yangel, a German rocket specialist brought to the Soviet Union at the end of World War II, became a leading missile designer from 1954 until his death in 1971, shortly after Khrushchev's death.
2. Sergei Pavlovich Korolyov (1907–1966), since the early 1930s a designer of rocket and space systems, including the Vostok and Voskhod, the first spaceships used in manned space flight and space walks. He oversaw the development of ballistic missiles (including the Semyorka, or T-7) and headed the Soviet space program from the 1950s until his death.

to secure our defense. There were objections that the acid would erode the fuel tank and therefore the missile could not sit long in a state of readiness on the launching pad. That was true. But we could let the missiles stay on the launch pad until the acid eroded the metal fuel tanks and then throw the tanks away and install new ones. It would be worthwhile, because we would be moving toward our goal: to have our combat missiles in a state of readiness.

I want to say with all my respect to Sergei Pavlovich Korolyov that even geniuses — and he was one — have their weaknesses. When he learned of Comrade Yangel's proposal, Sergei Pavlovich said, "I propose that you give this acid-fueled missile project to me. Besides that, I will also make an oxygen-fueled missile that will be capable of nearly instantaneous action. This missile will not require any supplementary equipment, like those guidance stations that have to be located every five hundred kilometers along the missile's flight path."

I said, "That sounds excellent. Take on the project and build it, but only the missile using oxygen. Improve the missile you are working on now. I can't transfer the acid-fueled missile to you. The concept was his and he would be insulted. You have to understand that you turned this down, while Yangel took it upon himself. Now you want to take everything into your own hands and shove Yangel aside. That is more than an insult, it is impossible. Let's do it this way: since the acid-fueled project is his idea and he developed it in his design bureau, let him solve that problem and you solve yours. Let it be a competition. You will do your missile of instant readiness with oxygen, and he will do his with an acid."

Sergei Pavlovich was strong-willed and decisive, and I could see that he greatly disliked my reasoning. I could see it in his face, but he was also smart, and he understood that I was right. Besides, he was dealing with the chairman of the Council of Ministers. Later my words were part of a formal decision.

That's how the problem of producing long-range combat rockets — so-called intercontinental ballistic missiles — was solved. We had come a long way. The United States could reach our missile sites. We were under a military blockade, encircled by American bases. Now, at least, Yangel had an idea that would allow us to solve the problem.

I would like to name one comrade who played a large part in

developing our missiles. That was Glushko, who built the rocket engine for Korolyov.[3] Later, differences of opinion started to pull them apart and the two of them couldn't seem to work together. I even invited them to my dacha with their wives. I wanted them to make peace with each other, so that they could devote more of their knowledge to the good of the country, rather than dissipate their energy on fights over details. It seemed to me that they were both talented, each in his own field. But nothing came of our meeting. Later Korolyov broke all ties with Glushko. He switched to [N. O.] Kuznetsov, a young, talented engine designer. Korolyov went down in history as the man who first dared to break the bounds that tie us to Earth.

Yet Glushko made no less a contribution than Korolyov. While Korolyov was working on the missile, Glushko was coming up with an engine that shook the world.[4]

There was still another missile, being worked on by Lavochkin. The day came when Lavochkin reported that his new rocket was ready for launching, and he wanted to carry out a test.[5] It was a very complicated piece of equipment. We later learned that the United States developed a missile along the same lines. The Americans probably proceeded from scientific data that were available to all designers and scientists. I do not think it was the result of espionage — that somebody stole the idea. No. However, I do not exclude it altogether because espionage existed, still exists, and will always exist as long as there are antagonistic socialist and capitalist states with different social and political systems.

We carried out a test. I do not remember now whether it was successful or whether, as we say, "the first pancake turned out lumpy" — that is, whether the missile blew up. I do remember that it was difficult to launch and that it was inferior in its technical and military characteristics. It was multistaged, designed like a

3. Academician Valentin Petrovich Glushko (born 1908) is one of the pioneers of Soviet rocket technology. He played a major role in liquid fuel development for rocket engines.

4. The engine was used in *Sputnik 1*, the first man-made satellite to orbit the Earth, in 1957.

5. Air Force Major General Semyon A. Lavochkin (1900–1960) designed high-speed fighters with air-cooled engines which proved highly effective against the Luftwaffe in World War II. Then he moved to missile design.

glass fitted within a glass. The engines ascended on gasoline, and only in the second stage did they start using oxygen. It was named either Burya [Tempest] or Uragan [Hurricane]. He worked with a large team that drained state resources terribly. It would be ready to go on line only after Korolyov's missile was finished.

Through these programs we decided to rely on intercontinental ballistic missiles as our weapon of choice for use against the United States. We turned away from another solution to this problem, a long-range bomber that could reach the United States but could not return. We stopped further work on the bomber, which had been designed by [V. M.] Myasishchev, the Mya-4, and limited ourselves to the few that had already been produced. They took part in an air show, and Western correspondents baptized them the Bison.[6] They really made an impression during the demonstrations, standing out from other bombers by their size, shape, and speed, but we were not satisfied with them.

We decided that the best thing would be to accelerate work on the creation of an ICBM by three different design bureaus. If one failed, then another one would have a different design, and the third bureau would have still another. Thus we would have a choice of the best design for the mass production of an ICBM, and we could have a way of delivering a retaliatory strike against the potential enemy. That would keep the enemy from attacking the USSR. By the enemy we meant, of course, the United States of America, because it was the only country whose power was comparable to the Soviet Union's.

When we became convinced that Korolyov had solved the problem of designing a rocket for space exploration, we were able to step into the international political arena and show that now even the territory of the United States of America was vulnerable to a strike by our missile forces. It became, as they say, a balm to the soul, and our position had improved.

Although we solved the ICBM problem, we needed a defense against nuclear attack. We decided to create an antimissile force. We needed to build a missile that could destroy an incoming missile with an atomic warhead. It was a very costly luxury and an

---

6. Bison is the NATO designation for the bomber.

extremely complex task; but we needed to solve the problem. A design office was established with Kisunko as its head.[7] Comrade Chelomei also worked on this problem.[8] I listened to him and to Comrade Kisunko.

I liked Chelomei and I met more often with him than with Kisunko. I'm not ashamed to say that I gave Chelomei my support back then. He fulfilled many of the hopes we placed in him, but in the end we were not able to create an antimissile system that would let us sleep peacefully at night. An absolute system of anti-missile defense is impossible to create. Therefore, the need to reach agreement with the other nuclear missile powers on the cessa-tion of efforts to create antimissile technology was dictated by circumstances.[9]

I made speeches to bolster the morale of my people. I wanted to give our enemy pause by saying that we had antimissile weap-onry. I exaggerated a little. I said that we had the capability of shooting a fly out of space with our missiles. In fact, absolute destruction of all missiles after launching, especially if there are many, is impossible.

During my time in office I had influence in the decision not to cooperate in international space research. We were unprepared to do so because we would have had to reveal our methods of opera-tion, our secrets, and our scientific and technical solutions for these problems. We had as yet not reached absolute parity with regard to nuclear weapons. We felt that the United States had amassed more nuclear weapons than we had. It was true that the United States relied primarily on bombers as the means of delivery, but missiles had begun to catch on with them and they had already created missiles.

The American astronauts have already reached the moon [July 20, 1969]. Now our radio, press, and television all say that we are ahead, but the evidence of this is not serious. I feel that it is good

7. Grigory V. Kisunko, born in 1918, is a Soviet scientist with expert creden-tials in the field of radio engineering and electronics who played a major role in the development of Soviet antimissile weaponry.

8. Vladimir N. Chelomei (1914–1984) was a full member of the USSR Academy of Sciences and a specialist in aviation propulsion.

9. A treaty limiting antiballistic missile defense sites to one each in the United States and the Soviet Union was signed at the same time as the SALT I treaty in 1972.

to hear things, but much better to see things. Our *Luna 16* was a big project undertaken by our scientists. The *Luna 17*, which is now operating on the moon, exploring the lunar surface, and sending information back to Earth, was even bigger. Still, man is really the lord of nature.

For this reason it was important for man to get to the moon, rather than an unmanned system, no matter how independent or smart it might be. Such a system is a creation of man, and so when man himself — the creator of an unmanned system — visits the moon and looks all around for himself, he understands better and more deeply than would have been possible with technological means.

I would like to say a few words about Academician P. L. Kapitsa so that people will understand properly after my death. Kapitsa is a great scientist but an offensive man.[10] That's why during Stalin's time he was not particularly well thought of, and why after Stalin's death we continued to show restraint toward him.

Was there anything that might have made us distrust him and think he might be a spy? It was very popular at the time to toss such phrases around. We had no facts of and we did not think of him in this way. In any case, I did not.

I happened to be a witness when the decision was made on how to keep Kapitsa in the Soviet Union. At that time he was relatively unknown and I had heard nothing about him. Stalin called in Mezhlauk, chairman of Gosplan. Because of my position [as a Moscow city party secretary] I had frequent contact with both Gosplan and Mezhlauk. Mezhlauk impressed me as a good statesman and as a man who knew his job well. I respected him a lot and am very sorry that his life and work came to such a tragic end — Stalin had him arrested and shot.[11]

Mezhlauk conducted a conference of scientists [in 1934] and

10. Pyotr L. Kapitsa was born in Russia in 1894 and after the revolution went to England, where he did pioneering work in low-temperature physics at Cambridge in the laboratory of Ernest Rutherford.

11. Valery Mezhlauk believed his arrest to be a mistake that would be corrected, and he continued to think about the problems that occupied him when he was free. He wrote "On Planning and Ways to Improve It" just before he was shot. See Medvedev, *Let History Judge*, p. 674.

Kapitsa was invited to come from England, where he was working at the time. Kapitsa had Soviet citizenship and held a Soviet passport. Stalin asked Mezhlauk to have a talk with Kapitsa and try to get him to stay here and work. Mezhlauk told Stalin that Kapitsa had expressed great reluctance to stay. Primarily, Kapitsa argued — and he was probably right — that in order for him to use and apply his knowledge, he needed to have the right conditions and equipment; everything without which a scientist could not work. At the time he was working in Rutherford's laboratory, under his guidance. Kapitsa had excellent working conditions there.

Stalin instructed Mezhlauk, "Tell Kapitsa we'll do everything to give him the material conditions he wants. We'll build him a special institute. But tell him he is definitely not returning to England. We will not allow him to leave." So that's what Mezhlauk did, and Kapitsa stayed.

Kapitsa was somewhat removed from me. I had heard he was a good scientist, and I felt Stalin had done the right thing. In our country's interests we had to use any opportunity to increase our defense capabilities. For this reason, we had to direct scientists into defense work.[12]

I want to relate another episode that took place during my time in office. It concerns defending our country in the most reliable way. In his time Stalin had decided to create an underground factory for producing nuclear energy and atomic bombs. Later, after his death, it was suggested we build a similar plant to assemble missiles. There were, after all, no ICBMs yet.

I then raised the question of an underground factory complex in the government. This made it possible for me to fly to Siberia to see for myself how the construction of the underground plant was progressing. During the war I was a great supporter of building underground plants. I even sent a report to Stalin when I worked in the Ukraine suggesting that coal mines be turned into underground workshops or even plants. However, now I consider this kind of thing obsolete. It solved nothing. Since the end of World War II, new means of war have appeared, and war will take place under different conditions and at a much different pace of events.

12. Kapitsa refused to work on the atomic bomb after quarreling with Beria, who was in charge of its production.

I went to Siberia and inspected these underground works. They were very well done, but they were still much smaller than what we needed, and the cost was very high. I saw that this plant did not solve the problem. I began asking, "What was the idea? How were they going to use such plants?" It turned out that this plant was meant for missile materials.

I said, "Comrades, this is an absolutely bankrupt idea, because if a nuclear war starts it will be over in an instant. How can we count on having enough time to produce rockets and use them as war weapons? Besides that, we need a steady supply of metal, instruments, and other devices. A missile might as well be stuffed with gold in terms of its cost. It is unthinkable; our means of transportation will also be destroyed. You'll be doomed. How can you count on having enough supplies for this plant to feed us with missiles? We could lose the war in a few days. Then the war can continue only in the form of guerrilla operations, or the people's resistance; the plants will be out of commission."

During World War II the Flying Fortresses made by the United States dominated the skies over Germany; they bombed by day and by night. Although they appeared to be impregnable, they suffered some losses, but these losses were justified because choice industrial facilities were destroyed. Missiles provide even more possibilities than aircraft because they can be aimed more accurately at their targets. The United States was a rich country and it was far away from us. The Americans would produce enough missiles to incapacitate an adversary within the first few days, or even hours. Therefore, this whole idea of underground plants couldn't be sustained. We would end up wasting money and material resources, without any certainty that the defense of the country would be secured. That was the wrong course. We had to look for something else.

Then I had an idea: to take a few plants that produced fighters and shift them to the production of missiles. The fuselages of fighters and rockets both used the same metals. We should refit these factories for missile production. For the instruments, we'd have to allocate a few plants or maybe build new ones. We had to make these allocations right away because we couldn't tolerate delays. We had to secure the defense of the country and not get ourselves into the same situation we found ourselves in during World War

II, when we didn't have factories to produce enough machine guns and we had no antiaircraft guns at all. I want to repeat that this was a case of scatter-brained stupidity on the part of Stalin and Voroshilov, who was the people's commissar for defense. It was his responsibility to fight for the proper armament for the Soviet army.

Today the determining factor in a war will be nuclear weapons. There is no better carrier for atomic bombs than missiles. We had to expend resources on the production of missiles. We in the leadership discussed all these possibilities and nobody objected. We ordered preparation of the necessary documents and they were signed and accepted. Some fighter and bomber plants were designated for the production of missiles. I will not give the locations of these plants, although it is no longer a secret. The history of producing missiles is well documented in the archives.

Vannikov was responsible for the building of these plants. He was the minister of medium machine building.[13] It was the ministry that dealt with nuclear power and the production of atomic bombs. That ministry also dealt with building the underground plant for producing missiles at the time I rejected the idea. Nearly half the budget for the plant had already been spent. The total was about 600 million rubles, and 300 million had already been spent.

When this idea occurred to me, I put it before Vannikov. "What is your opinion, Comrade Vannikov, concerning this matter?" I asked. I had a very good opinion of Vannikov and respected him. He was a clever man. He looked at me with cunning eyes, and I noticed a smile cross his face. He said, "I completely agree with you."

I said, "Then why did you . . . ?"

Vannikov replied, "It was Stalin's idea."

Probably it was I who had suggested this idea to Stalin when I sent him my report. However, now, when it is clear that future wars will be different and different weapons will be used, such underground factories are not going to save us.

Comrade Vannikov said to me, "I completely share your point of view. We have to reject the project." This strengthened me even

13. Boris L. Vannikov (1897–1962) was a protégé of Stalin's in the 1920s and rose to become commissar of the defense industry and commissar of armaments and ammunition during World War II. He was chosen by Stalin to play a key role in the Soviet nuclear program, and is buried in the Kremlin Wall.

more. We adopted a government and party decision on the change of direction in the production of means for defense and attack — nuclear missiles.

During this period we also were building up our stock of atomic bombs. We were able to produce them cheaper after each experimental test explosion. In order to lower the cost per bomb we had to increase the number of bombs we could get from a given amount of material. Still, we lacked the capacity to produce nuclear bombs on a large scale. However, we made progress in that direction. Our scientists learned to make better atomic bombs from a smaller quantity of fissionable material.

Again, the person directly in charge was Vannikov. His people dealt with nuclear energy and they did a good job. Now that we've started talking about that, I will share a secret with you: we got some assistance on a number of issues through some good people who helped us to master the production of nuclear energy faster and to produce our first atomic bomb. These people suffered; they were people committed to ideas. They were neither agents nor spies for the Soviet Union. Rather, they were people sympathetic with our ideals. They acted on their progressive views, without seeking any payment. I say progressive because I believe that they were not Communists. They did what they could in order to help the Soviet Union to arm itself with the atomic bomb and thus to stand against the United States of America. That was the issue of the times.

This does not diminish the merits and initiative of our own scientists, but one must not discount the help that was provided to us by our friends. The names of those friends are known to thinking people and to those who follow events in the newspapers. Those friends suffered; they were punished. But their names are known.

Let this be a worthy tribute to the memory of those people. Let my words be like words of thanks to those people who sacrificed their lives and who provided help to the Soviet state for that great cause when the United States was ahead of us and was blackmailing us. Finally, exerting all our strength and all our capacities, we built the atomic bomb; but it must be understood that we did it to become equal.

Since I was present at the talks that Stalin had in a limited circle when he mentioned the Rosenbergs with warmth, I feel it is my duty to speak of them now. I cannot specifically say what kind of help the Rosenbergs provided us, but both Stalin and Molotov were informed. Molotov knew because he was then the minister of foreign affairs. I heard from both Stalin and Molotov that the Rosenbergs provided very significant help in accelerating the production of our atomic bomb.[14]

Probably the time will come when it will be possible to reveal all this openly and to pay the deepest respect to these people who gave their lives to help the proletarian state, the Soviet state, to produce an atomic bomb and thus to stand up to the imperialist world, primarily the United States. I mean the aggressive world, those who fostered and still foster the idea of undermining the Soviet state.

I remember when I was in England [1956] Academician Kurchatov accompanied us. A British scientist received Kurchatov and took him to visit various scientific and research institutes.[15] We were then obliged to extend an invitation to this British scientist to visit our country. To show this British scientist something of ours in return was exceedingly difficult for us. We had been inculcated for decades with the belief that the imperialists were our sworn enemies. They would spy on and sneak a look at everything of ours and not show us anything of theirs. They would recruit our people and worm their way in. To a great extent this was true, of course, but we cannot take such an absurdity to the extreme of scaring even ourselves and losing all faith in our own people. We must not lose sight of the fact that our people were fighting to build socialism, that they had their own integrity and national pride, their own worth. All these feelings had been smothered within us. For Stalin such emotions did not exist at all. With us, only police measures existed, to restrain and not let go. To put our international scientific relations in simple words: "You can't take a step toward me, and I am forbidden to take a step toward you."

14. Julius and Ethel Rosenberg were executed in the electric chair in 1953 after being convicted of conspiracy to commit espionage for passing American atomic bomb secrets to the Soviet Union.

15. Academician Igor V. Kurchatov, the famous atomic physicist, was the father of the Soviet A-bomb.

And so we had only one choice: to steal — though, of course, you have to be smart enough to do that. True, everyone steals. All countries steal, even if they can buy licenses and obtain what they need legally. Given the chance, they steal instead. I do not say this to condemn this method of contact. I feel that it is better, of course, to maintain contacts on a basis of licensing exchanges and payments for obtaining them. This is so much more simple and beneficial than theft. When you buy stolen property you don't always get exactly what you need, and a thief sometimes is a stooge. Sometimes what he thinks he is stealing has actually been sold to him by order of an intelligence agency. I know of one such case myself.

When Grechko commanded our troops in East Germany [1957–1960], we purchased an American missile from West Germany. When it had been delivered to our researchers for analysis they began to laugh. What had happened? The agent who sold it probably became suspicious and realized that the man he was dealing with was a Soviet intelligence officer. He palmed off an inferior missile on our man to humiliate us with a piece of junk.

THERE was a terrific commotion in Moscow and in the Politburo about Boris Pasternak's *Doctor Zhivago* [in 1958, when Pasternak won the Nobel Prize for literature]. I recall that there had been a report to the Politburo, probably by Suslov. In such cases the reports were prepared by the Central Committee Department of Agitation and Propaganda, and Suslov was in charge of the department. Even if somebody else presented the report, Suslov played a decisive role. The report said the book was of poor quality and very strange, not Soviet in tone; therefore, it would be harmful to print it. I won't give you the arguments, since I do not remember them and don't want to invent them now. I don't think anyone read it apart from Suslov. Actually, Suslov probably didn't read it either, but only was briefed on it by an aide. He was probably given a summary of the book that consisted of one, or at the most, three pages. Of course, to assess a creative work and to reach a judgment in this manner is entirely unacceptable.

Now that I'm approaching the end of my life as a pensioner, I feel sorry that I didn't support Pasternak. I regret that I had a hand in banning his book and that I supported Suslov. We should have given the readers the opportunity to reach their own verdict. Judgments should depend on the readers. I'm truly sorry for the way I behaved toward Pasternak. My only excuse is that I didn't read the book.

We banned *Doctor Zhivago*, trusting those whose job it was to read and monitor artistic works. As a result we caused much harm to the Soviet Union. Because of the step we took, the intelligentsia abroad rose up against the Soviet Union, including those members of the intelligentsia who were not against socialism. These were people who believed that creativity in the expression of personal feelings and personal views should not be limited.

It is inadmissible to interfere with the creative work of artists and writers. They say we have no censorship. That's nonsense. That's talk for children. We have the most real — and I might even say the most cruel — censorship. We should not turn criticism into censorship. In such cases critics and ideologues turn into police bullies.

I feel proud and pleased of the way we dealt with Aleksandr Solzhenitsyn's *One Day in the Life of Ivan Denisovich*. We decided at the "highest level" — on the fifth and sixth floors of the Central Committee, where the commissions convened.

It began when Comrade Tvardovsky arranged a meeting with me. He brought the work to me, briefed me on the contents, and gave me his opinion. Tvardovsky said, "Comrade Khrushchev, I think this work is very good. From this work I can see that its author is going to become a great writer." He thought this was his first work.[16]

Tvardovsky said, "The theme raised in the book may, of course, evoke a range of different attitudes both to the work and to the author. Please read it yourself and make your own judgment. I ask you not to interfere with its publication. I will publish it in my magazine."

I did not know the biography of Solzhenitsyn. We knew from

16. Solzhenitsyn's manuscript for *One Day in the Life of Ivan Denisovich* was delivered to *Novy Mir*, the literary magazine, in November 1961. After reading the novel, editor Aleksandr Tvardovsky was so enthusiastic that he said, "I've got a manuscript by a new Gogol." When Tvardovsky met Solzhenitsyn he asked him what else he had written, but Solzhenitsyn was evasive. See Michael Scammell's biography *Solzhenitsyn* (London: Hutchinson, 1985), pp. 410–416 and 427–449.

his work and reports I received that he had been in the camps for a long time — in Kolyma, probably.[17] What he describes in his work is derived from his own experiences in the camps, and it is possible that he modeled the main character after himself.

I read the book. It is very heavy, but it was written well, in my opinion. The life of Ivan Denisovich and his surroundings are well described and deeply disturbing. This is the main quality required in a work of art. It evokes revulsion toward what existed in the camps and the conditions under which Ivan Denisovich and his friends lived while they served their terms in the camp.

I know that readers really went after this book and devoured it with pleasure. It was as though they were searching for something. They were looking for an explanation of what had happened. They were trying to find an answer to how Ivan Denisovich, an honest man, could find himself in such conditions in our socialist time, in our socialist state. I think that this already says something good about the author. He made people aware of how many had been in the camps.

After I became a pensioner I read the book by General Gorbatov, who was also in the camps and in exile.[18] I knew Gorbatov during the war; he had been freed by that time. He came to Kharkov, the headquarters for our front, at the end of October 1941. We were sitting together and he told us about the people who were left behind in the camps, people of his rank, generals, and he named them. Marshal Timoshenko, who was the commander of the front then, knew those people mentioned by Gorbatov. I remember now that we petitioned Stalin to free one or two of them and send them to our front. In Timoshenko's estimation they were worthy people and good generals. It seems to me that one or two of them were sent to us.

After Stalin's death there was an investigation into the cases of

17. Solzhenitsyn was arrested in 1945 and after interrogation and processing was sent to Marfino Special Prison No. 16, on the outskirts of Moscow. His time there is described in *The First Circle*. From August 1950 to February 1953 he was at Ekibastuz, part of a large complex of labor camps based in Dzhezkazgan, in the semiarid steppes of Kazakhstan in Soviet Central Asia. Then he was sent into internal exile in Kazakhstan and finally returned to his home in Ryazan in 1957.

18. General Aleksandr V. Gorbatov (1891–1973) was given full general's rank in 1955 by Khrushchev. His book was titled *My Times and Wars*.

those who died in the camps. That's why I considered it necessary not to interfere with the publication of Solzhenitsyn's book *One Day in the Life of Ivan Denisovich*.

I proceeded from the following premise: the evil inflicted on the Communist party — on the Soviet people, on workers, peasants, and the intelligentsia — had to be condemned. The best way to condemn is to lance the boil, show the conditions under which people lived, and provoke anger against the one who caused it all. In other words, to brand it with shame so that it cannot be repeated again. That is what drove me when I made the decision that we had to allow the publication not only of Solzhenitsyn's *One Day*, but of other books like it.

At that time, almost all my comrades agreed with me. We had discussions, and there were some differences. Actually, only one voice, Suslov's, squawked in opposition. His words were like a policeman's. He wanted to hold everything in check. "You cannot do this. That's all there is to it," he said. He distrusted the people. "How will the people perceive this? How will the people understand?" The people will understand correctly — that was my reply. The people will always distinguish good from bad.

Therefore, in order to prevent a repetition we had to brand the truth firmly into literature. That is the whole story. Solzhenitsyn is still writing, but they do not publish his works for us here in the Soviet Union. His books are only being published abroad.[19] I can see from the press that he is now in peculiar circumstances. The intellectuals, or at least some part of them, sympathize with him and take risks on his behalf. They say that he lives in Rostropovich's dacha. Rostropovich is a great artist, a great musician and cellist. He himself, of course, has taken a very risky step and put himself into a very precarious position with the leadership, if I may say so. That is unfortunate, but it also speaks well for the dignity and strong spirit of Rostropovich.[20]

19. In the spring of 1990, three volumes of Aleksandr Solzhenitsyn's *Gulag Archipelago* were published in the Soviet Union.
20. Cellist Mstislav Rostropovich and his wife, the soprano Galina Vishnevskaya, defended Solzhenitsyn against censorship in a letter printed in 1970 in the Western press. As a result they were ostracized by Soviet authorities and forbidden to travel until 1974, when they left the Soviet Union on a two-year visa. In 1976 they decided to remain in the West and Rostropovich became the music director and conductor of the National Symphony Orchestra of Washington, D.C.

Solzhenitsyn is not guilty of any crime. He speaks of his suffering. He assesses his life and the conditions in which he found himself when he was in camp. He speaks about people who were in camp with him.

Stalin was to blame for all this. He was a criminal in this respect, and criminals should be tried. They should be tried not only in a courtroom by a judge, but by society as well. The strongest trial is to brand Stalin a criminal in literature.

If any author is guilty of abuses and slanders, then he must be put on trial. Even then it should be a legal trial on a legal basis. If there is no crime, then, according to our constitution, which provides freedom of speech and the press, he has the right to express himself, like every Soviet citizen. Therefore, it is stupid to create those conditions in which Solzhenitsyn finds himself now.[21] In this way we undermine Lenin's principles of freedom of speech and freedom of press, Lenin's norms for Socialist society.

I remember also when the issue of Kazakevich's book *The Blue Notebook* came up.[22] It was well written and was eventually made into a film. I saw it at least twice on television. To be frank, Lenin and Zinoviev are portrayed as rather weak characters, despite their stature. The events took place when Zinoviev and Lenin were together in a straw hut at Razliv [north of Petrograd, in Finland] during the summer of 1917. Lenin was in hiding, planning for the October Revolution.

The author wrote me a short note asking me to explain why the

Rostropovich said he and his wife were not defecting but were in exile until the Soviet Union restored his citizenship and that of Nobel Prize winner Aleksandr Solzhenitsyn. Rostropovich's citizenship was restored in January 1990 and he returned in triumph in March with the National Symphony for concerts in Moscow and Leningrad. Solzhenitsyn's citizenship has still not been restored.

21. Solzhenitsyn was deprived of his Soviet citizenship and deported on February 13, 1974. He lives in Cavendish, Vermont, with his family and has said he will not return until his works are published in full in the Soviet Union.

22. Emmanuil G. Kazakevich (1913–1962) derived the title from the blue notebook in which Lenin wrote the notes and draft for his book *State and Revolution* in the summer of 1917. Lenin was planning an armed uprising against the Provisional Government in Petrograd (now Leningrad), which had taken power after the February 1917 revolution. *State and Revolution* is a handbook for seizing and consolidating power; it describes how to take over and control the army and the bureaucracy without destroying them. Kazakevich won the Stalin Prize for Literature in 1948 and in 1950. *The Blue Notebook* was published in 1961.

work had not been accepted for publication. He sent a copy of the manuscript too. I read the work and liked it. I noticed nothing in its contents that would preclude its being published. I was vacationing at the time in the Caucasus, and Mikoyan was there too. I called him up and said, "Anastas Ivanovich, I'm sending you a manuscript, please read it. Then we'll get together, and I'd like to hear what you think."

Mikoyan read it and I asked him, "So what do you think?"

He replied, "I don't understand. I think the man wrote a good little book. I don't understand why they don't publish it."

"All right, then," I said, "when we get back to Moscow, let's discuss it in the Presidium of the Central Committee."

That's what we did. I put it on the agenda. I asked everyone, "What do you all think about this book? Who objects? Who feels this book should not be published?"

Suslov stuck his neck out. He looked around and began, "Well, Comrade Khrushchev, how can we print a book that says that when Lenin and Zinoviev were together they called each other 'comrade'? Zinoviev is an enemy of the people!"

I was amazed at how reality could be distorted and historical facts altered. Let the reader judge for himself! Regardless of whether or not he was an enemy of the people, the fact remains that Lenin and Zinoviev really did spend some time together in that hut. They had to have talked to each other, discussing the events that were going on, even if only over tea, and needed to address one another in some way. That's most probably what they called each other: Comrade Lenin and Comrade Zinoviev. I even think Lenin called Zinoviev by his first name, Grigory, because they were very close for a time. Lenin, Zinoviev, and Kamenev were considered to be a troika. At the beginning of the revolution, they were always seen as a single unit. They were of one mind and of one point of view regarding the revolution. It's true they later split over differences on how to prepare for the revolution, but this happened after their time together in the cabin.

I realized the foolishness of the censors. I asked for an explanation for the members of the Presidium. The arguments against publishing the book were laughably insubstantial. Everyone had his say, and I won their support. We did not block the work, and sent it to the publisher. The book did come out.

Does the book cause doubt or concern today? I don't know. Perhaps there are critics who are displeased, but that is another problem. A critic states his opinion in order to help an author bring his work closer to perfection. Such criticism is beneficial. It raises the level of an author's literary skill. What we were discussing was not criticism, it was politics: whether to block a book or to let it through. That is red tape. Those red-tape functions were performed and still are performed mainly by Suslov.[23]

He is an honest man and undoubtedly loyal to Communist ideals, but his political limitations are very harmful. People might ask me, "How did you tolerate Suslov when you were leader?"

Well, a man makes many mistakes in his lifetime. I think that Suslov is a good, reliable worker and member of the collective. That's why I never raised the issue with any others about whether or not to replace him, although many individuals did come to me privately to suggest such a change. They came to express their criticism of Suslov, that he was performing poorly and that his relations with the intelligentsia were very bad. I kept him on because I could control him.

I just wish I had handled *Doctor Zhivago* the same way I did *The Blue Notebook*. There was a difference, of course. This is not an excuse, but there was a difference!

I am now of an age to repent, but what I am repenting is not absolute. I made mistakes in judgment about what to support and what to forbid. I recognize the mistakes I made in my time when I was in a position to determine the direction of events. It was often not a creative direction, but an administrative one.[24] We were too concerned with what to support, what to restrain, what to forbid. When I was in that position I shared the responsibility, but now I'm against this form of governing. We must not conduct the struggle in this way.

Nowadays they wear short skirts, but already longer dresses are coming back into fashion. Everything changes. The same is true in music, too; everything changes. Therefore, you have to show tol-

23. Suslov died on January 27, 1982.

24. The term "administrative command system of government" is used by Mikhail Gorbachev to describe the Brezhnev era of stagnation. It is a label for the pre-*perestroika* system of socialism controlled from the top down with commands emanating from the Politburo.

erance, be tolerant. Do these changes really affect Communist ideology? In my opinion, no.

The revolution was made for a piece of bread. We must provide that bread. We cannot say yet that economically we hold God by his beard. I know that people are looking for every opportunity to get the food they need. Through the existing system of shops it is not possible to acquire food on time and in the quantity needed. I know that people from other regions come to Moscow to find the products they need. Moscow, which cannot satisfy the needs of its own population, is singled out and is better off than other cities of the Soviet Union, even places like Kiev, to say nothing of other regional capitals. Kiev was always a mirror that reflected the state of agricultural production. Now this mirror shows us a very unattractive image.

All this says that the production of grain in our country lags behind the demand. This somewhat astonishes me because when I read newspaper articles and reports of the ministries that control agriculture it appears that we have very high achievements and that the production of grain and agricultural products has increased. You'd never know that from the markets.

The Soviet Union has to use the services of capitalism, the system which we have made it our goal to defeat — I mean to defeat economically. We cannot yet create sufficient grain reserves to permit us to be independent of weather conditions. This task requires high productivity of labor and a scientific approach. Defeating capitalism is also a matter of providing for material and cultural needs. We have to give our people more than the capitalist world gives. This is the principal issue.

You cannot only promise, you have to deliver. The Soviet socialist system is the most progressive, but even after fifty years, nowhere is the Communist party yet able to win in a parliamentary election. This is something to think about. People refuse to follow us.

In the East European countries socialism is the result of the defeat of Germany and of assistance from the Soviet Union. In other countries, where the Soviet army did not penetrate, socialism did not come about. Therefore, we must follow the path of peaceful coexistence. We have to show in a peaceful way the advantages of socialism, its capability to fulfill the cultural and material needs of man.

The Soviet people have achieved a much better life than before the revolution; there is no question about that. However, we are not yet a mirror into which the West wants to look. We have to create tangible advantages and therefore create conditions for the victory of our way of life. This is the question of questions. The solution will come through the productivity of labor, through science, technology, and education.

Paradise is a place where people want to end up, not a place they run from! Yet in this country the doors are closed and locked. What kind of socialism is that? What kind of shit is that when you have to keep people in chains? What kind of social order? What kind of paradise? Some curse me for the times I opened the doors. If God had given me the chance to continue, I would have thrown the doors and windows wide open.

Lenin opened the doors during the civil war and many did leave. Shalyapin, the singer, left; so did Averchenko, Andreyev, and other great writers.[25] More would have left, but do you really think the whole country would have left? Impossible. Why should we be afraid of that? Many people leave their countries and never return. It's nothing to be afraid of.

MY time has passed and I am very tired. I am at the age when I have nothing before me but the past. My only future is to go to my grave. I am not afraid of the grave, I want to die. It is so dull — so dull and boring for me to live in my situation. But I did want this opportunity to express my opinion one last time.

25. Fedor I. Shalyapin (1873–1938), the celebrated bass singer and actor, emigrated in 1921. Arkadi T. Averchenko (1881–1925) was a humorist noted for making fun of middle-class, philistine life. He settled in Prague and wrote stories against the Soviet regime. Leonid N. Andreyev (1871–1919) wrote on what were then considered shocking themes of death, solitude, and sex. He died in exile in Finland.

Appendix
Chronology of Khrushchev's Career

1894 April 17. Born in Kalinovka, Kursk Province, near Ukrainian border.

Accession of Czar Nicholas II.

1904–5

Russo-Japanese War.

1905

The 1905 revolution.

1909 Moves to Yuzovka (later Stalino, now Donetsk) in Donbass region of Ukraine, where father works in mine.

1909–12 Learns metal fitter's trade at Bosse factory in Yuzovka.

1912–18 Works as metal fitter in generator plants of French-owned Ruchenkov and Pastukhov mines.

1914

Outbreak of World War I.

1915–17 Represents miners at political meetings and rallies, meets Lazar Kaganovich.

February Revolution (1917): abdication of czar; formation of Provisional Government.

October Revolution; Lenin overthrows Provisional Government and establishes Soviet rule.

1918 Becomes Bolshevik.

Treaty of Brest-Litovsk (March); Russia concludes peace with Germany.

1919 Joins Red Army.

Revised and updated from Nikita Khrushchev, *Khrushchev Remembers*, edited and translated by Strobe Talbott (Boston: Little, Brown, 1970), pp. 529–534.

1919–21	Soldier and party worker in ranks of Ninth Rifle Division, then attached to Budyonny's First Mounted Army for offensive to Black Sea.	*Civil war and Allied intervention.*
1921	Death of first wife in famine.	*Famine; introduction of New Economic Policy (NEP).*
1922	Back to Yuzovka from army.	
	Assigned by Yuzovka party organization to be deputy director of Ruchenkov mines.	
	Offered directorship of Pastukhov mines but asks permission to study at Yuzovka Workers' Faculty.	
1923	Student and political leader at Yuzovka Workers' Faculty.	
1924	Holds various posts in Yuzovka party organization.	*Death of Lenin.*
	Marries Nina Petrovna.	
1925	Appointed party secretary of Petrovsko-Marinsk district of Stalino (formerly Yuzovka) region.	
	Attends Ninth Ukrainian Party Congress with Kaganovich in chair.	
	Consulting (i.e., nonvoting) delegate to Fourteenth All-Union Party Congress in Moscow; first exposure to Stalin.	*Stalin moves against Zinoviev and Kamenev.*
1926	First recorded public speech at Ukrainian party conference in Kharkov.	
1927	Delegate to Fifteenth All-Union Party Congress in Moscow.	*Defeat of Zinoviev and Kamenev.*
	Promoted from Stalino district to regional party apparatus.	
1928	Promoted by Kaganovich to be deputy chief of organizational section of Ukrainian central committee in Kharkov.	*First Five-Year Plan; start of collectivization.*
	Promoted by Kaganovich to be chief of organizational section of Kiev party apparatus.	

1929   Thirty-five years old; requests permission to study metallurgy at Industrial Academy in Moscow.

Kaganovich transferred to Moscow.

1929–30   Political worker and student at Industrial Academy.

Trotsky banished.

Voted down as academy delegate to Sixteenth Party Congress.

Associated with Nadezhda Alliluyeva, Stalin's wife and group organizer at academy.

Sent to inspect collective farm in Samara (now Kuibyshev) region; first glimpse of conditions caused by collectivization.

Recruited to lead pro-Stalin forces at academy.

1931   Elected first secretary of Bauman district; six months later promoted to first secretary of Krasnaya Presnya district.

1932   Leaves academy without graduating; promoted to second secretary under Kaganovich of Moscow city party committee.

Death of Nadezhda Alliluyeva, Stalin's wife.

1933   Becomes second secretary of Moscow regional committee.

Active in reconstruction of Moscow and building of Metro under Kaganovich.

1934   Elected to Central Committee at Seventeenth Party Congress.

Kirov murdered.

1935   Takes Kaganovich's place as first secretary of Moscow city and regional committees.

Years of Stalin's blood purges of party apparatus, Great Terror, and show trials begin.

1936

Zinoviev and Kamenev tried and executed (August).

Yezhov replaces Yagoda as secret police chief (September).

1937

Execution of Tukhachevsky and generals (June).

1938 Appointed first secretary of Ukrainian central committee.	*Bukharin and Rykov tried (March).* *Beria becomes head of secret police (December).*
1939 Made full member of Politburo (March).	*Molotov-Ribbentrop pact (August).*
As Ukrainian first secretary and civilian member of Kiev military council, moves into western Ukraine (occupied Poland).	*Germany invades Poland (September); World War II begins.*
1939–40	*Winter War with Finland (November–March).*
1940 Supervises sovietization of western Ukraine.	
1941–43 As member of Military Council and Politburo representative, serves on various fronts as commissar with wartime rank of lieutenant general.	*Germany invades Russia (June 1941).* *Fall of Kiev (September 1941).* *Battle of Moscow (winter 1941–42).* *Kharkov (Barvenkovo) disaster (May 1942).* *Battle of Stalingrad (July 1942–winter 1943).* *Battle of Kursk (summer 1943).*
Begins reconstruction of Ukrainian economy and party.	*Liberation of Kiev (November 1943).*
1944 Appointed chairman of Ukrainian council of ministers while retaining position as first secretary of Ukrainian party.	*Soviet offensive toward Berlin (spring).* *Allied invasion of France (June).*
1945 Leads commission of experts to help Poles with reconstruction of Warsaw.	*Yalta Conference (February).* *Soviet troops capture Berlin (May).* *Germany surrenders (May).* *Potsdam Conference (July–August).* *Japan surrenders (August).*
1946–47 Temporary eclipse and demotion; replaced by Kaganovich as first secretary of Ukraine; near-fatal bout with pneumonia.	*Famine in Ukraine.*
1948 Restored to full power in Ukraine.	*Stalin breaks with Tito.*
1948–49	*Berlin airlift (June–September).*

1949   Recalled by Stalin to Moscow, made   *The Leningrad Affair.*
       head of Moscow party organization
       (December).

1950   In charge of agriculture; amalga-   *Jewish conspiracy trial.*
       mates collective farms and pushes
       agro-town scheme.   *Outbreak of Korean War (June).*

1952   Delivers report on amendments to
       Party Statutes at Nineteenth Party
       Congress (October).

1953   *Doctors' Plot: Stalin orders arrest of
                                                 Kremlin doctors (January–February).*

       Ranked behind Malenkov, Molotov,   *Stalin's death; Malenkov becomes prime
       Beria, and Kaganovich.   minister and first secretary (March).*

       Replaces Malenkov as first secre-
       tary (September).

1954   Visits Peking with Bulganin.

       Begins Virgin Lands campaign to
       open   vast   tracts   for   grain
       cultivation.

1955   Visits Yugoslavia (restores relations   *Bulganin replaces Malenkov as prime min-
       with Tito); Geneva for summit   ister (February).*
       meeting; Afghanistan; and India.
                                                 Warsaw Pact created (May).

1956   Delivers secret speech on crimes of
       Stalin at Twentieth Party Congress
       (February).

       Visits London (April).   *Defiance of Poland (June–October).*

                                                 Suez crisis (October–November).

                                                 Hungarian revolt (October).

1957   Begins decentralization of industry
       (May).

       Smashes opposition of Antiparty
       Group: Malenkov, Molotov, Kagano-
       vich, Shepilov, and others (July).

       Dismisses Marshal Zhukov from   Sputnik I *launched (October).*
       post   of   minister   of   defense
       (October).

1957   *Moscow meeting of world Communist
                                                 parties, attended by Mao Zedong
                                                 (November).*

1958   Takes over premiership from Bul-
       ganin (March).

                                                 First Berlin crisis: Western powers told to
                                                 evacuate city in six months; they refuse
                                                 (autumn).

1959   Refuses to give China atomic weap-
       ons information (summer).

       First visit to United States, consul-
       tations with Eisenhower at Camp
       David (September).

1960   Announces downing of U-2 recon-
       naissance plane and capture of Gary
       Powers (May).

       Wrecks Paris summit meeting
       (May).

       Attacks China behind closed doors
       at Romanian Party Congress in
       Bucharest (June) and at Moscow
       Conference of World Communist
       Parties (November).

1961   *Major Y. Gagarin, first man in space*
                                                 (April).

       Meets with Kennedy in Vienna   *Second Berlin crisis: Flood of refugees to*
       (June).   *West increases (June).*

       Makes public attack on China,   *Construction of Berlin Wall (August).*
       thinly disguised as Albania, at
       Twenty-second Party Congress
       (October).

       Has Stalin's body removed from
       mausoleum.

1962   Goes to brink of war over missiles
       in   Cuba — and   steps   back
       (October).

1963   Cracks down on writers and artists.   *Nuclear test-ban treaty (August).*

                                             Disastrous harvest.

1964   Prepares for showdown with China
       at world party conference sched-
       uled for December.

       Resigns all offices; succeeded by
       Brezhnev as first secretary and
       Kosygin   as   prime   minister
       (October).

1966   Begins dictating memoirs.

1967   *Six-Day War in Middle East (June).*

1968   *Warsaw Pact forces invade Czechoslovakia (August).*

1970   First volume of memoirs published in United States.

1971   Dies (September 11). Buried in Novodevichy Cemetery, Moscow.

1974   Second volume of memoirs published in United States.

Index

Adreasian, Comrade, 19
Albania, 69–70, 105–8, 109–11, 127–28
Albanian Communist party, 105, 107
Alekseyev, Aleksandr I., 176
Alexander I, czar of Russia, 144
Allied Council for Japan, 82n–83n
Alliluyeva, Nadezhda Sergeyevna, 14–17
Alliluyeva, Svetlana, 16–17
Anderson, Rudolf, Jr., 178n
Andreyev, Leonid N., 203
Andropov, Yuri, 111
Antiparty Group, 10n, 17n, 62n–63n, 103n
Antipov, N. K., 37
anti-Semitism, 10n, 19, 26–27, 101–2, 113
Arabs, 95–96, 97–98, 127
Archangel invasion (1918), 97–98
atomic weapons. See nuclear weapons
Attlee, Clement, 101n
Austria, 85, 125
    Soviet peace treaty with, 72–80
Austrian Communist party, 74, 78
Averchenko, Arkadi T., 203

Bagramyan, I. K., 62–63, 64
Baku, 59
Balluku, Bequir, 107
Baltic republics, annexation of, xiii, xiv, 46, 51
Batista, Fulgencio, 170

Bay of Pigs invasion (1961), 171–72, 181
Beck, Józef, 129
Beneš, Edvard, 130n
Beria, Lavrenty P., 17, 38–39, 40–41, 42, 53, 63n, 65, 66, 67, 86–87, 104, 135, 136
Berlin, 161, 163–67, 169–70
Berlin Wall, 169–70
Bessarabia, 46, 51, 108
Bevan, Aneurin, 67
Bierut, Boleslaw, 43–44, 113, 114
Bierut, Mme., 113
Bison bomber, 187
Black Sea, 120
Blue Notebook, The (Kazakevich), 199–201
Bolsheviks, 7, 9–10, 11n, 24n, 25, 35
Brezhnev, Leonid, xii, xiii, 140n, 201n
Bukharin, N. I., 41, 44n
Bukovina, 108
Bulganin, Nikolai, 39, 46n, 85, 115, 146
Bulgaria, 65, 70n, 105, 111–12, 132, 166
Byelorussia, 46, 65–66
Byrnes, James, 67

Castro, Fidel, xii, xiii, xiv, 170, 171, 172, 176–77, 178, 181–83
Central Committee, 1, 2, 9n, 18, 21, 25, 30, 31, 32, 38, 40, 41, 42, 43, 62n, 73, 111n, 128, 196

Central Committee (*continued*)
    Presidium of, 36, 41, 42–43, 62n–
        63n, 69, 76, 77, 123, 200
Charles XII, king of Sweden, 95
Cheka (Extraordinary Commission to
    Combat Counterrevolution and
    Sabotage), 21, 23, 30–31, 116n,
    132–33, 136, 155
Chelomei, Vladimir N., 188
Chiang Kai-shek, 142, 150–51
China, 52, 71, 83n, 105n, 142–44,
    147–54
    Albania and, 107–8
    Czechoslovak economy and, 153–54
    and Japan's claims against Soviet
        Union, 90–92
    Mao's Stalinist policies in, 159–60
    Vietnam and, 156–58, 159n
    Yugoslavia and, 152–53
Chinese Communist party, 143, 147,
    150, 156, 160
Chubar, V., 31, 35–36
Churchill, Winston, 67, 68, 81n, 82,
    97–98, 101n
Cold War, 134
    Berlin crisis and, 163–67, 169–70
    Cuba and, 170–83
    Warsaw Pact formation and, 68–72
collectivization, 159, 163
Comintern (Communist
    International), 37, 128, 150
Communist Party of the Soviet Union,
    11, 17–18, 25, 50, 107, 156. *See
    also* Central Committee;
    Politburo
Council of Ministers, 1, 2, 9n, 38–39,
    73, 111n, 169
Cuba, 170–83
Cuban missile crisis (1962), xii, xiii,
    170–80, 182–83
Cultural Revolution, 159
Czechoslovak Communist party, 129,
    132, 133, 134, 139, 141
Czechoslovakia, 48, 70n, 112–13, 117,
    120–21, 128–41
    China and, 153–54
    purges in, 133, 135–37
    Soviet invasion of (1968), xiv, 139–
        41

Dayan, Moshe, 96–97
de Gaulle, Charles, 99–100
Deng Xiaoping, 152
Denmark, 54
Doctor Zhivago (Pasternak), xi, 195–
    96, 201
Donbass, 4, 5, 6–13, 27, 32, 33, 35,
    128
Dubček, Alexander, 140n
Dulles, John Foster, 68
Dzerzhinsky, Felix E., 116

Egypt, 95
Eideman, R. P., 56n
Eisenhower, Dwight D., viii
Estonia, 46, 51

Fierlinger, Mme., 130
Fierlinger, Zdenek, 130
Finland, 46, 51, 54–55, 71
Fomenko (mine worker), 7
Forefathers' Eve (Mickiewicz), 117
France, 11n, 73, 98, 99–100, 129,
    154, 155, 165–66
    World War II and, 46, 48, 49n, 50,
        51, 54
French Communist party, 44, 100

Gamarnik, Yan, 28
German Democratic Republic (GDR)
    (East Germany), 69, 70, 114, 120,
    161–64, 165, 167–69, 195
Germany, Federal Republic of (West
    Germany), 93, 112, 120, 163–64,
    165, 167, 168, 169, 174, 195
Germany, Nazi, 65–66, 72, 80, 81,
    102, 117–18, 129, 135
    attack on Soviet Union launched by,
        49–52, 54–56
    Kharkov campaign of, 57–62, 63–64
    Soviet pact with, xiii, xiv, 45–48,
        49–52, 53, 55, 108
Germany, unification of, 99, 162
Gero, Enro, 121–22
Gheorghiu-Dej, Gheorghe, 103, 109,
    111, 112
glasnost, vii, xiv
Glushko, Valentin Petrovich, 186

Gomulka, Wladyslaw, 114, 115, 116–17, 118, 119–20
Gorbachev, Mikhail, vii, xiv–xv
Gorbatov, Aleksandr V., 197
Gosplan (Czechoslovakia), 154
Gosplan (Hungary), 122
Gosplan (Soviet Union), 111*n*, 154, 189
Gottwald, Klement, 128–29, 130–32, 133–34, 136, 141
Gottwald, Mme., 128–29, 130–31
Great Britain, 11*n*, 73, 84, 100*n*, 129, 165–66, 174, 190, 194
  World War II and, 46, 48, 49*n*, 50, 51, 54, 67
Great Leap Forward, 153, 159
Great Terror, viii, 16*n*, 17–38, 52, 101–2, 104*n*, 114, 116–17, 135–37
  estimated casualties of, 40*n*
  Khrushchev's secret speech on, 30*n*, 39–44, 104*n*, 135
Grechko, Andrei Antonovich, 113, 195
Greece, 100, 166
Gromyko, Andrei Andreyevich, 174–75
Groza, Petru, 109–10
Gusev, Dmitri N., 16*n*
Gusev, Nikolai I., 16*n*
Gusev, Sergei Ivanovich, 16*n*
Guseva, Mme., 16–17

Hatoyama, Ichiro, 88
Hitler, Adolf, 46, 48–51, 53–60, 65, 70, 84, 108, 129, 144, 161
Hitler-Stalin pact. *See* Molotov-Ribbentrop pact (1939)
Ho Chi Minh, 154–58
Holland, 54, 84
Hoxha, Enver, 105, 107, 127–28
Hungarian Communist party, 121
Hungary, 54, 70*n*, 132
  uprising in (1956), 120–27
Husak, Gustav, 140

Industrial Academy (Moscow), 14*n*
intercontinental ballistic missiles (ICBMs), 184–87
Iosifovna, Anna, 94–95
Israel, 95–98, 127

Italian Communist party, 44
Italy, 72*n*, 76, 99, 100, 105, 168, 174, 179, 182

Japan, xiii, xiv, 28, 52–53, 80–94, 142, 150
  Soviet military conflicts with, 11*n*, 52–53, 80–83
  Soviet peace treaty with, 80, 83–90
Jews, 10*n*, 19, 26–27, 95, 101–2, 110, 113
Johnson, Lyndon B., 180–81

Kádár, János, 122, 123*n*, 124, 127
Kaganovich, Lazar M., 9–10, 13*n*, 14–15, 18, 33, 34, 39, 42, 62*n*, 115, 135, 136–37
Kalinovka, 4–6
Kameney, L. B., 24*n*, 25*n*, 41, 200
Kang Sheng, 152
Kapital, Das (Marx), 7
Kapitsa, Pyotr L., 189–90
Katzenelenbogen, Misha, 19
Kazakevich, Emmanuil G., 199–201
Kuzakov, M. I., 124–25
Kennedy, John F., viii, 175*n*, 176–77, 178, 179 81, 182
Kennedy, Robert, 178, 179
KGB (Committee for State Security), 40*n*, 111*n*, 116
Khalkhin-Gol River, battle at (1939), 52–53
Kharkov offensive (1942), 57–62, 63–64
Khrushchev (grandfather), 4, 5, 6
Khrushchev, Sergei (father), 4–5, 6–7, 8–9
Khrushchev, Sergei (son), x–xi, xii, xiv, 16
Khrushcheva, Aksiniya (Ksenya) (mother), 4–5, 6–7
Khrushcheva, Irina Sergeyevna (sister), 5, 6–7
Khrushcheva, Nina Petrovna (wife), 94, 109, 112
Khrushchev on Khrushchev (S. Khrushchev), x–xi, xii
Khrushchev Remembers (N. Khrushchev), vii–xiii

Khrushchev Remembers: The Last Testament (N. Khrushchev), viii–xiii, 63n
Kiev, 56–57
Kim Il Sung, 144–47
Kin Jong Il, 145n
Kireyevsky, Ivan, 128n
Kirov, Sergei Mironovich, 19n, 20–25, 31n, 103
Kisunko, Grigory V., 188
Kliszko, Zenon, 114, 115n
Komsomol (Young Communist League), 29–30, 34
Konev, Ivan S., 115, 123–24
Kono, Ichiro, 88
Korea, 81, 82
Korea, Democratic People's Republic of (North Korea), 143, 144–47
Korea, Republic of (South Korea), 144, 145, 146
Korean War, 144–47
Korolyov, Sergei Pavlovich, 184, 185–86, 187
Korytny, Mme., 27–28
Korytny, Semyon Zadharovich, 27–28
Kosarev, Aleksandr, 29–30, 34
Kosior, S. V., 31–32, 34
Kosygin, Aleksei, 111
Kultikhov, Yakov Isaakovich, 96
Kurchatov, Igor V., 194
Kuril Islands, 81, 88–89, 90–92
Kuznetsov, A. A., 26n
Kuznetsov, N. O., 186

Latvia, 46, 51
Lavochkin, Semyon A., 186
Le Duan, 156, 157, 158
Lend-Lease, 84
Lenin, Vladimir Ilyich, 11n, 17n, 20, 21, 24n, 25, 46, 101, 153, 159, 160, 168, 199, 200
Leningrad, 56
Leningrad Affair (1949–1950), 26, 101
Lenin's testament, 20, 21
Lesechko, Mikhail, 111
Lithuania, xiv, 46, 51
Loga-Sowinski, Ignacy, 114, 115n
Lozovsky, Solomon A., 101
Luca, Vasile, 110
Luna missions, 189

Luxembourg, 54
Lyubchenko (chairman of people's commissars in Ukraine), 31–32, 33

Makhachkala, 59
Malenkov, Georgi M., 9n–10n, 38, 39, 56, 59, 62, 65, 66, 85, 103, 122, 124–25
Malinovsky, Rodion Y., 63n, 170, 171, 177, 181–82
Manchuria, 52, 53n, 81–82
Mannerheim Line, 55
Mao Zedong, 90–92, 105n, 142–43, 147–50, 152–54, 159–60
Marshall Plan, 164n
Marshal Zhukov's Greatest Battles (Zhukov), 62–64
Marx, Karl, 7, 153
Marxism-Leninism, 2, 3, 85, 100, 102, 121, 124, 136, 139, 140, 165
Masaryk, Tomáš, 128
Matsu, 148n, 150
Maurer, Ion Gheorghe, 112
Medved, F. D., 23–24
Mein Kampf (Hitler), 50, 51
Mezhlauk, Valery, 189–90
Mickiewicz, Adam, 117
Mikhailovna, Lydia, 5–6
Mikhoels, Solomon M., 101
Mikoyan, Anastas Ivanovich, 15, 16, 19, 31n, 46n, 53, 60–62, 75, 85, 103, 115, 122–23, 143, 178–79, 200
Ministry of Foreign Affairs, 73
Mishakova, Olga, 34–35
Moldavia, 108–9
Molotov, Vyacheslav Mikhailovich, 17, 18, 22, 36, 42, 46n, 49n, 53, 62n, 69–70, 97–98, 135, 194
fraternal Communist countries and, 103, 110, 113, 115, 134
and peace treaty with Austria, 73, 74–78
and peace treaty with Japan, 85–87
Molotova, Mme. (Comrade Zemchuzhina), 101
Molotov-Ribbentrop pact (1939), xiii, xiv, 45–48, 49–52, 53, 55, 108
Mongolia, 52–53

Moscow, 18, 58, 69
Moskalenko, Kirill, 63*n*
Muller, Henry, xi
Munnich, Ferenc, 123*n*, 124
MVD (Ministry of Internal Affairs),
    40–41, 111*n*
Myasishchev, V. M., 187
My Times and Wars (Gorbatov), 197

Nagy, Imre, 121, 122, 123*n*, 124, 125–
    26
Napoleon I, emperor of the French,
    144
NATO (North Atlantic Treaty
    Organization), 68, 70–71, 120,
    125*n*, 148, 174
Nikolaenko (Ukrainian party
    member), 34, 35
Nikolayev, Leonid Vasilievich, 21–22,
    24
Nixon, Richard M., 94
NKVD (People's Commissariat of
    Internal Affairs), 23, 24*n*, 30, 38*n*
Nobel Prize, 195
Norway, 54
Novotný, Antonín, 134, 135–37, 140*n*,
    153
nuclear energy, 193
nuclear weapons, xiii, 71, 82, 86, 101,
    118–19, 190–95
    Cuban missile crisis and, xii, xiii,
        170–80, 182–83
    defense against, 187–88
    factories for manufacture of, 190–93
    ICBMs, 184–87

Ochab, Edward, 43*n*, 113, 114, 115
October Revolution (1917), 11, 14
Okinawa, 86, 94*n*
*One Day in the Life of Ivan
    Denisovich* (Solzhenitsyn), xiii,
    196–99
Osoaviakhim, 56

Pan-Slavism, 128
Pasternak, Boris, x, 195
Pauker, Anna, 110
perestroika, xiv, 1
Pervukhin, Mikhail G., 169
Pétain, Philippe, 54

Peter I (Peter the Great), czar of
    Russia, 95, 97, 98
Petlura, S. V., 33
Pilsudski, Józef, 37–38
Pliyev, Issa Aleksandrovich, 171, 178
Poland, 70*n*, 96, 144*n*
    postwar relations with, 113–20, 121
    purges in, 37–38, 43–44, 114
    World War II and, 46, 48–49, 50,
        51, 54, 117–18, 129
Polish Communist party, 43–44, 113,
    115*n*, 132
Politburo, xii, 1, 2, 18, 21, 30, 36*n*,
    38–39, 40, 45, 53, 103, 122*n*,
    133, 136, 195, 201*n*
Popov, G. M., 26
Popovic, Koca, 104
Port Arthur, 71, 81
Pospelov, Pyotr, 42, 43
Pospelov Commission, 42, 43
Postyshev, P. P., 31–32, 34
Potsdam Conference (1945), 100–101,
    166
Pravda, 7, 32, 42, 103
Presidium of Central Committee, 36,
    41, 42–43, 62*n*–63*n*, 69, 76, 77,
    123, 200
Presidium of Supreme Soviet, 1, 2,
    10*n*, 15*n*, 77
Purkayev, M. A., 56
Pu Yi, Henry (Emperor Hsuan Tung),
    82
Pyatakov, Yuri, 35

Quemoy, 148*n*, 150

Raab, Julius, 78–79
Rákosi, Mátyás, 121, 122*n*, 124, 125,
    126
Rankovic, Aleksandr, 152
Red Army, 11, 15*n*, 33, 39
Rhee, Syngman, 145
Ribbentrop, Joachim von, 45, 46, 48,
    53
Rokossovsky, Konstantin K., 114*n*–
    15*n*, 119
Romania, 51, 51, 54, 70*n*, 108–11,
    112–13, 120–21, 126*n*, 127, 132,
    138
Romanian Communist party, 110

Roosevelt, Franklin D., 80, 81*n*, 82
Rosenberg, Ethel and Julius, xiii, 193–94
Rostropovich, Mstislav, 198
Rudenko, R. A., 35, 41–42
Rudzutak, Jan, 30
Rusk, Dean, 174–75
Russo-Japanese War (1904–1905), 81
Rykov, A. I., 41

Sakhalin Island, 81, 82, 90–92
Sato, Eisaku, 94
Savinkov, Boris V., 97–98
Scherf, Adolf, 79
Seventeenth Party Congress (1934), 18–20, 25
Shalyapin, Fedor I., 203
Shchusev, Aleksei Viktorovich, 29
Sheboldaev, B. P., 20–21
Sheku, Mehmet, 107
Shepilov, Dimitri T., 103
Shvernik, Nikolai M., 19*n*
Shvernik Commission, 19, 21, 22, 23–24
Siberia, 190, 191
Sinkiang, 142–43
Sino-Soviet split, 90–92, 105*n*, 107–8, 142–44, 150–54, 156, 158*n*–59*n*
Six-Day War (1967), 95, 97, 98
Slansky, Rudolf, 133, 134*n*, 136
Slavophile movement, 128
Solzhenitsyn, Aleksandr, xiii, 196–99
Soong Ch'ing-ling, 152
Sovrom (Soviet Romanian Society), 110
space program, 188–89
Spain, 168
Sputnik 1, 186*n*
Spychalski, Marian, 114, 115*n*
Stalin, Joseph, viii, 3–4, 71, 74–75, 77, 86, 87, 92, 107, 121, 141, 159–60, 165, 166, 189–90, 197, 199
  China and, 142–44, 147, 150
  fraternal countries of West and, 102–5, 109–10, 130–34
  Khrushchev's secret speech on crimes of, 30*n*, 39–44, 104*n*, 135
  Korean War and, 144–47
  nuclear weapons and, xiii, 193–94
  postwar politics and, 69, 72–73, 75, 79–80, 83–85, 99–101
  purges and, 17–38, 101–2, 114, 116–17, 135–37
  succession plans of, 38–39
  Vietnam and, 154–56
  wife's death and, 14–17
  World War II and, 45–48, 49–51, 53–62, 64–67, 80–83, 108, 192
Stalingrad, 57, 59, 60, 149
State and Revolution (Lenin), 199*n*
Supreme Soviet, xiv
  Presidium of, 1, 2, 10*n*, 15*n*, 77
Suslov, Mikhail A., 103, 122, 195, 198, 200, 201
Svoboda, Ludvík, 140
Sweden, 95, 97

Taiwan Strait crisis (1958), 148–49
TASS, 73, 170
Thorez, Maurice, 44, 99–100
Timoshenko, Semyon K., 48, 49, 55, 57, 58, 60, 63, 64, 197
Tito, Marshal (Josip Broz), 72, 76, 102, 103, 105, 127, 128, 152*n*
Togliatti, Palmiro, 44, 100
Transylvania, 127
Trieste, 72, 75, 76, 78
Trotskyites, 17–18, 24
Truman, Harry S., 67, 82, 83, 86, 100*n*–101*n*, 134
Truman Doctrine, 100*n*
Tukhachevsky, Mikhail, 27, 28, 33*n*, 56*n*
Turkey, 100*n*, 166, 168, 174, 179, 182
Tvardovsky, Aleksandr, 196
Twentieth Party Congress (1956), 30*n*, 39–44, 104*n*, 107, 110, 135, 159
Twenty-second Party Congress (1961), 22, 159

Uborevich, I. P., 27
Ukraine, 10, 13*n*, 25, 26, 31–32, 33–34, 46, 51*n*, 56–59, 65–66, 77, 103, 104*n*, 129, 190
Ulbricht, Walter, 161, 167, 168, 169
United Nations, 174, 182

United States, 11n, 16, 68–69, 71,
72n, 73, 75, 92, 96, 100–101,
110–11, 120, 125n, 134, 157, 158,
164–66, 185, 186, 187, 188, 193,
194, 195
China and, 148–51
Cuba and, 170, 171–83
Japan and, 83–90, 94
Korean War and, 145, 146, 147
World War II and, 52, 67, 80, 81–
83, 191
USSR Under Construction, 155
Ustinov, D. F., 184
U Thant, 182
U-2 incident (1962), 178

Vannikov, Boris L., 192–93
Vareikis, I. M., 32–33
Vasilevsky, A. M., 58
Vienna, occupation of, 73, 78
Vietnam, 154–58, 159n, 181
Vietnamese Communist party, 156,
157
Vishnevskaya, Galina, 198n–99n
Vlasik, Nikolai, 15–16
Voroshilov, Kliment Y., 15, 18, 22, 36,
39, 42, 45, 46n, 49n, 52, 64, 103,
109–10, 135, 192
Voznesensky, N. A., 26n
Vukmanovic-Tempo, Svetozar, 105

Warsaw Pact, 68–72, 112, 118–21
Winter War (1939–1940), 15n, 54–55
World War I, 11n, 50, 51n, 57, 72n,
100, 164
World War II, xiii, 45–67, 70, 72n,
102, 105, 117–18, 129, 149, 164,
191
German attack on Soviet Union in,
49–52, 54–56

Japanese aggression in, 52–53, 80–
83
Kharkov offensive in, 57–62, 63–64
memoirs about, 62–64
Molotov-Ribbentrop pact and, xiii,
xiv, 45–48, 49–52, 53, 55, 108
Soviet lack of preparedness in, 15n,
52, 53–57, 191–92
Soviet peace treaty with Austria
after, 72–80
Soviet peace treaty with Japan after,
80, 83–90

Yagoda, Genrikh Grigorevich, 24,
38n, 41, 135
Yakir, Iona, 27–29
Yakubovsky, Ivan I., 169
Yalta Conference (1945), 80–81, 109
Yangel, Mikhail Kuzinich, 184–85
Yegorov, A. I., 28
Yezhov, Nikolai, 38, 104, 135, 136
Yudin, P. F., 103
Yugoslav Communist party, 126
Yugoslavia, 54, 69, 72, 76, 102–4, 105,
111, 126–28, 152–53, 168
Yuzovka, 4, 5, 6–11, 13

Zambrowski, Roman, 113
Zápotocký, Antonín, 134, 135, 136,
137, 153
Zemchuzhina, Comrade (Mme.
Molotova), 101
Zhou Enlai, 147, 157
Zhukov, Georgi A. (Yuri), 176
Zhukov, Georgi K., 53, 57, 62–64
Zimmerwald Conference (1915), 11
Zinoviev, Grigory Yevseyevich, 24,
41, 199, 200
Zvezda, 7